The Flowers of Evil

Volume 9

Shuzo Oshimi

VERTICAL.

Contents

Chapter 43: That Was Your Soul

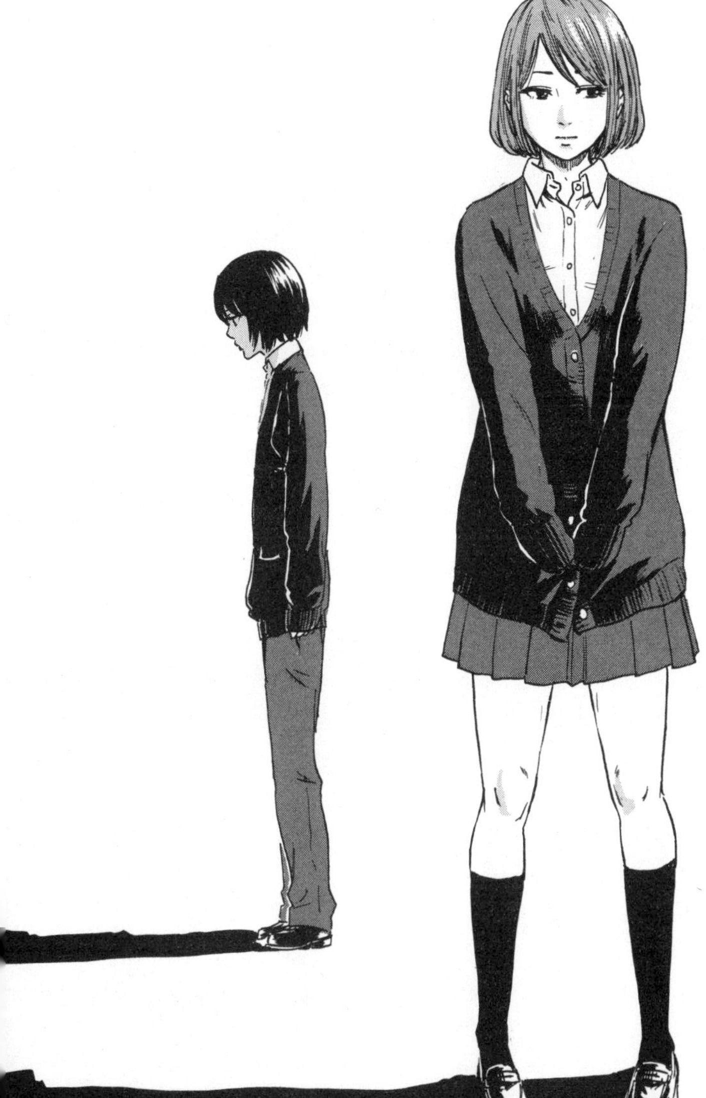

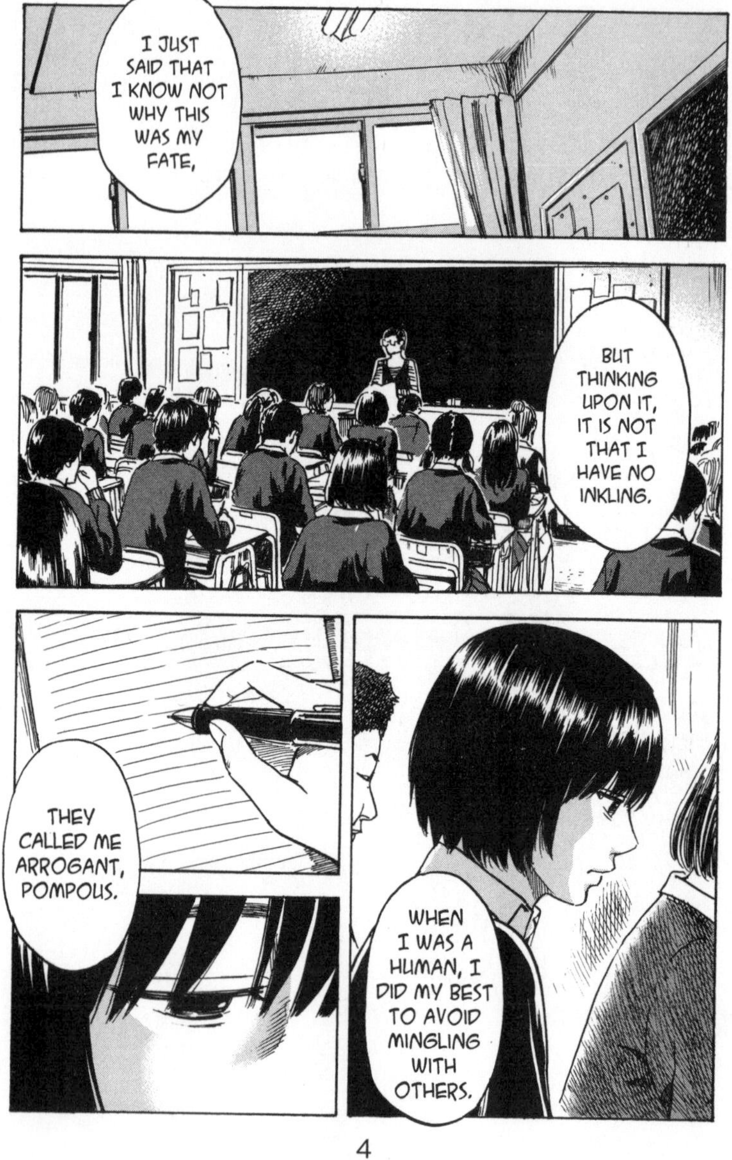
I JUST SAID THAT I KNOW NOT WHY THIS WAS MY FATE,
BUT THINKING UPON IT, IT IS NOT THAT I HAVE NO INKLING.
WHEN I WAS A HUMAN, I DID MY BEST TO AVOID MINGLING WITH OTHERS.
THEY CALLED ME ARROGANT, POMPOUS.

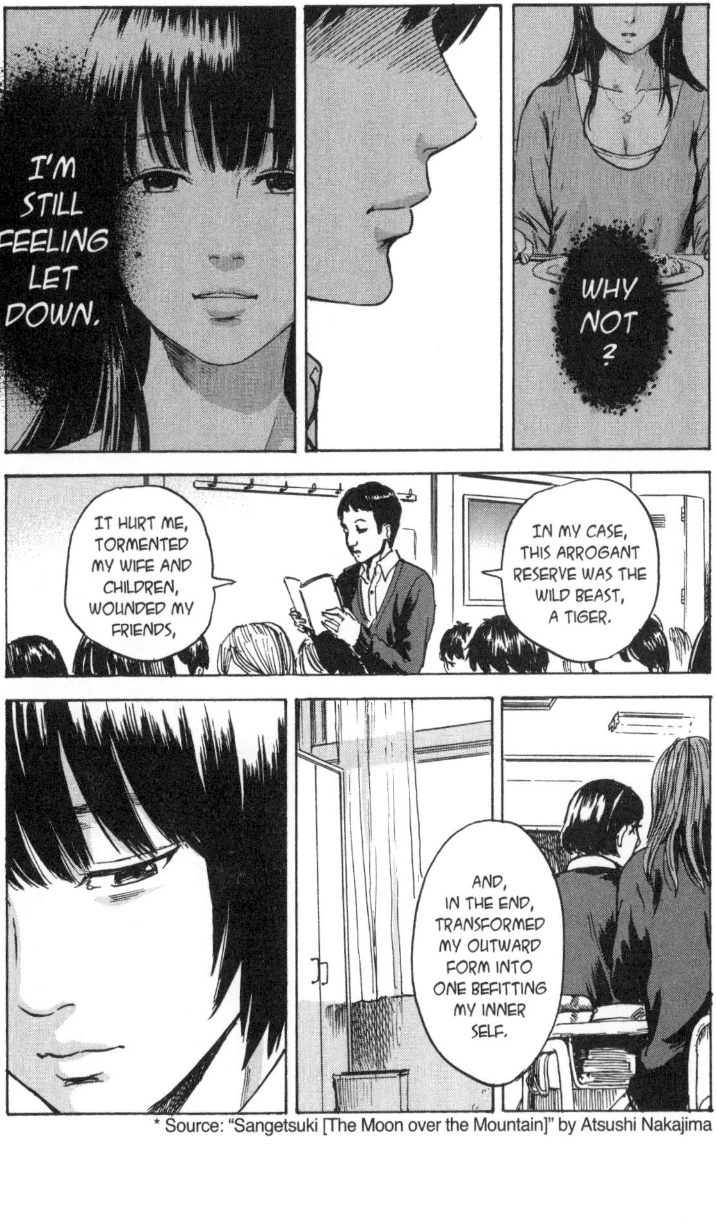
WHY NOT ?
I'M STILL FEELING LET DOWN.
IN MY CASE, THIS ARROGANT RESERVE WAS THE WILD BEAST, A TIGER.
IT HURT ME, TORMENTED MY WIFE AND CHILDREN, WOUNDED MY FRIENDS,
AND, IN THE END, TRANSFORMED MY OUTWARD FORM INTO ONE BEFITTING MY INNER SELF.

* Source: "Sangetsuki [The Moon over the Mountain]" by Atsushi Nakajima

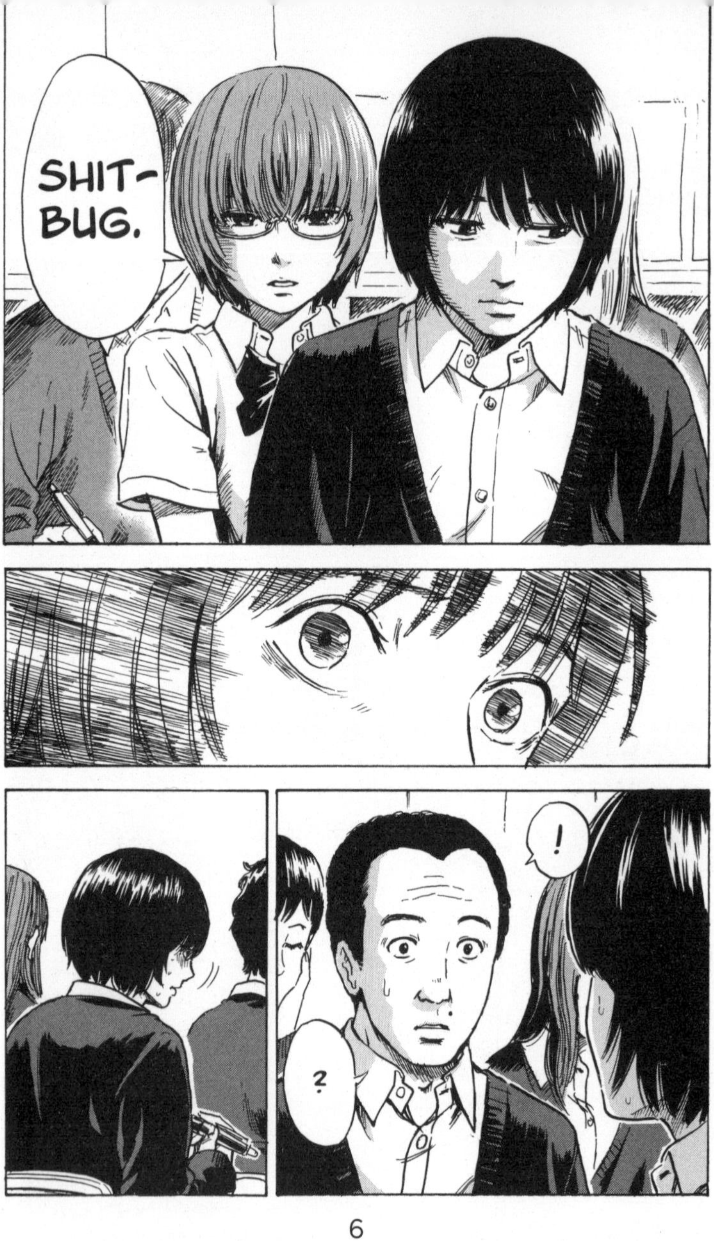
SHIT-BUG.
!
?

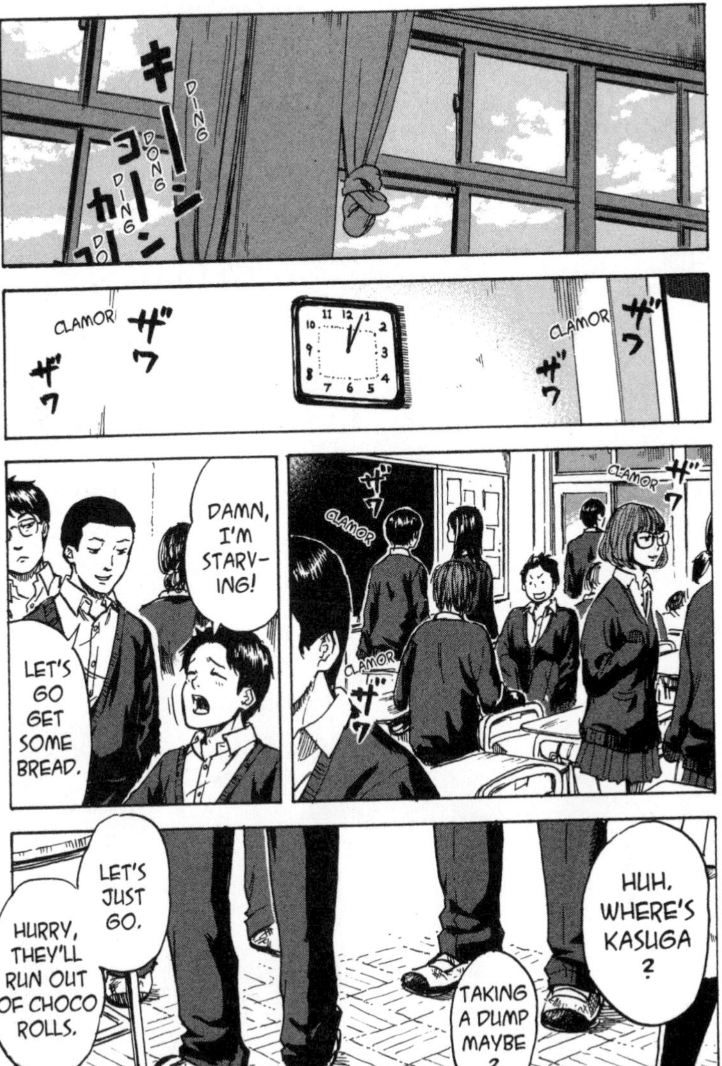
キーン
コーン
カーン
DING
DONG
DING
DO
ザワ
ザワ
CLAMOR
ザワ
ザワ
CLAMOR
ザワ
CLAMOR
ザワ
CLAMOR
ザワ
CLAMOR
DAMN, I'M STARVING!
LET'S GO GET SOME BREAD.
HUH. WHERE'S KASUGA?
TAKING A DUMP MAYBE?
LET'S JUST GO.
HURRY, THEY'LL RUN OUT OF CHOCO ROLLS.

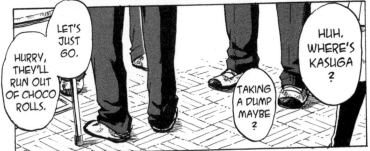

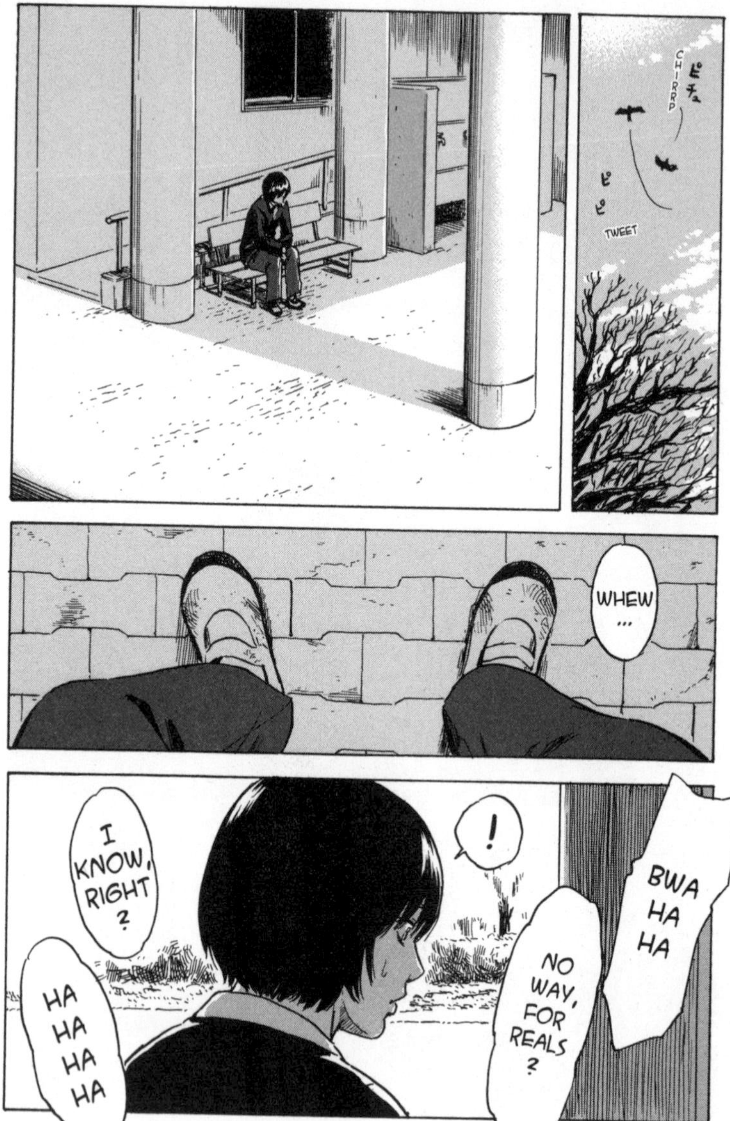
ピチュ
CHIRRP
ピピ
TWEET
WHEW ...
BWA HA HA
NO WAY, FOR REALS?
!
I KNOW, RIGHT?
HA HA HA HA

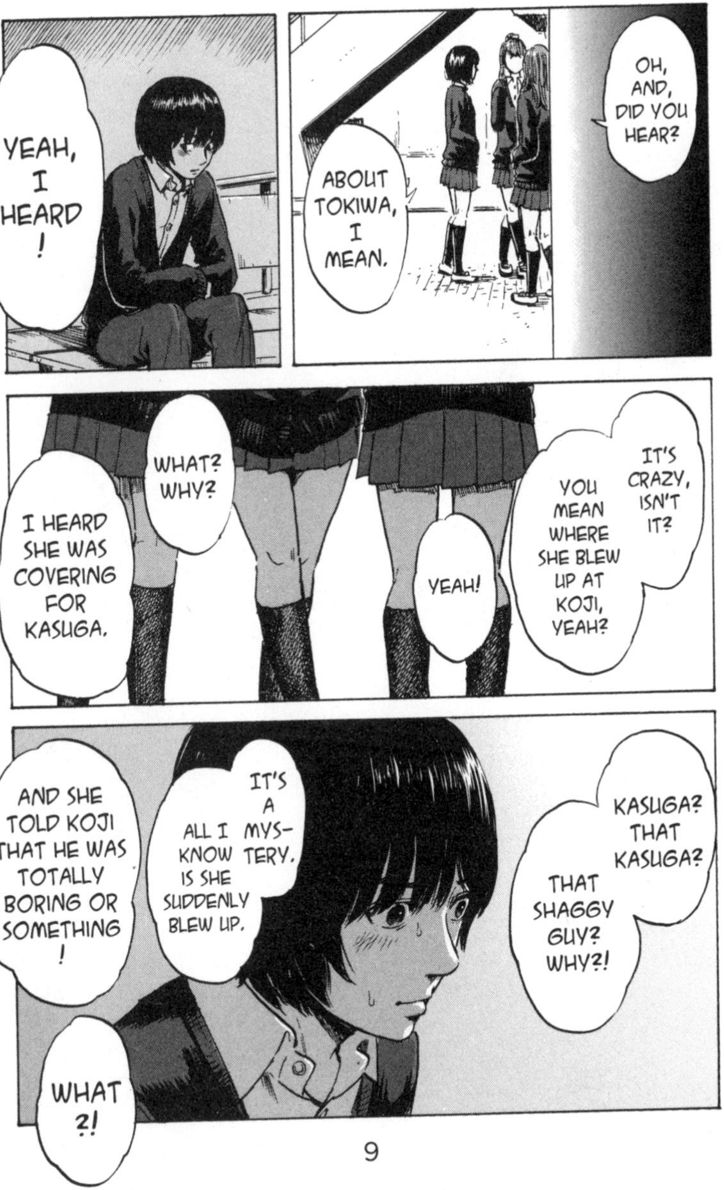

OH, AND, DID YOU HEAR?
ABOUT TOKIWA, I MEAN.
YEAH, I HEARD!
IT'S CRAZY, ISN'T IT?
YOU MEAN WHERE SHE BLEW UP AT KOJI, YEAH?
YEAH!
WHAT? WHY?
I HEARD SHE WAS COVERING FOR KASUGA.
KASUGA? THAT KASUGA?
THAT SHAGGY GUY? WHY?!
IT'S A MYSTERY.
ALL I KNOW IS SHE SUDDENLY BLEW UP.
AND SHE TOLD KOJI THAT HE WAS TOTALLY BORING OR SOMETHING!
WHAT?!

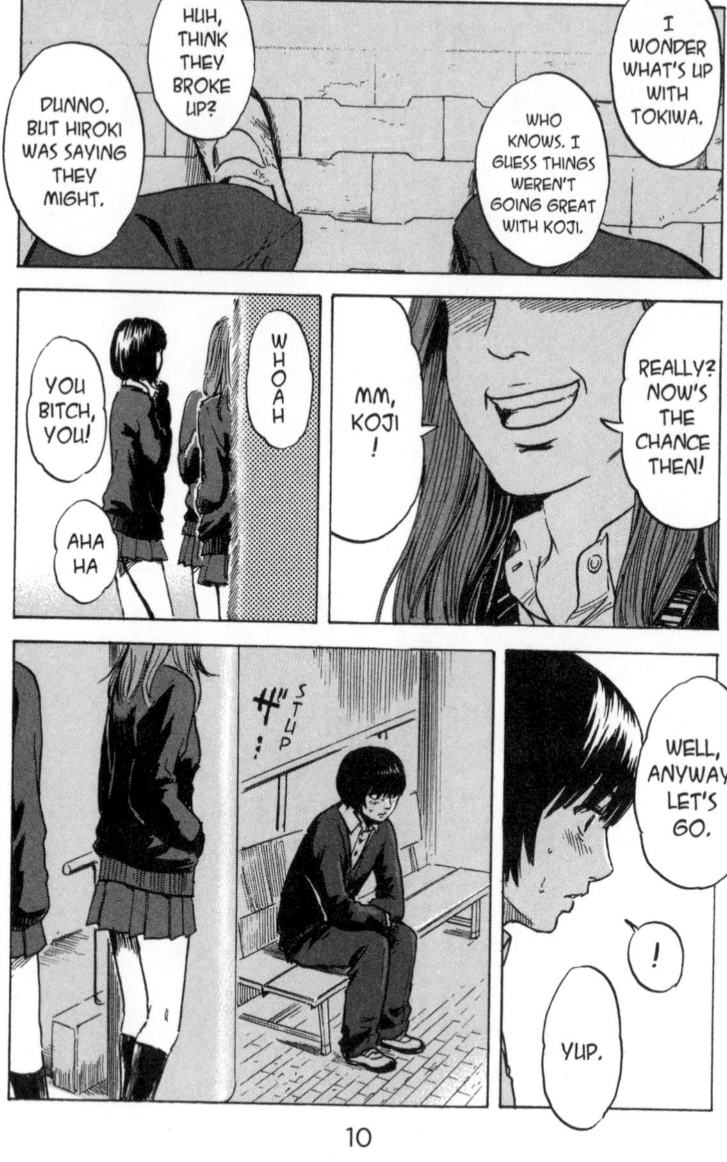
I WONDER WHAT'S UP WITH TOKIWA.
WHO KNOWS. I GUESS THINGS WEREN'T GOING GREAT WITH KOJI.
HUH, THINK THEY BROKE UP?
DUNNO. BUT HIROKI WAS SAYING THEY MIGHT.
REALLY? NOW'S THE CHANCE THEN!
MM, KOJI!
WHOAH
YOU BITCH, YOU!
AHA HA
WELL, ANYWAY, LET'S GO.
!
YUP.
STUP

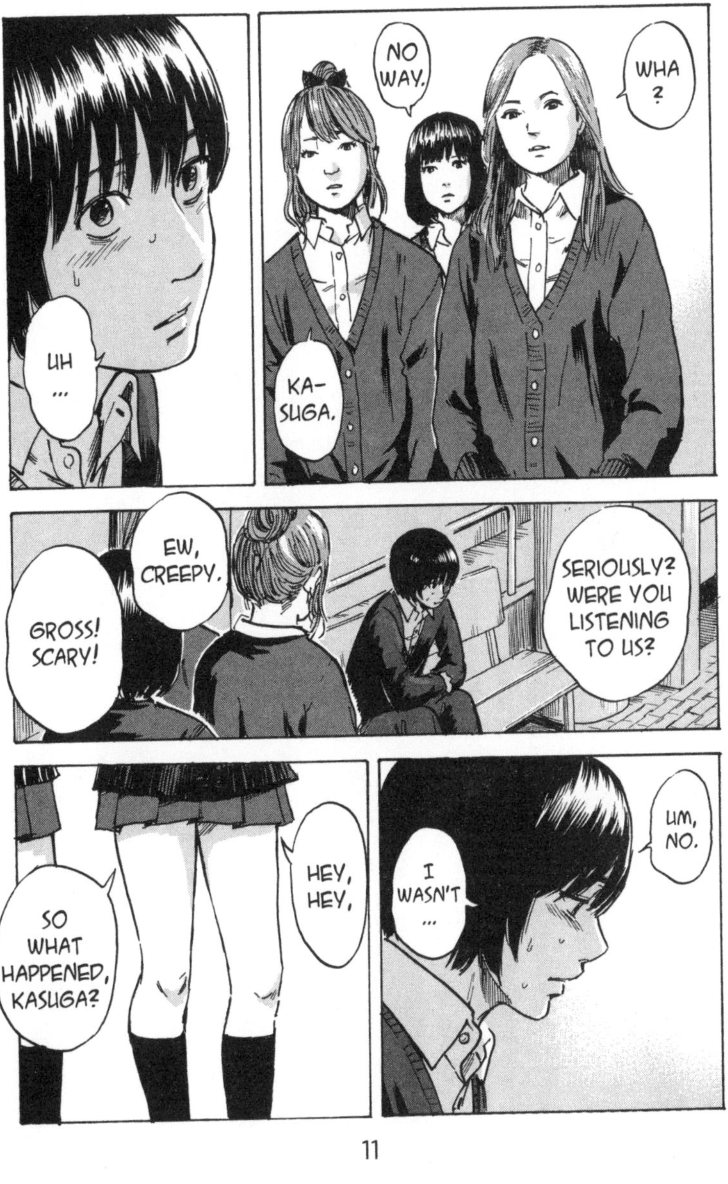
WHA?
NO WAY.
KA-SUGA.
UH ...
SERIOUSLY? WERE YOU LISTENING TO US?
EW, CREEPY.
GROSS! SCARY!
UM, NO.
I WASN'T ...
HEY, HEY,
SO WHAT HAPPENED, KASUGA?

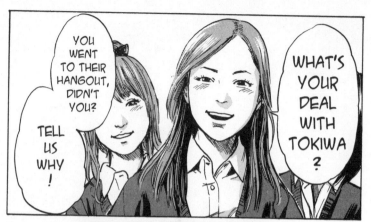

WHAT'S YOUR DEAL WITH TOKIWA?
YOU WENT TO THEIR HANGOUT, DIDN'T YOU?
TELL US WHY!
ONLY COOL PEOPLE GET TO GO THERE.
SO WHY?!
WHY WHAT?

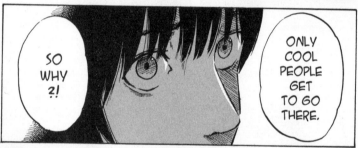

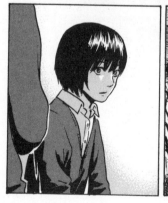

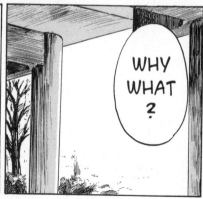

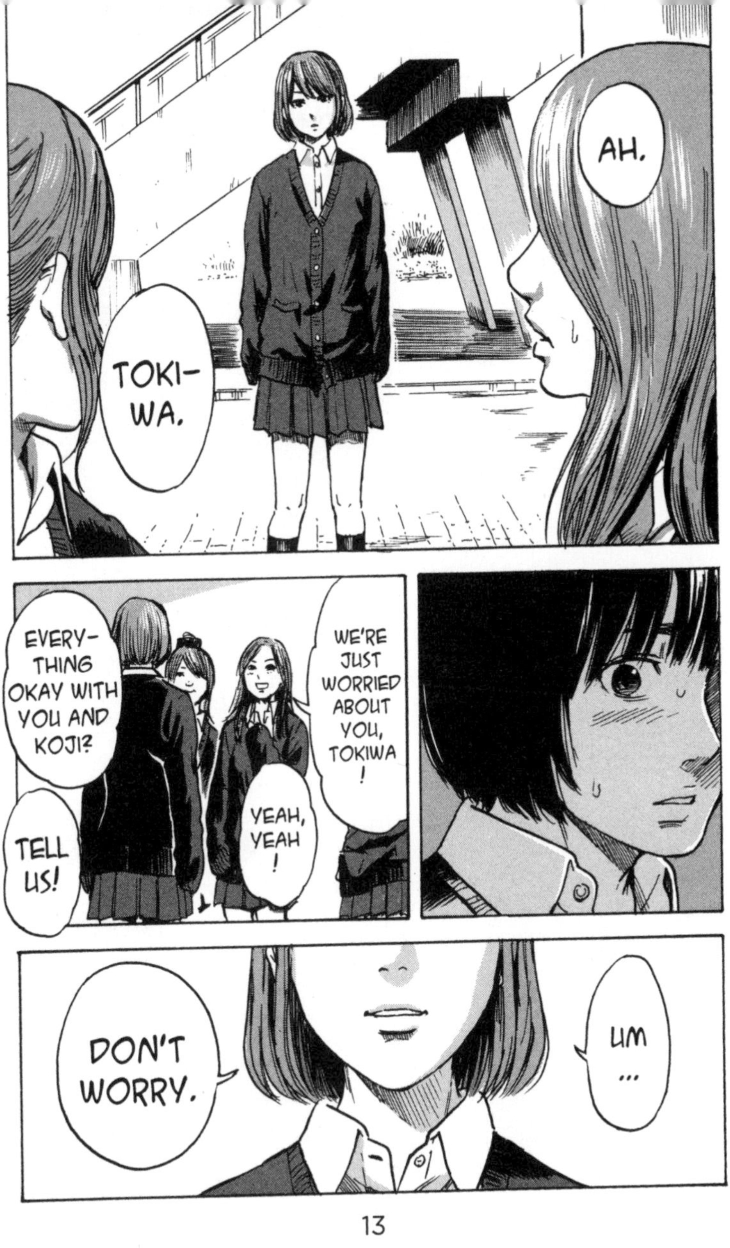
AH.
TOKI-WA.
WE'RE JUST WORRIED ABOUT YOU, TOKIWA!
EVERY-THING OKAY WITH YOU AND KOJI?
YEAH, YEAH!
TELL US!
UM ...
DON'T WORRY.

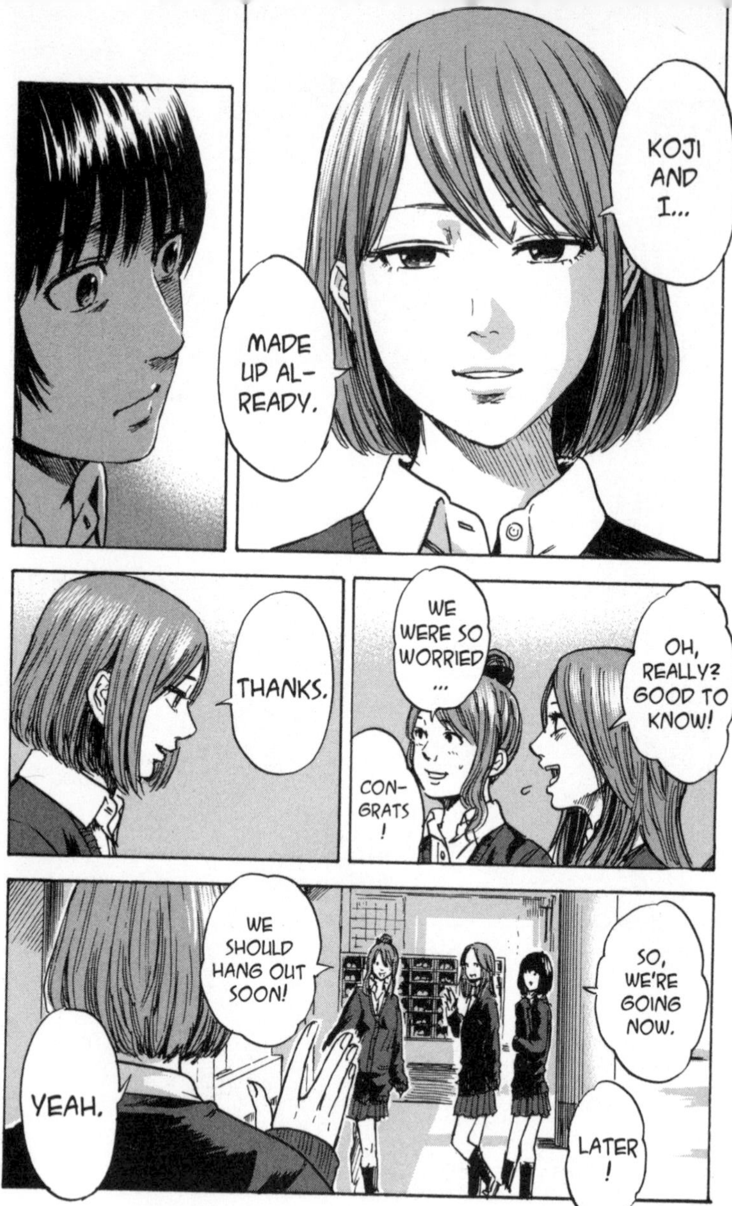
KOJI AND I...
MADE UP AL-READY.
OH, REALLY? GOOD TO KNOW!
WE WERE SO WORRIED ...
CON-GRATS !
THANKS.
SO, WE'RE GOING NOW.
LATER !
WE SHOULD HANG OUT SOON!
YEAH.

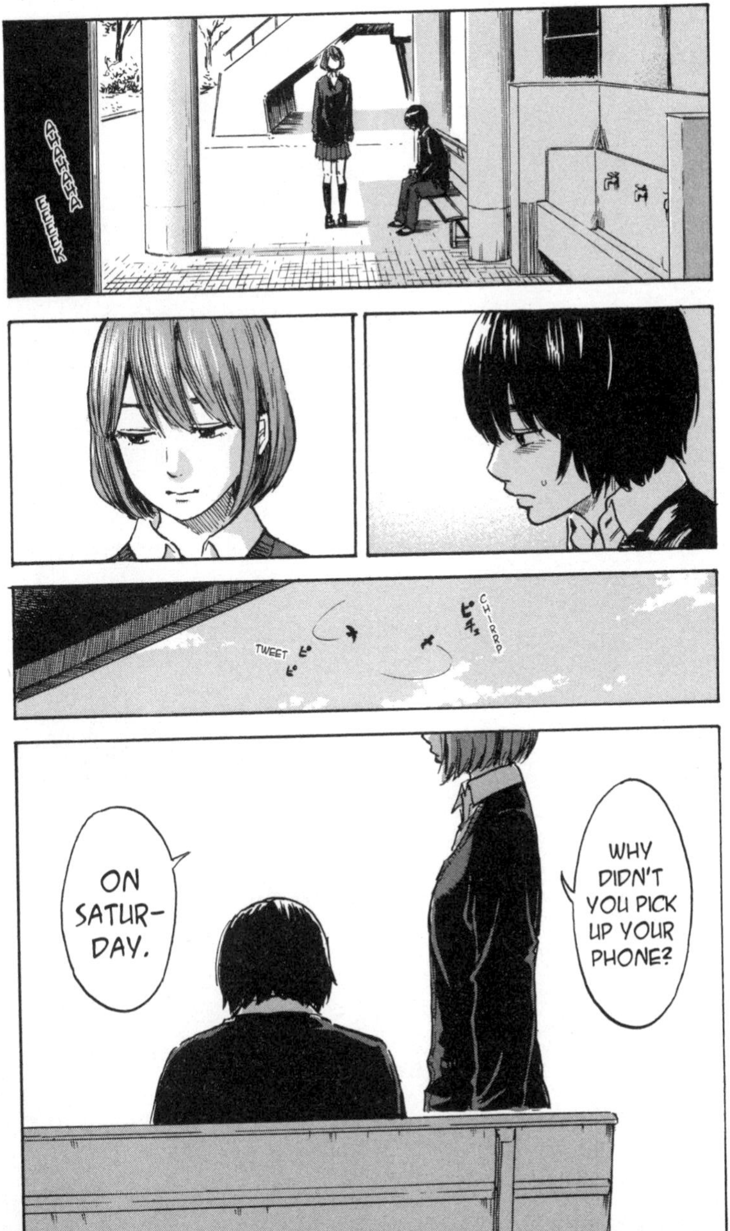
AHAHAHA
EEEEEK
ピチュ CHIRRP
ピピ TWEET
WHY DIDN'T YOU PICK UP YOUR PHONE?
ON SATUR-DAY.

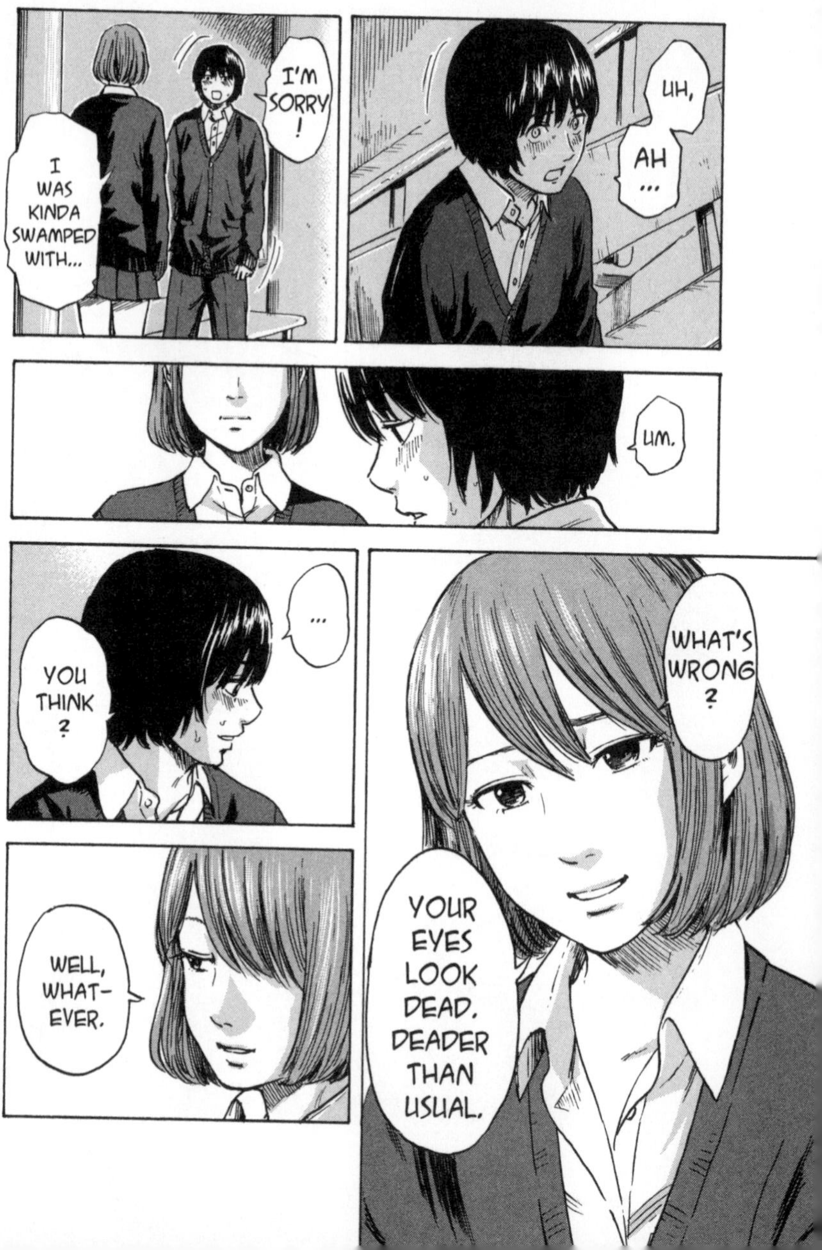
UH,
AH ...
I'M SORRY!
I WAS KINDA SWAMPED WITH...
UM.
WHAT'S WRONG?
YOUR EYES LOOK DEAD. DEADER THAN USUAL.
...
YOU THINK?
WELL, WHAT-EVER.

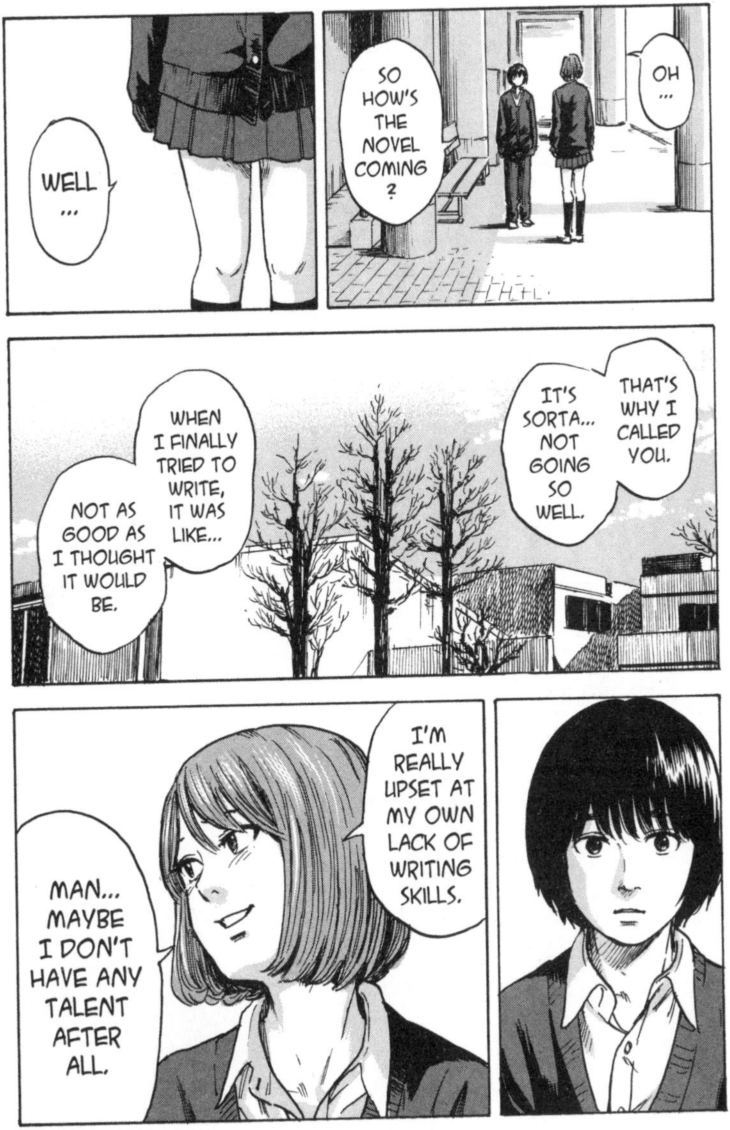
OH ...
SO HOW'S THE NOVEL COMING ?
WELL ...
THAT'S WHY I CALLED YOU.
IT'S SORTA... NOT GOING SO WELL.
WHEN I FINALLY TRIED TO WRITE, IT WAS LIKE...
NOT AS GOOD AS I THOUGHT IT WOULD BE.
I'M REALLY UPSET AT MY OWN LACK OF WRITING SKILLS.
MAN... MAYBE I DON'T HAVE ANY TALENT AFTER ALL.

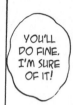

THAT'S NOT TRUE!
YOU'LL DO FINE. I'M SURE OF IT!
IT IS GOOD ...
ABSO-LUTE-LY!
MM.
THANKS.
SO...
KASUGA ...

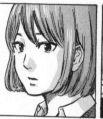

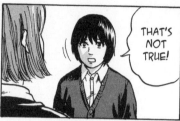

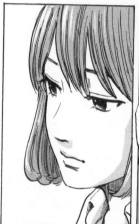

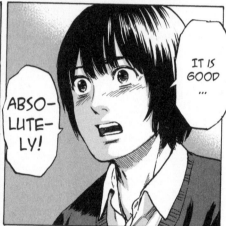

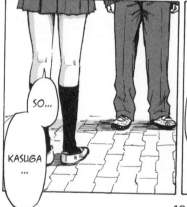

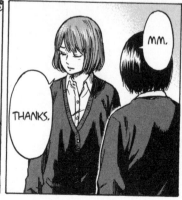

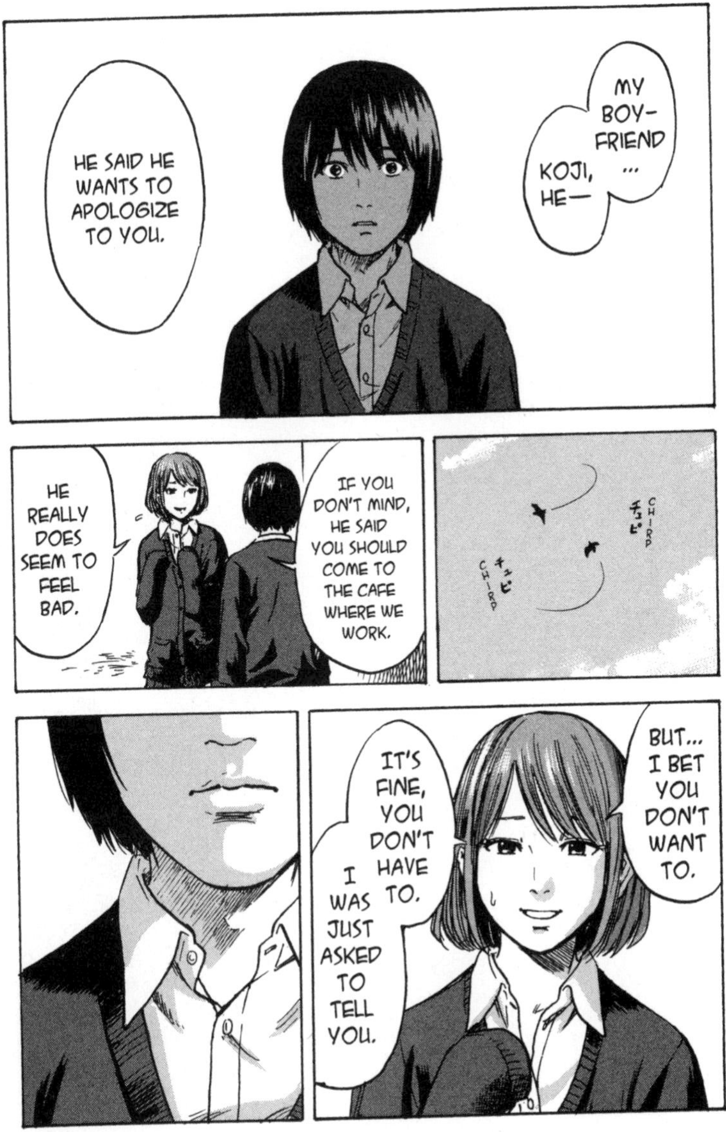
MY BOY-FRIEND ... KOJI, HE—
HE SAID HE WANTS TO APOLOGIZE TO YOU.
チュピ CHIRP
チュピ CHIRP
IF YOU DON'T MIND, HE SAID YOU SHOULD COME TO THE CAFE WHERE WE WORK.
HE REALLY DOES SEEM TO FEEL BAD.
BUT... I BET YOU DON'T WANT TO.
IT'S FINE, YOU DON'T HAVE TO.
I WAS JUST ASKED TO TELL YOU.

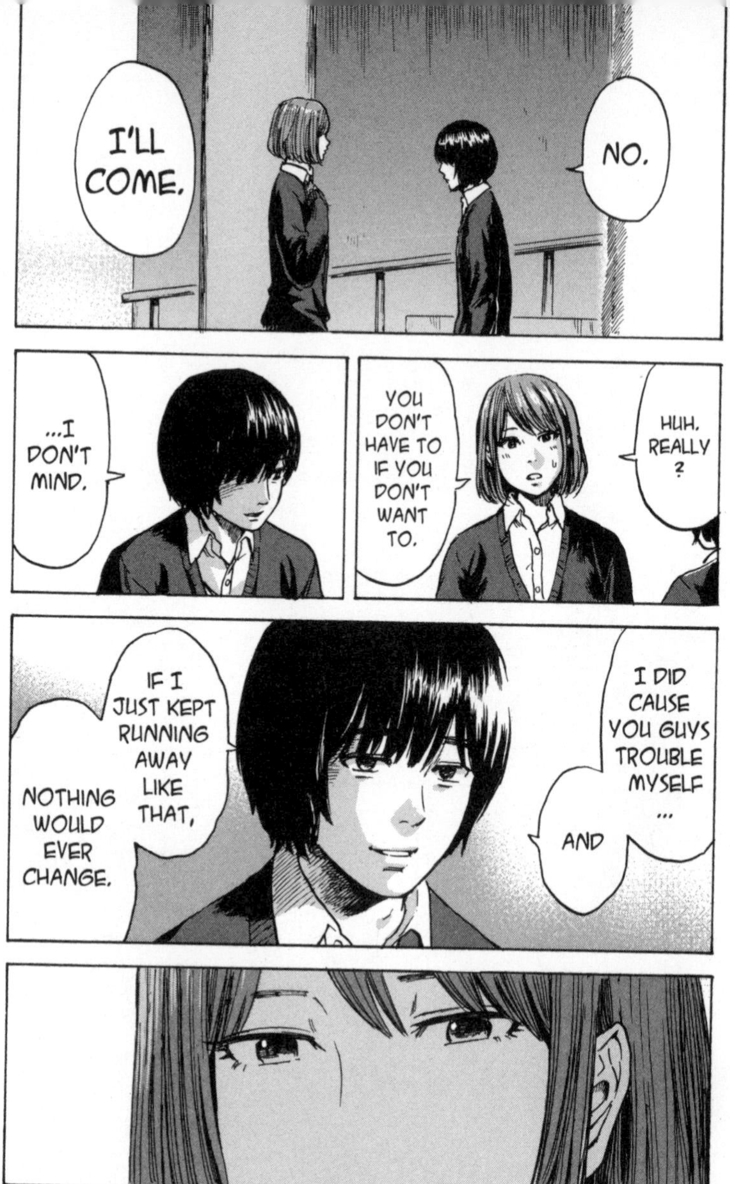
NO.
I'LL COME.
HUH, REALLY?
YOU DON'T HAVE TO IF YOU DON'T WANT TO.
...I DON'T MIND.
I DID CAUSE YOU GUYS TROUBLE MYSELF... AND
IF I JUST KEPT RUNNING AWAY LIKE THAT, NOTHING WOULD EVER CHANGE.

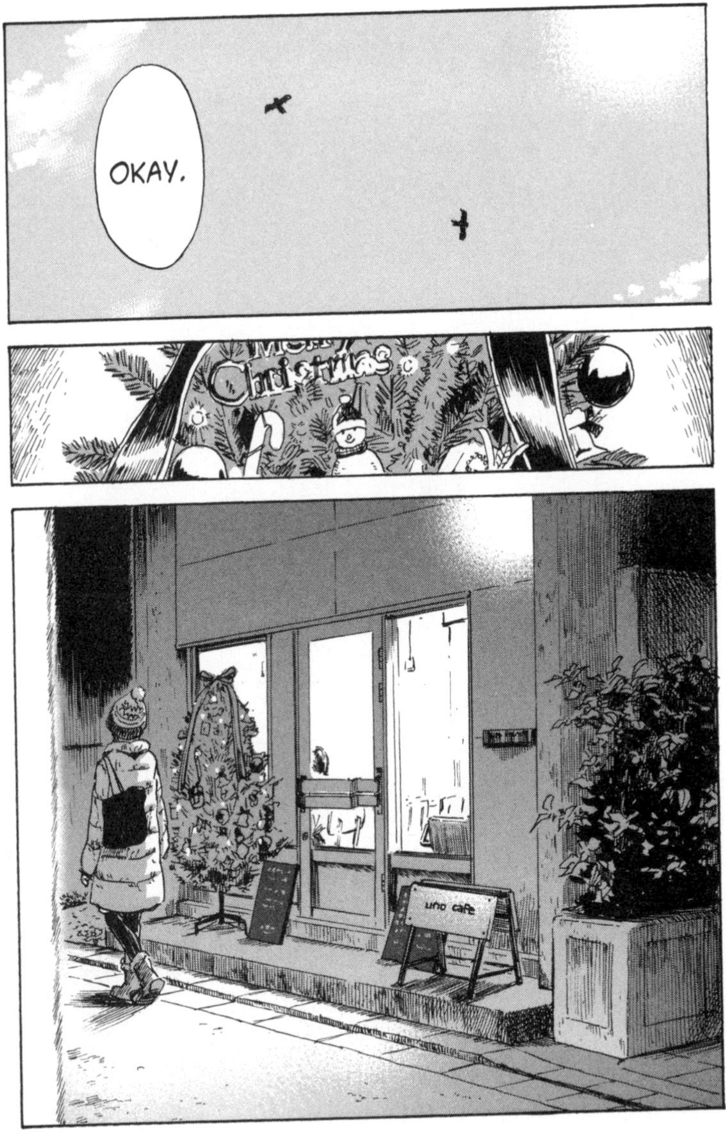
OKAY.
Christmas
uno cafe

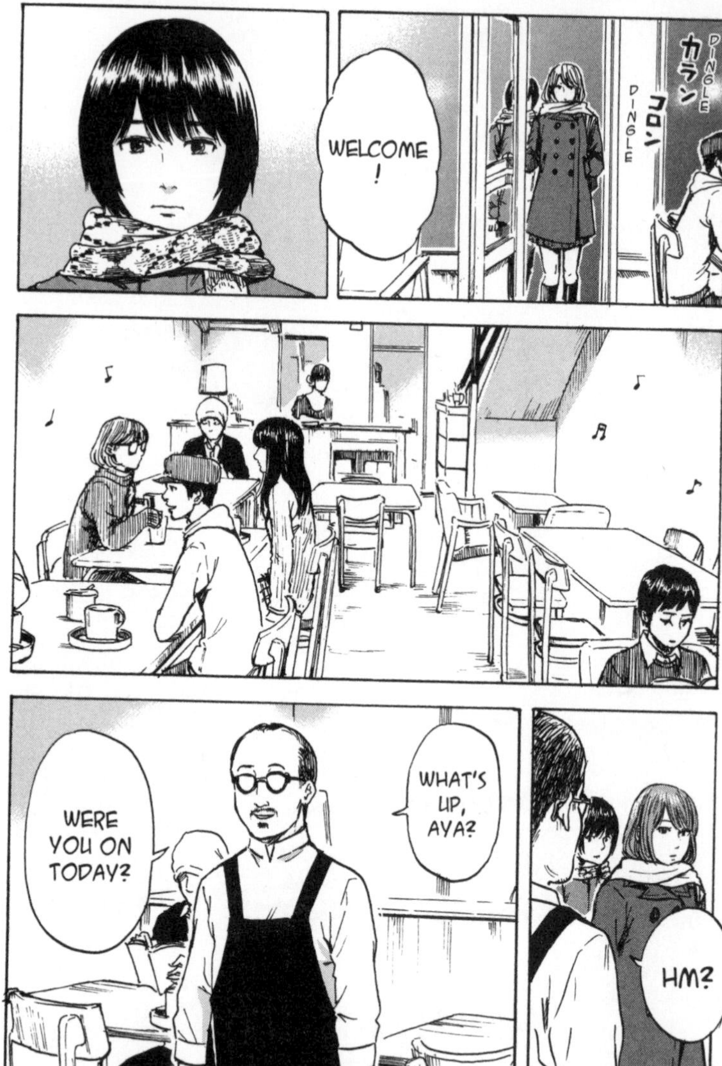
カラン
DINGLE
コロン
DINGLE
WELCOME!
HM?
WHAT'S UP, AYA?
WERE YOU ON TODAY?

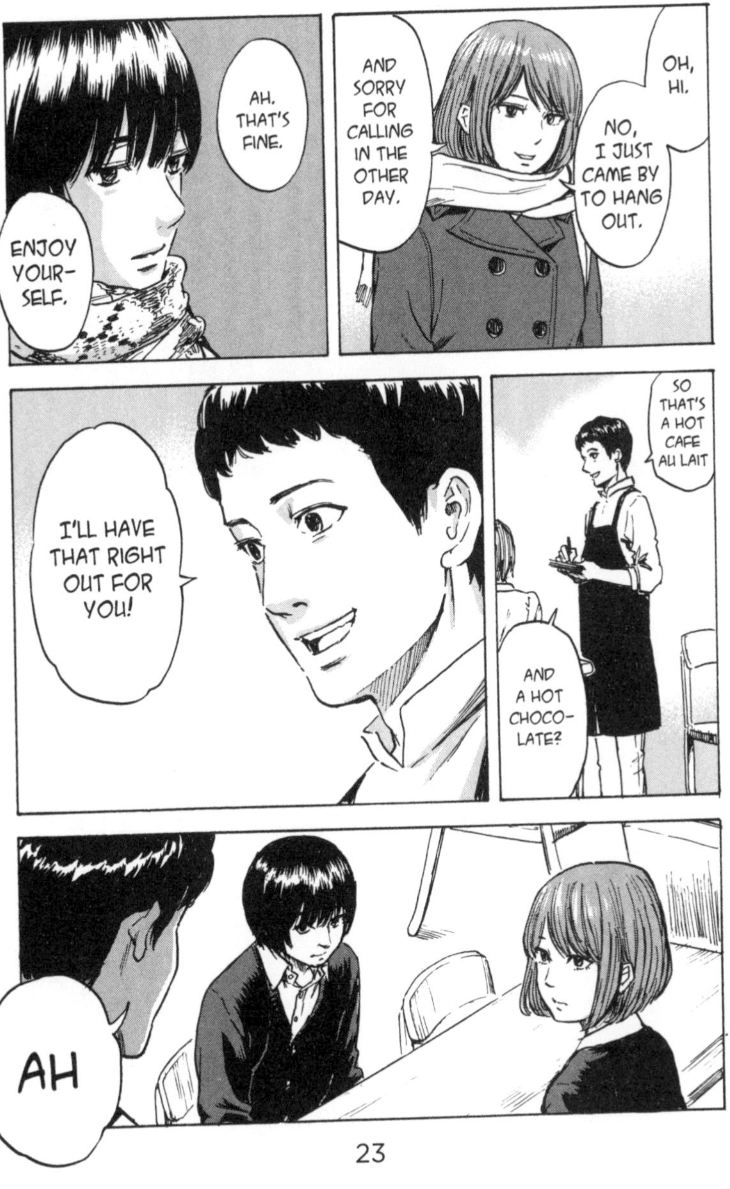
OH, HI.
NO, I JUST CAME BY TO HANG OUT.
AND SORRY FOR CALLING IN THE OTHER DAY.
AH. THAT'S FINE.
ENJOY YOURSELF.
SO THAT'S A HOT CAFE AU LAIT
AND A HOT CHOCOLATE?
I'LL HAVE THAT RIGHT OUT FOR YOU!
AH

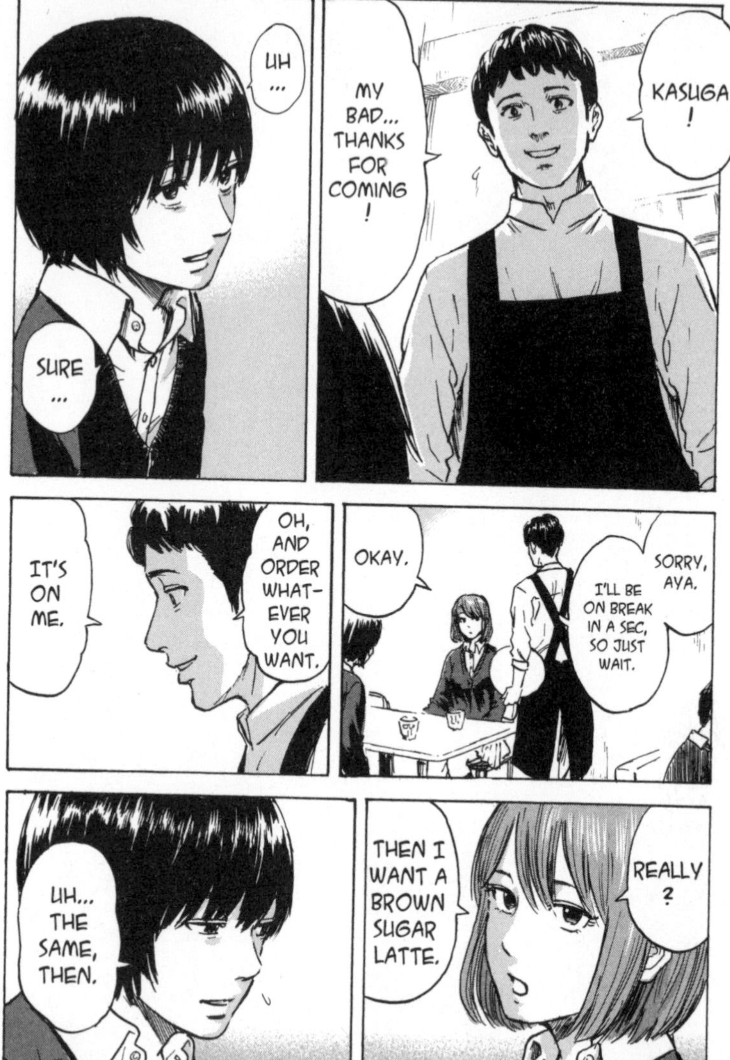
KASUGA!
MY BAD... THANKS FOR COMING!
UH...
SURE...
SORRY, AYA.
I'LL BE ON BREAK IN A SEC, SO JUST WAIT.
OKAY.
OH, AND ORDER WHAT-EVER YOU WANT.
IT'S ON ME.
REALLY?
THEN I WANT A BROWN SUGAR LATTE.
UH... THE SAME, THEN.

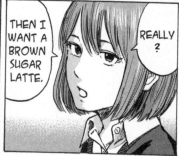

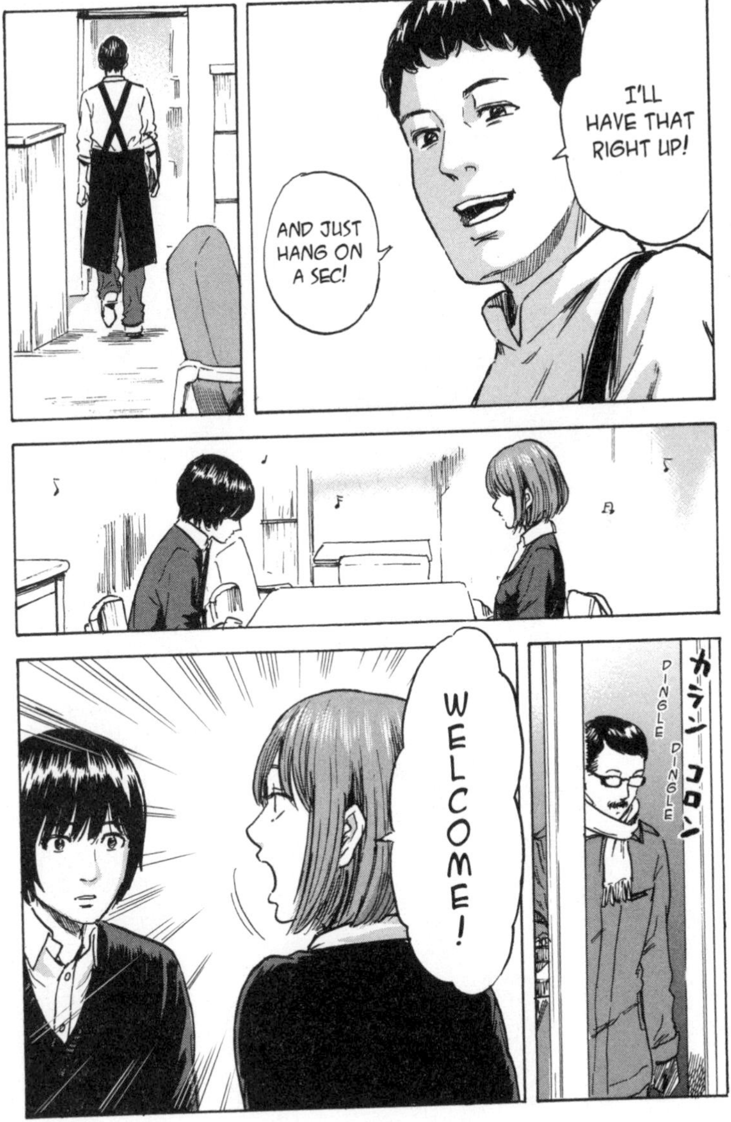
I'LL HAVE THAT RIGHT UP!
AND JUST HANG ON A SEC!
カラン コロン
DINGLE DINGLE
WELCOME!

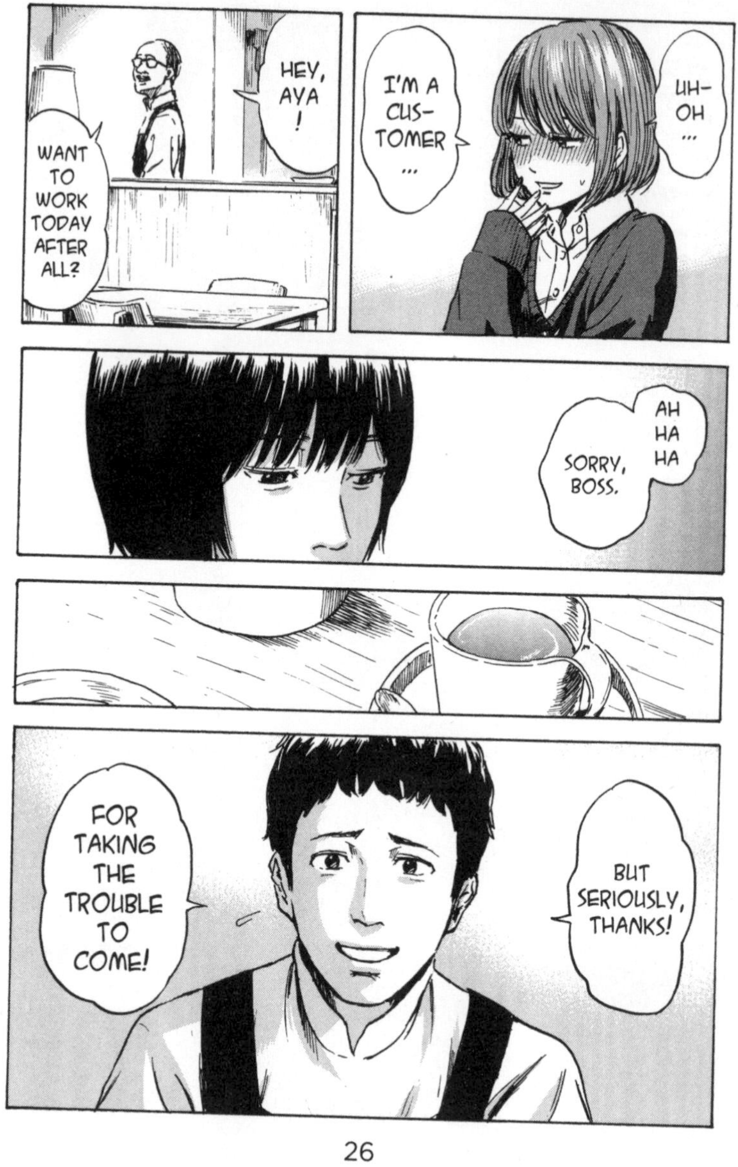
UH-OH ...
I'M A CUS-TOMER ...
HEY, AYA!
WANT TO WORK TODAY AFTER ALL?
AH HA HA
SORRY, BOSS.
BUT SERIOUSLY, THANKS!
FOR TAKING THE TROUBLE TO COME!

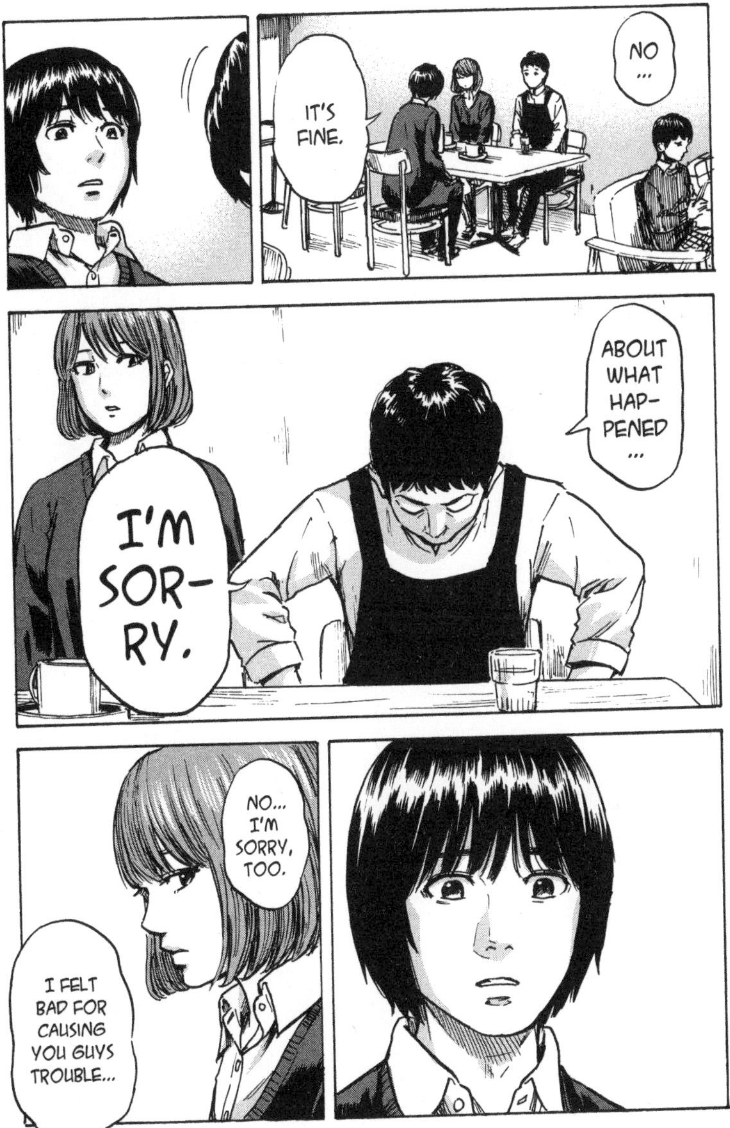
NO ...
IT'S FINE.
ABOUT WHAT HAP-PENED ...
I'M SOR-RY.
NO... I'M SORRY, TOO.
I FELT BAD FOR CAUSING YOU GUYS TROUBLE...

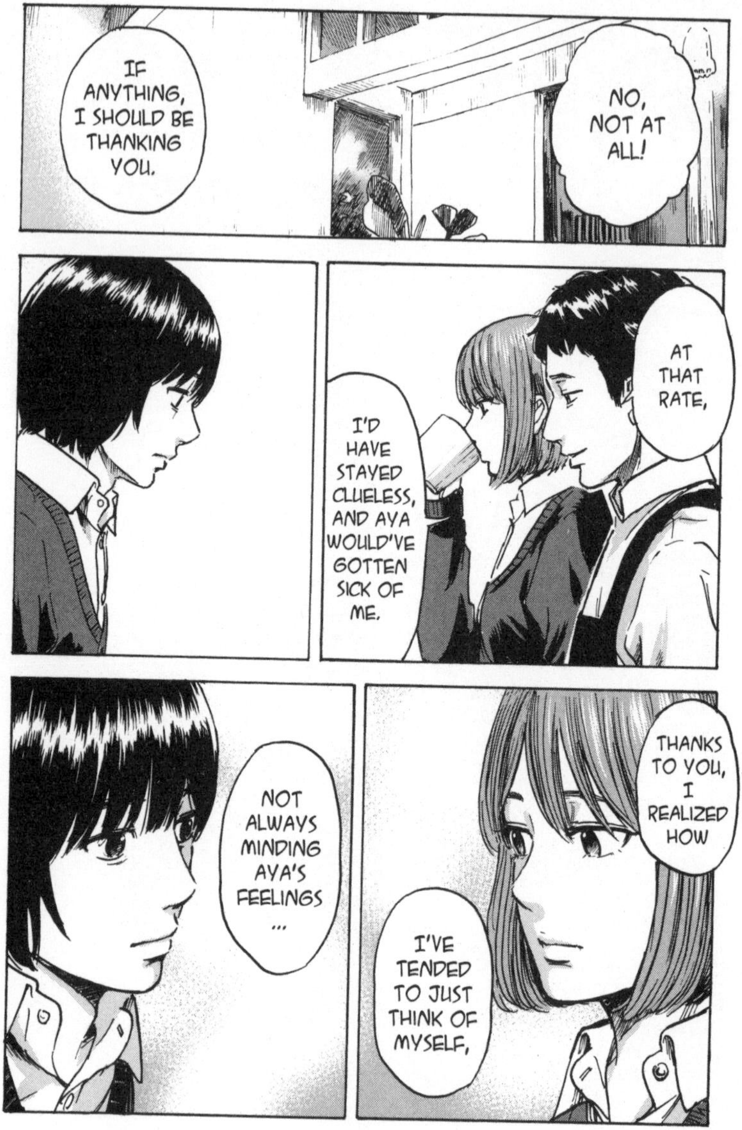
NO, NOT AT ALL!
IF ANYTHING, I SHOULD BE THANKING YOU.
AT THAT RATE,
I'D HAVE STAYED CLUELESS, AND AYA WOULD'VE GOTTEN SICK OF ME.
THANKS TO YOU, I REALIZED HOW
I'VE TENDED TO JUST THINK OF MYSELF,
NOT ALWAYS MINDING AYA'S FEELINGS ...

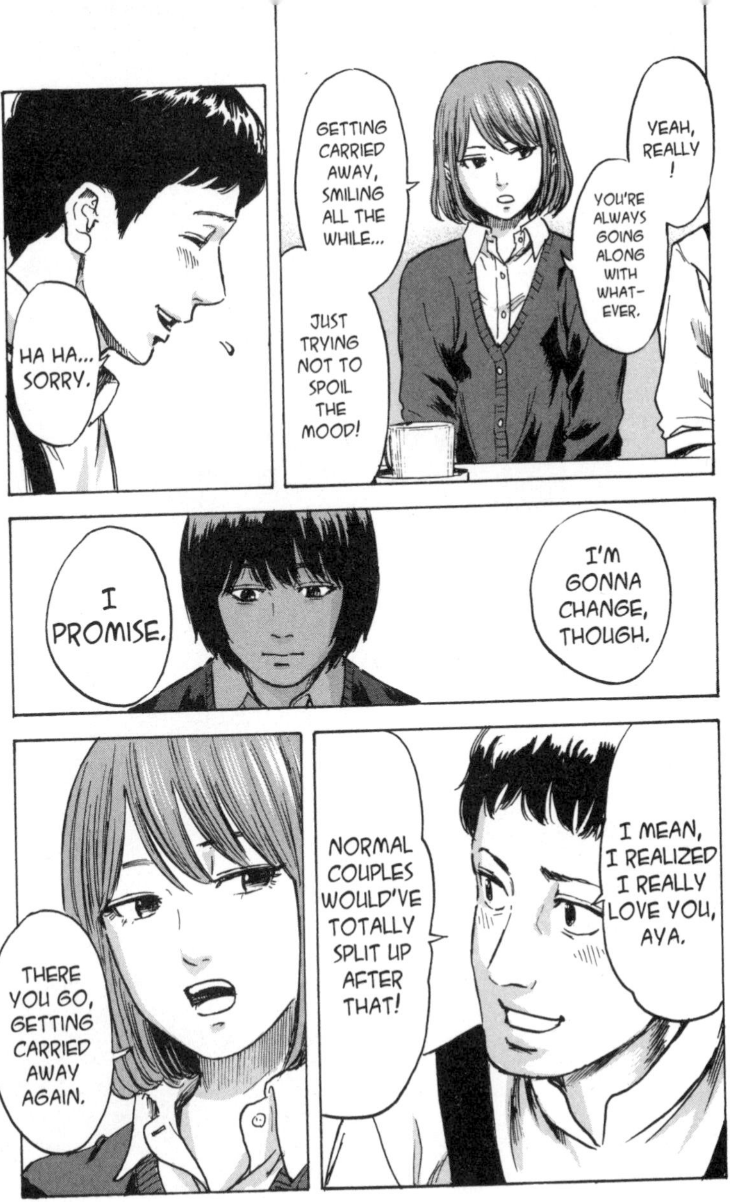
YEAH, REALLY!
YOU'RE ALWAYS GOING ALONG WITH WHAT-EVER.
GETTING CARRIED AWAY, SMILING ALL THE WHILE...
JUST TRYING NOT TO SPOIL THE MOOD!
HA HA... SORRY.
I'M GONNA CHANGE, THOUGH.
I PROMISE.
I MEAN, I REALIZED I REALLY LOVE YOU, AYA.
NORMAL COUPLES WOULD'VE TOTALLY SPLIT UP AFTER THAT!
THERE YOU GO, GETTING CARRIED AWAY AGAIN.

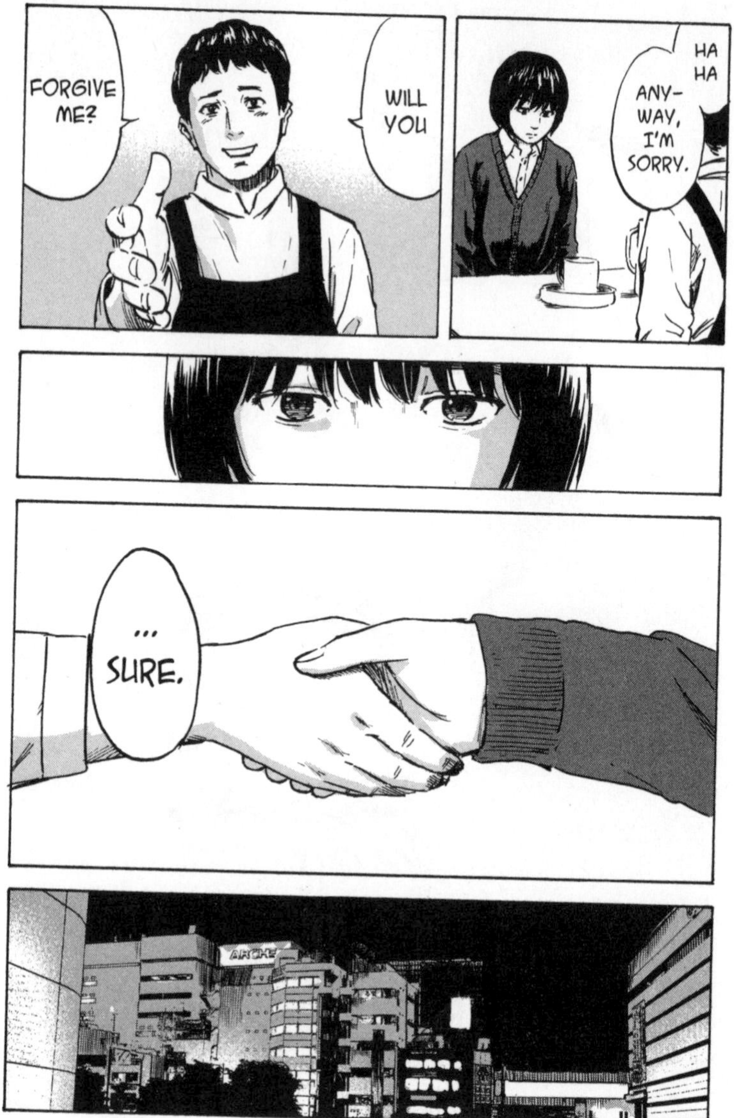
HA HA
ANY-WAY, I'M SORRY.
WILL YOU
FORGIVE ME?
... SURE.

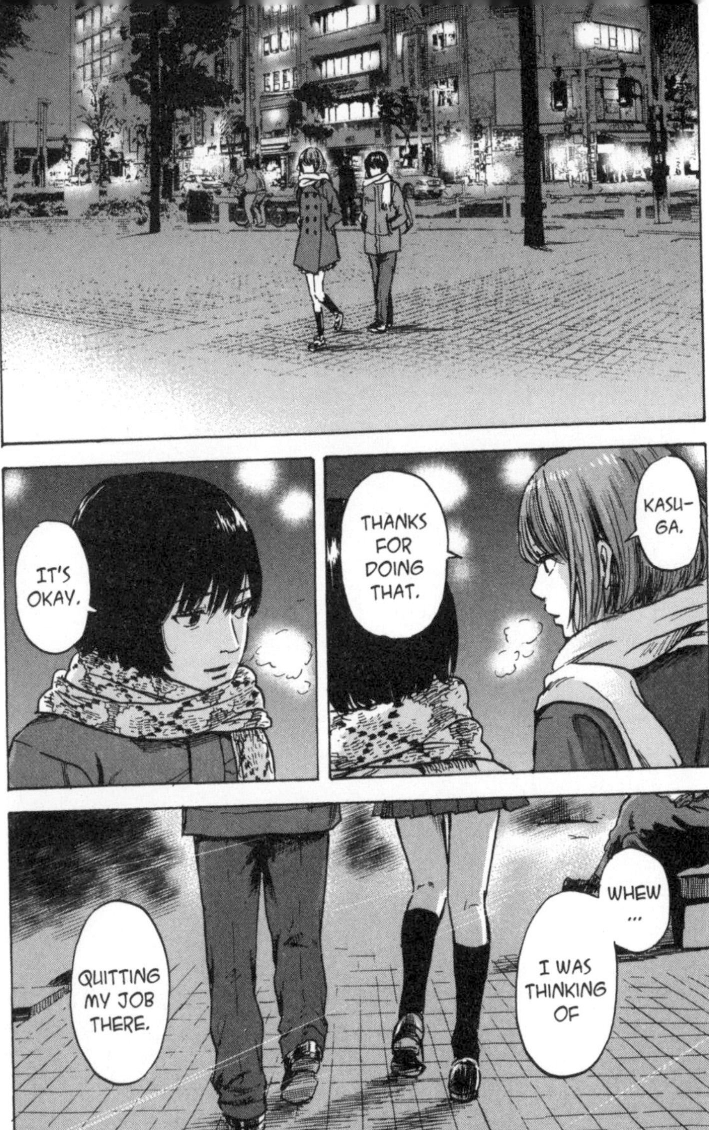
KASU-GA.
THANKS FOR DOING THAT.
IT'S OKAY.
WHEW ...
I WAS THINKING OF
QUITTING MY JOB THERE.

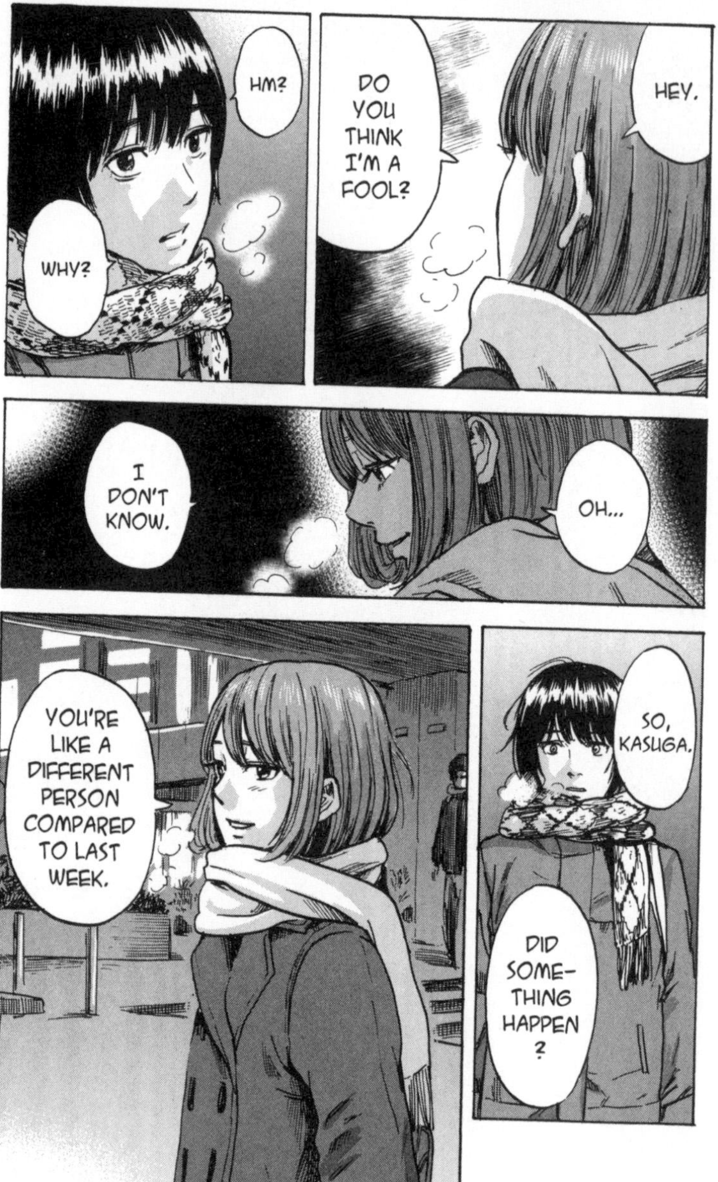
HEY.
DO YOU THINK I'M A FOOL?
HM?
WHY?
OH...
I DON'T KNOW.
SO, KASUGA.
DID SOME-THING HAPPEN?
YOU'RE LIKE A DIFFERENT PERSON COMPARED TO LAST WEEK.

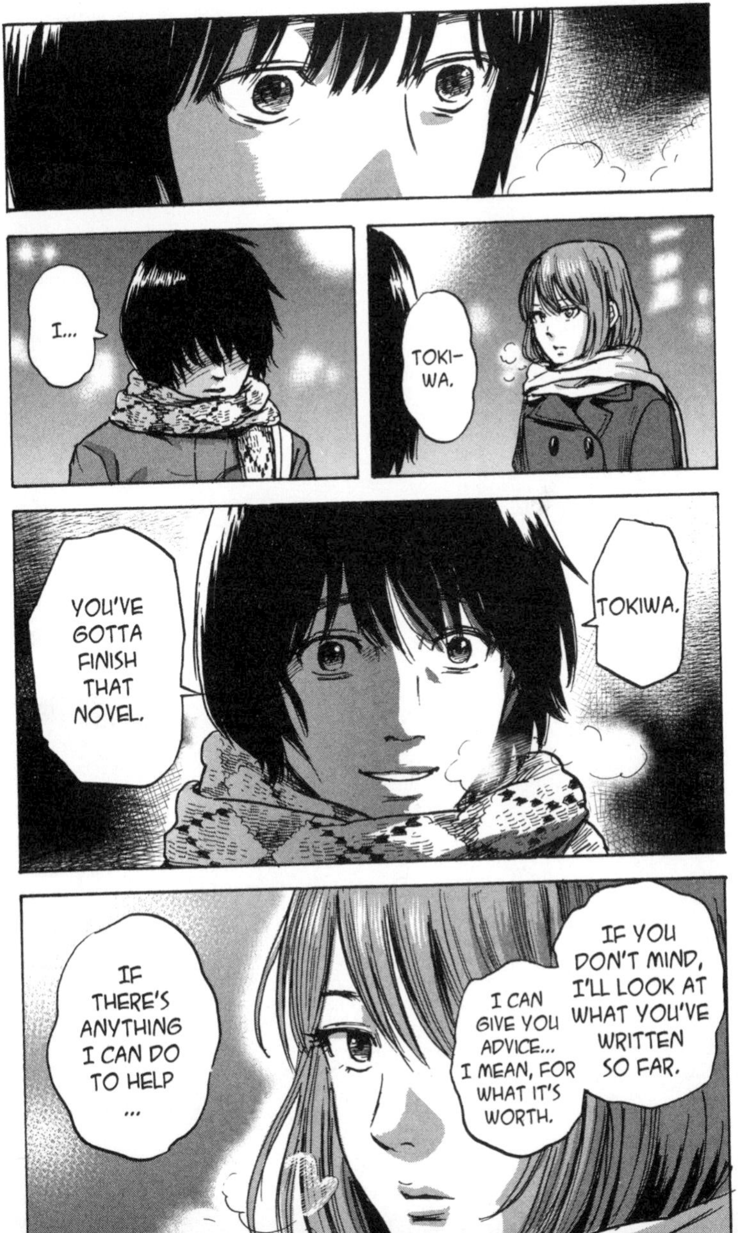
TOKI-WA.
I...
TOKIWA.
YOU'VE GOTTA FINISH THAT NOVEL.
IF YOU DON'T MIND, I'LL LOOK AT WHAT YOU'VE WRITTEN SO FAR.
I CAN GIVE YOU ADVICE... I MEAN, FOR WHAT IT'S WORTH.
IF THERE'S ANYTHING I CAN DO TO HELP ...

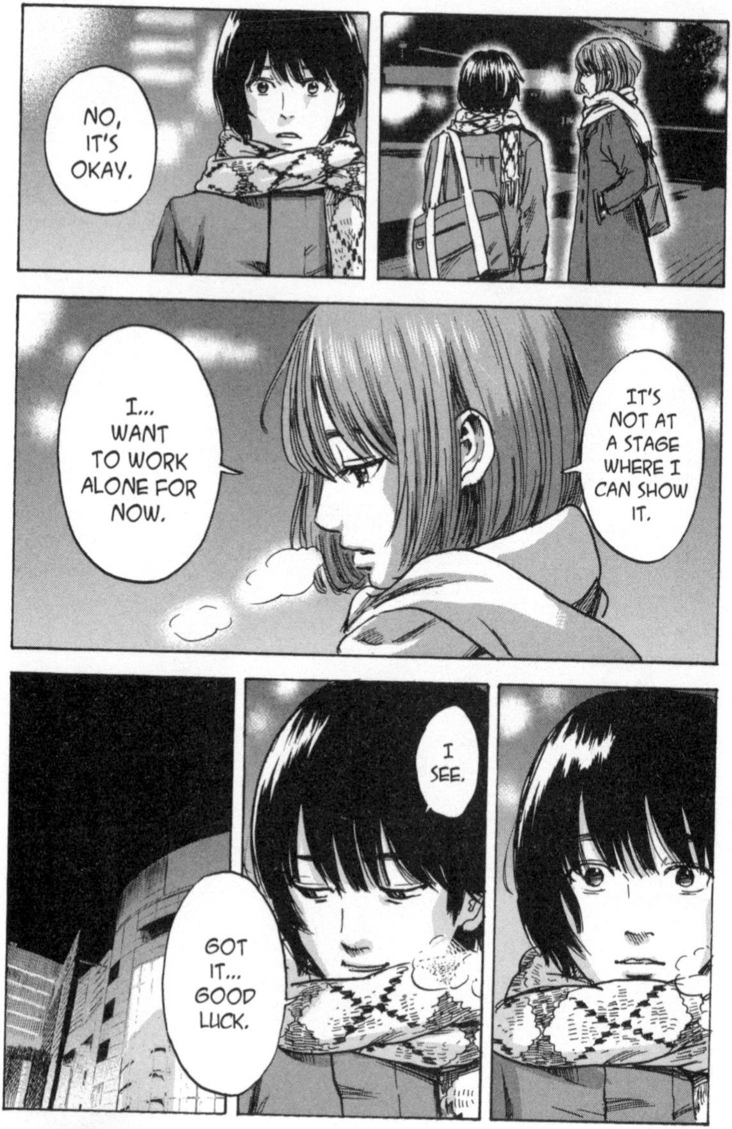
NO, IT'S OKAY.
IT'S NOT AT A STAGE WHERE I CAN SHOW IT.
I... WANT TO WORK ALONE FOR NOW.
I SEE.
GOT IT... GOOD LUCK.

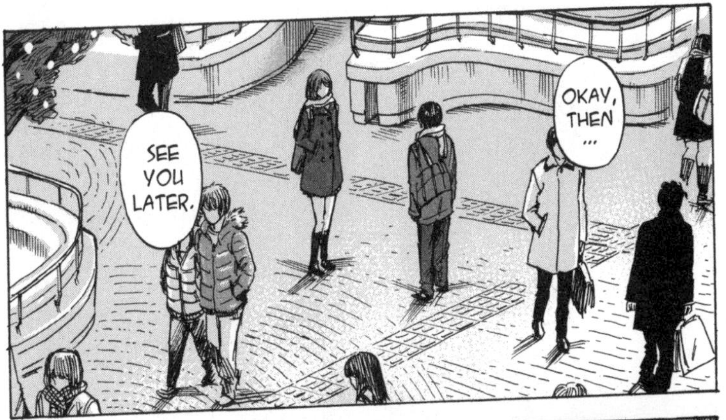
OKAY, THEN ...
SEE YOU LATER.

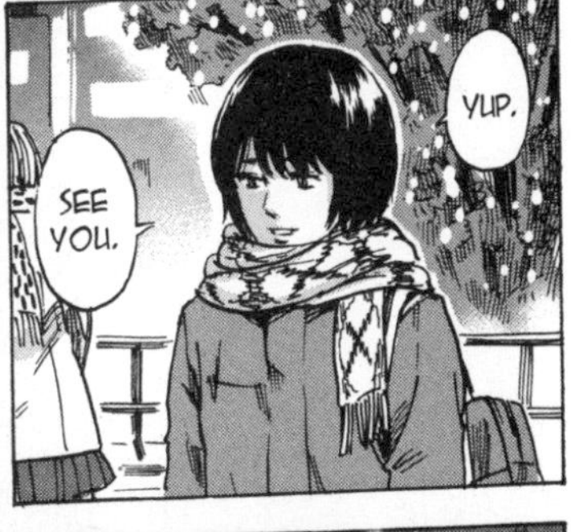
YUP.
SEE YOU.

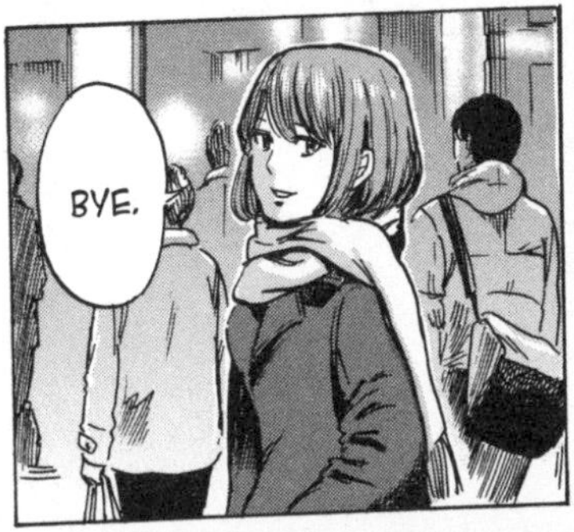
BYE.

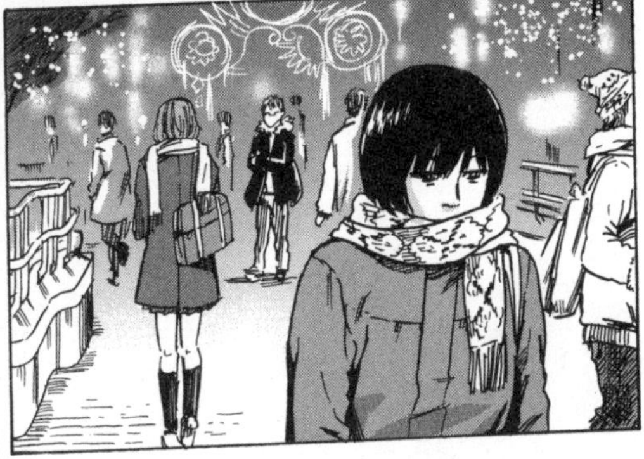

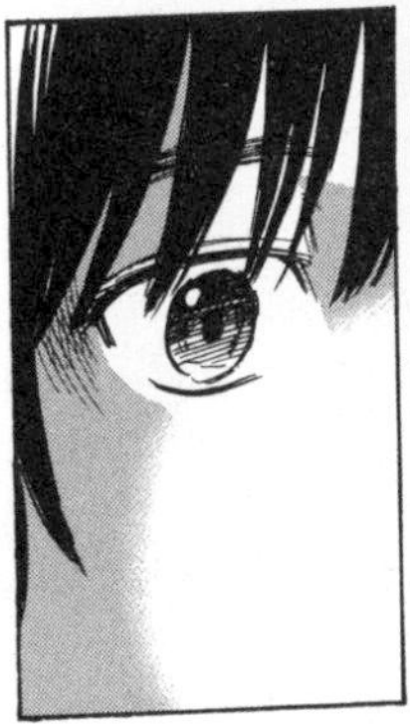

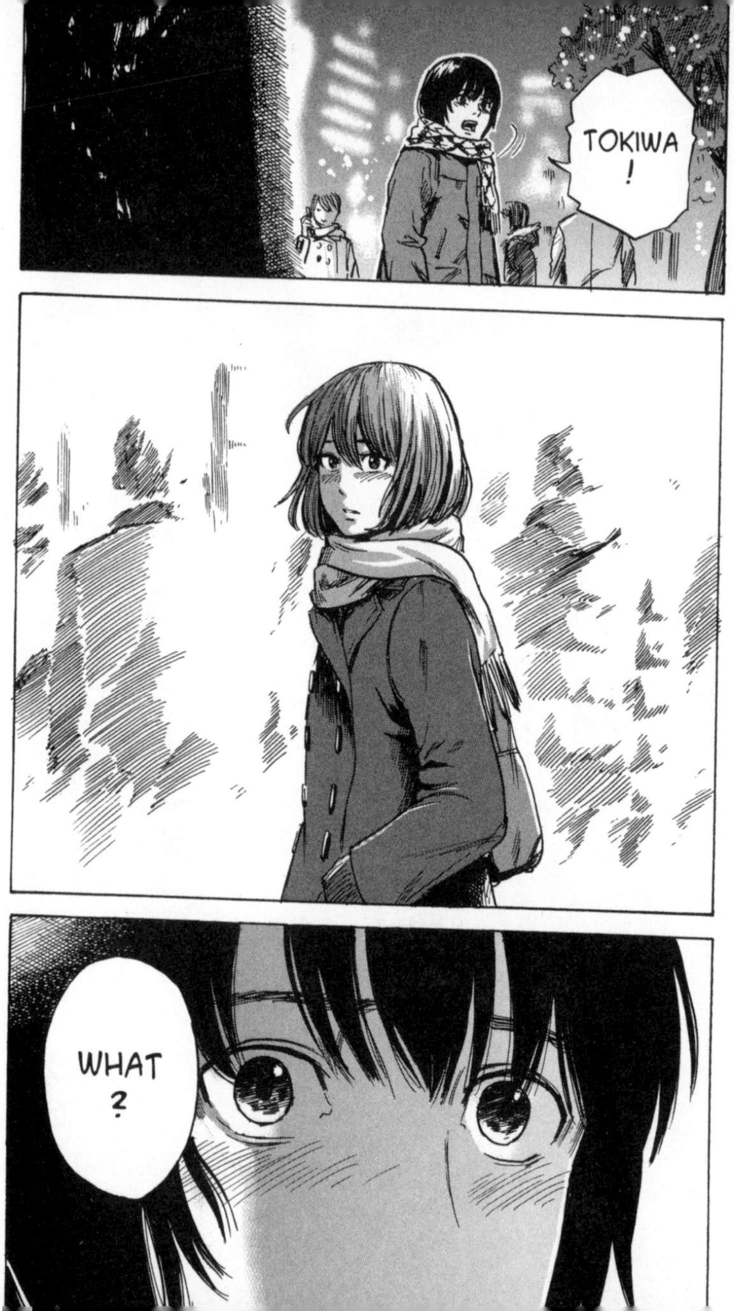
TOKIWA
!
WHAT
?

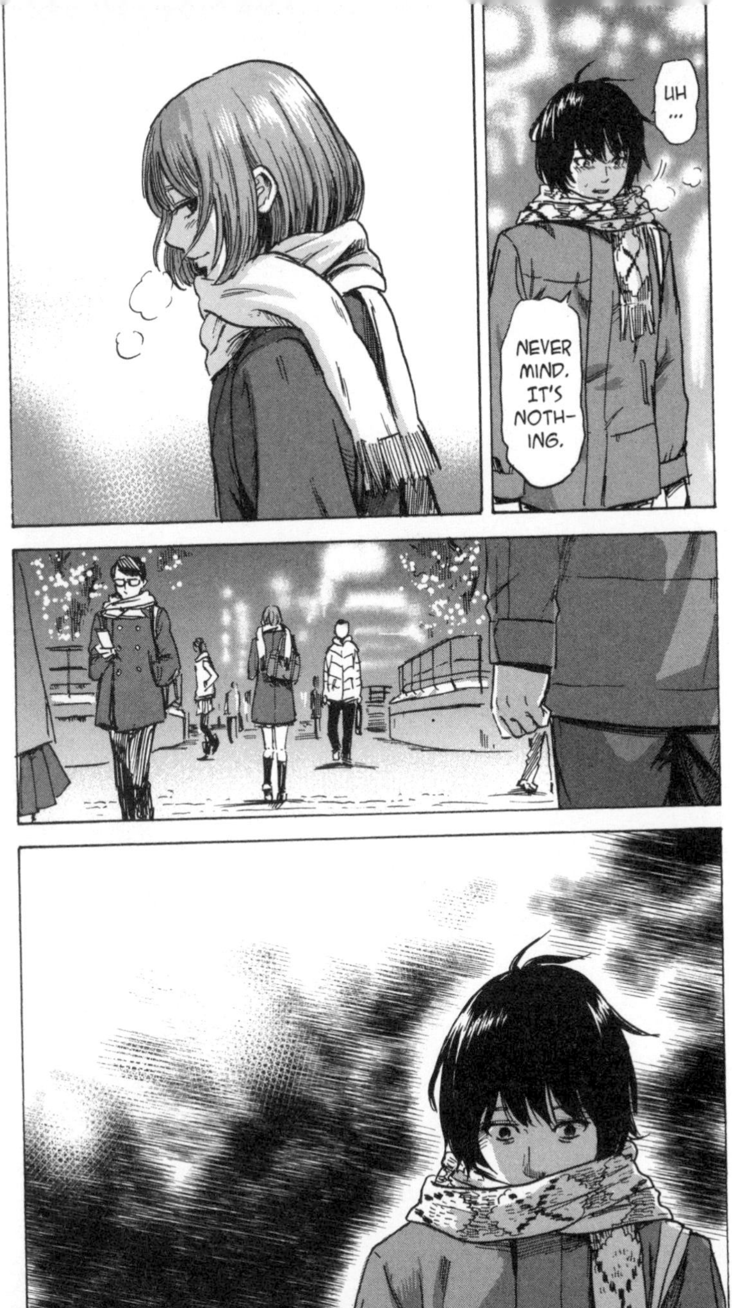
UH ...
NEVER MIND. IT'S NOTHING.

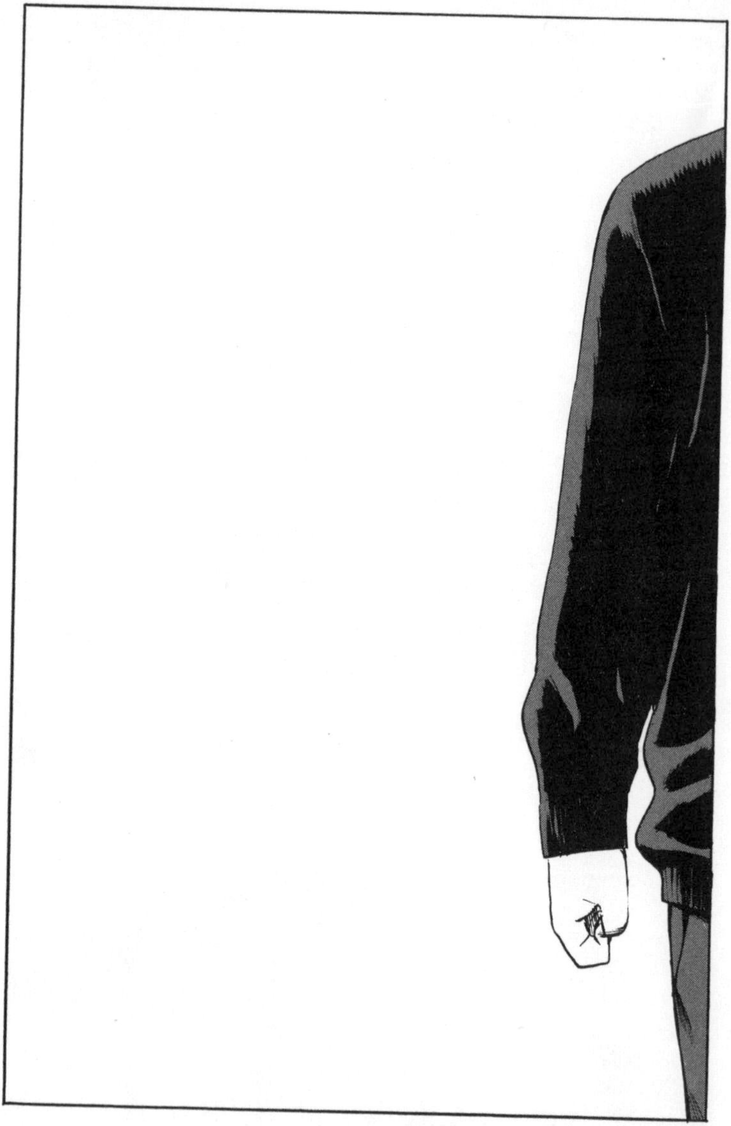

Chapter 44: What My Sinful Heart Seeks

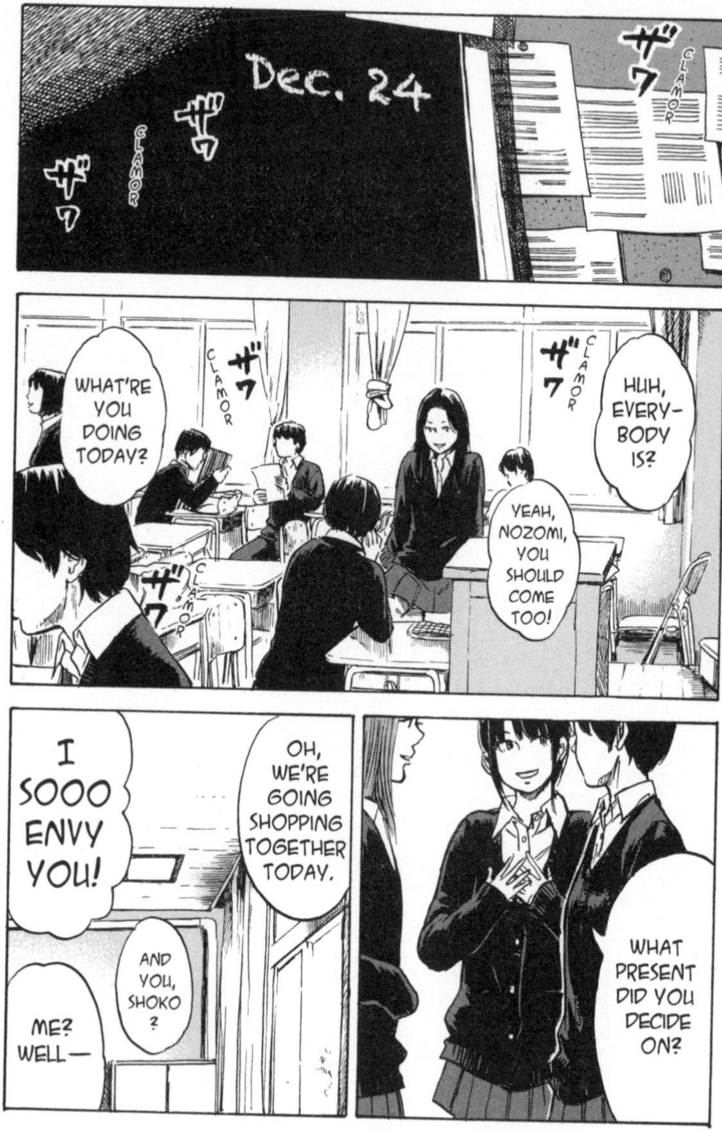
ザワ
CLAMOR
Dec. 24
ザワ
CLAMOR
ザワ
ザワ
CLAMOR
HUH, EVERY-BODY IS?
YEAH, NOZOMI, YOU SHOULD COME TOO!
ザワ
CLAMOR
WHAT'RE YOU DOING TODAY?
ザワ
CLAMOR
WHAT PRESENT DID YOU DECIDE ON?
OH, WE'RE GOING SHOPPING TOGETHER TODAY.
I SOOO ENVY YOU!
AND YOU, SHOKO?
ME? WELL—

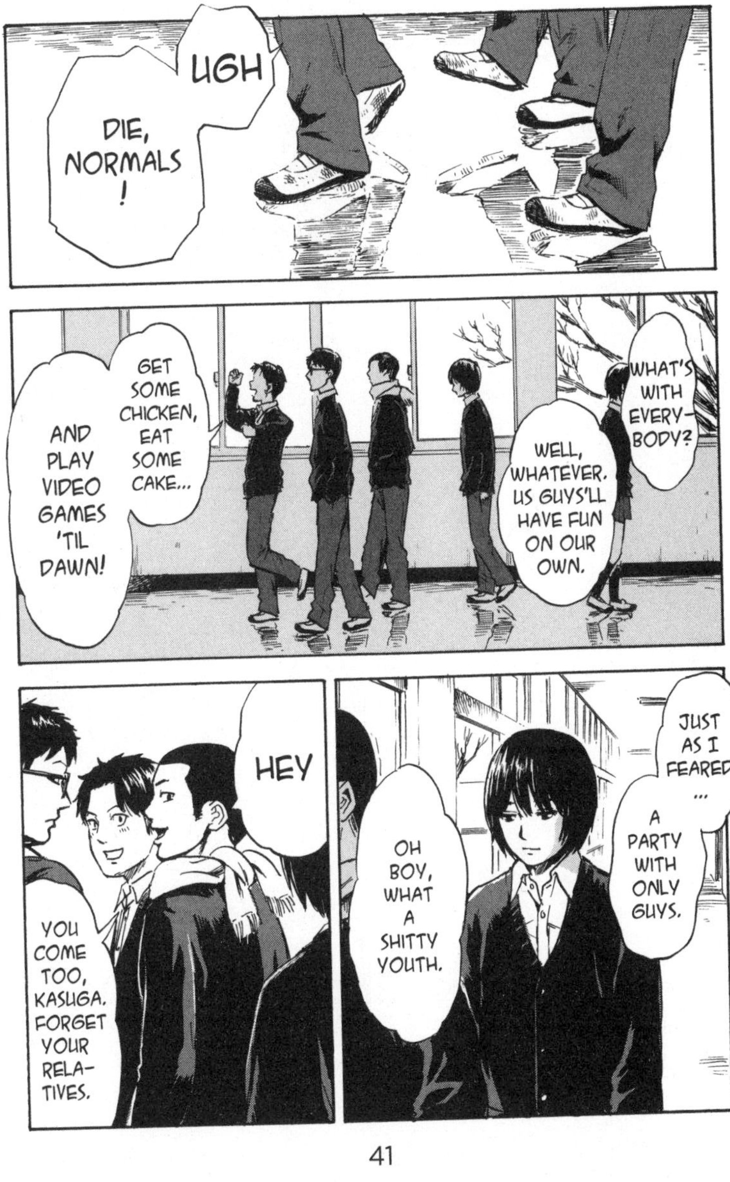
UGH
DIE, NORMALS!
WHAT'S WITH EVERYBODY?
WELL, WHATEVER. US GUYS'LL HAVE FUN ON OUR OWN.
GET SOME CHICKEN, EAT SOME CAKE...
AND PLAY VIDEO GAMES 'TIL DAWN!
JUST AS I FEARED...
A PARTY WITH ONLY GUYS.
OH BOY, WHAT A SHITTY YOUTH.
HEY
YOU COME TOO, KASUGA. FORGET YOUR RELATIVES.

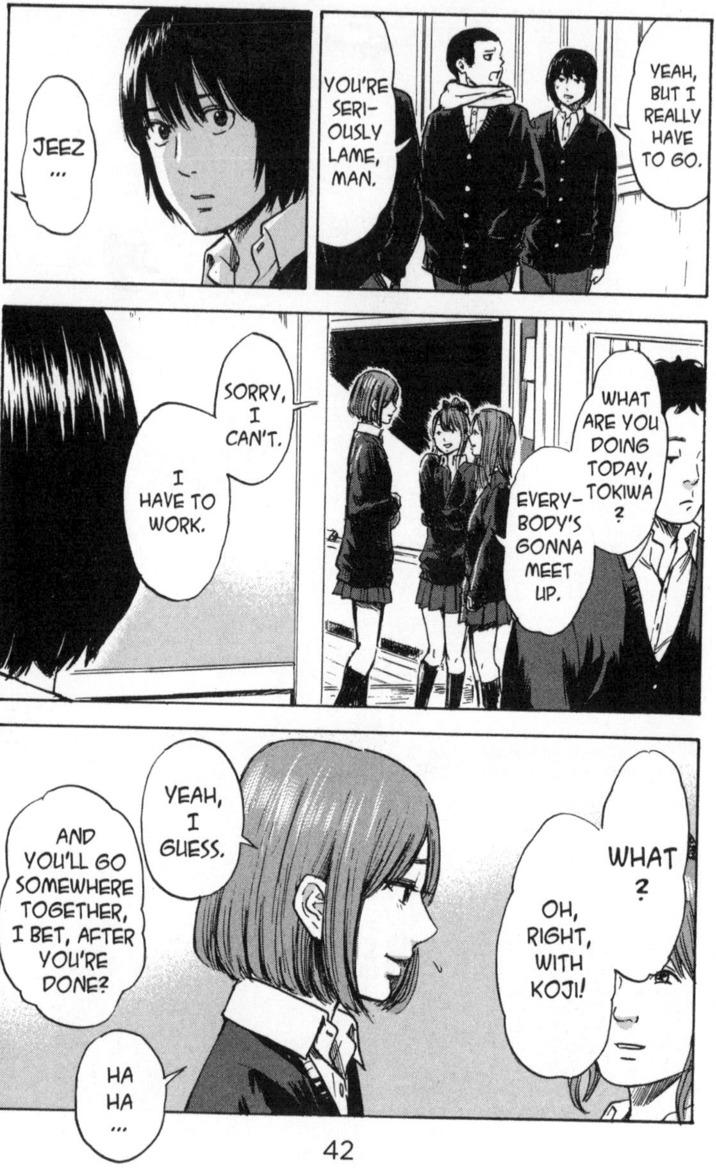
YEAH, BUT I REALLY HAVE TO GO.
YOU'RE SERI-OUSLY LAME, MAN.
JEEZ ...
WHAT ARE YOU DOING TODAY, TOKIWA?
EVERY-BODY'S GONNA MEET UP.
SORRY, I CAN'T.
I HAVE TO WORK.
WHAT?
OH, RIGHT, WITH KOJI!
YEAH, I GUESS.
AND YOU'LL GO SOMEWHERE TOGETHER, I BET, AFTER YOU'RE DONE?
HA HA ...

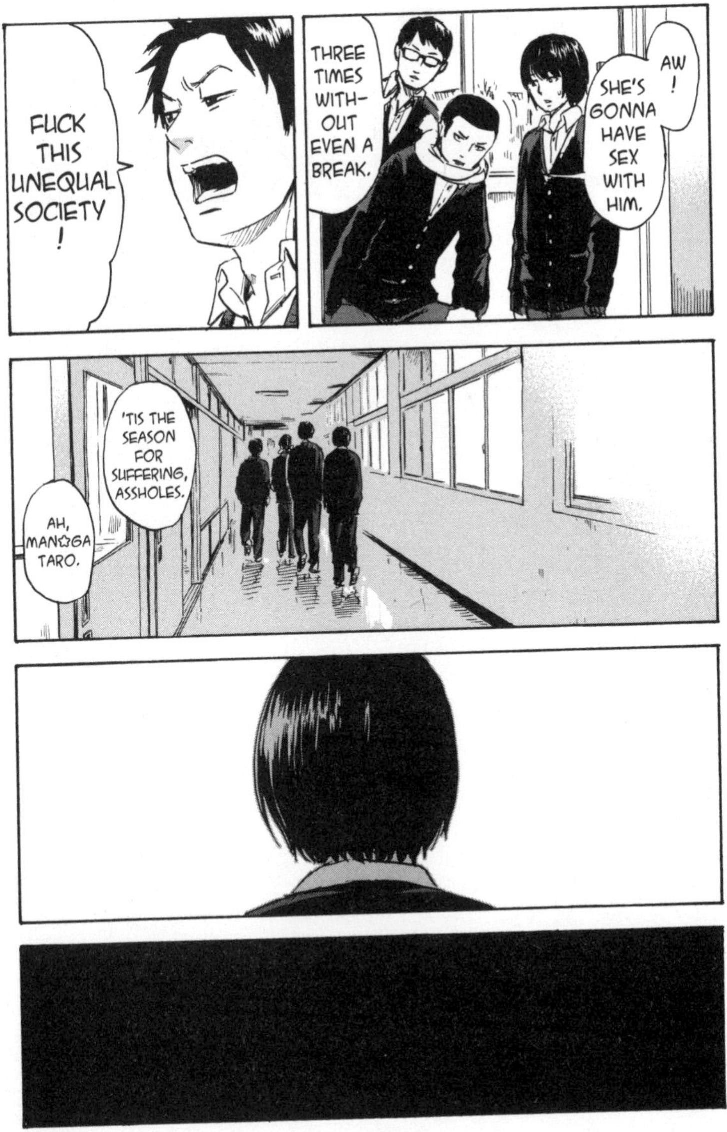
AW! SHE'S GONNA HAVE SEX WITH HIM.
THREE TIMES WITH-OUT EVEN A BREAK.
FUCK THIS UNEQUAL SOCIETY!
'TIS THE SEASON FOR SUFFERING, ASSHOLES.
AH, MAN☆GA TARO.

KAGOYAMA CONDOS. KAGOYAMA CONDOS.
ガオオオ!!
BRRM
まれ
コッ TOK TOK
コッ TOK TOK
コッ TOK

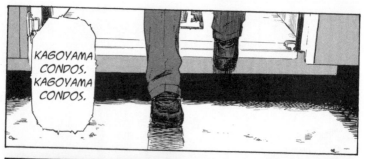

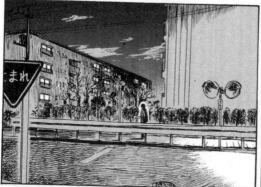

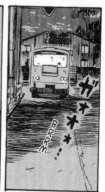

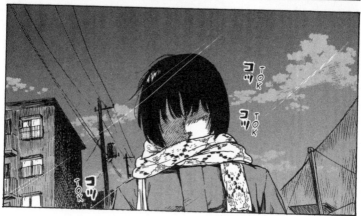

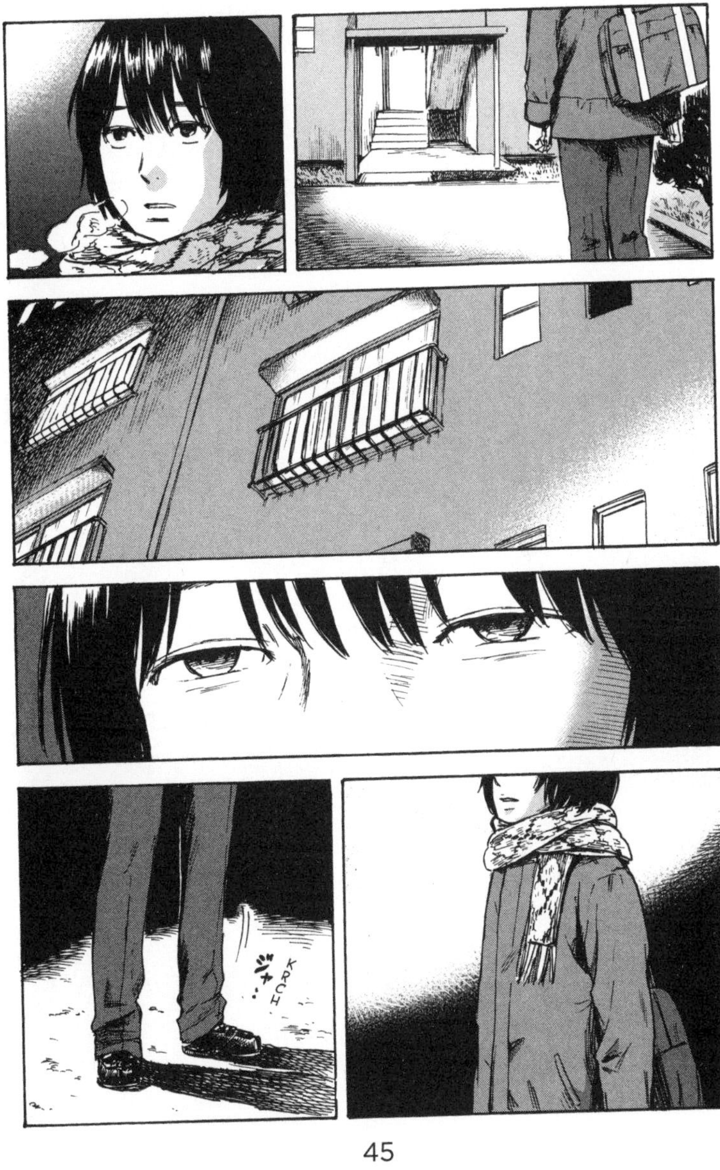
ジャ‥
KRCH

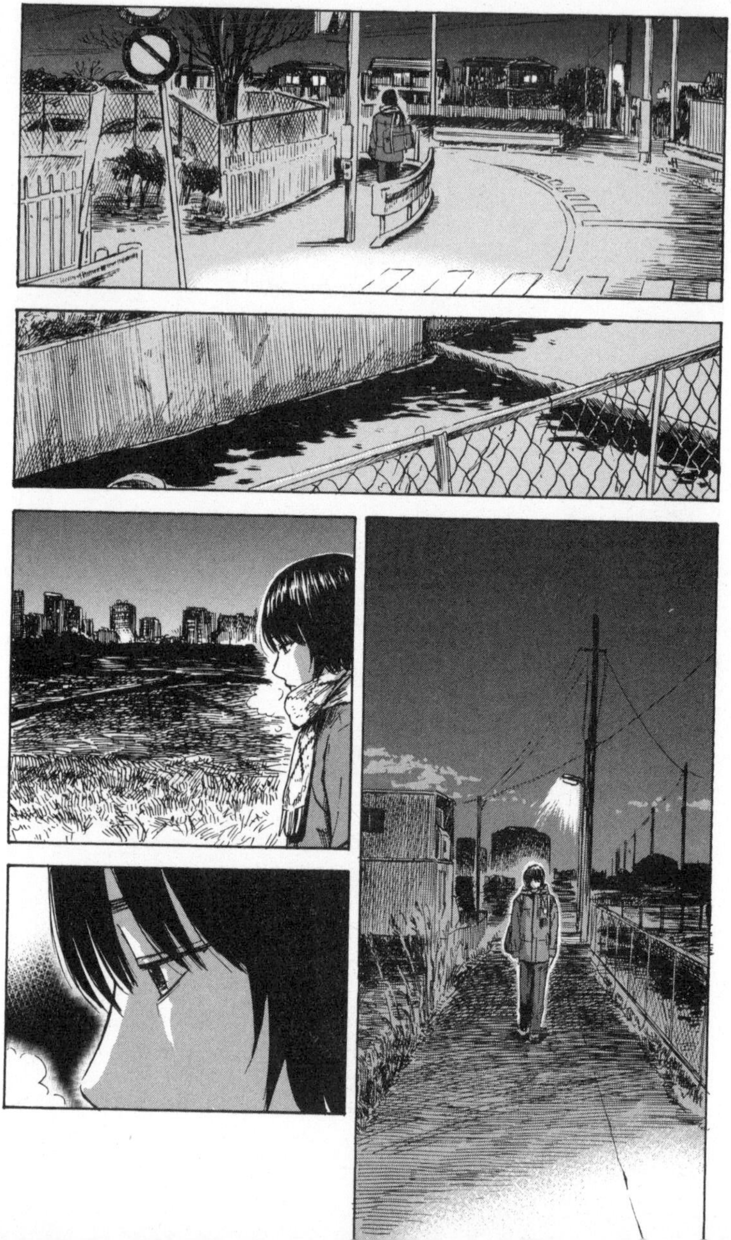

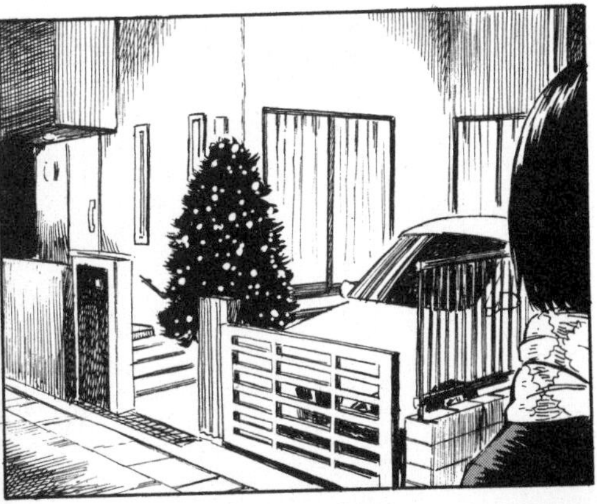

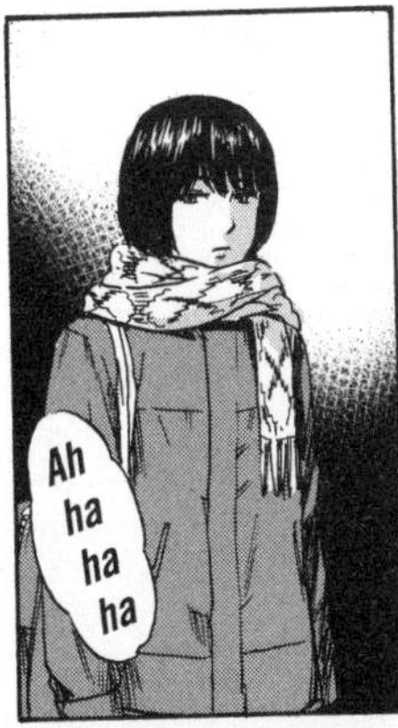
Ah ha ha ha

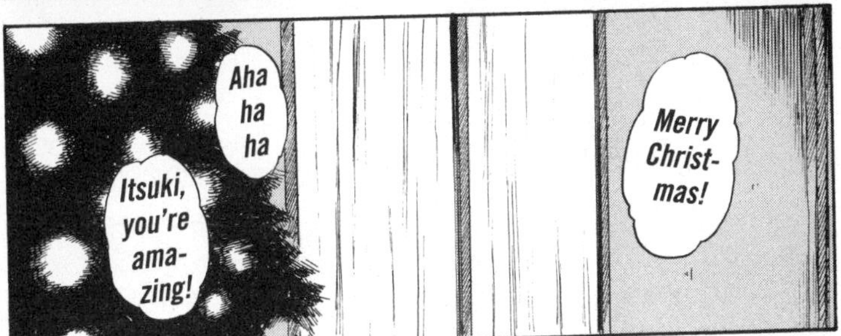
Merry Christmas!
Aha ha ha
Itsuki, you're amazing!

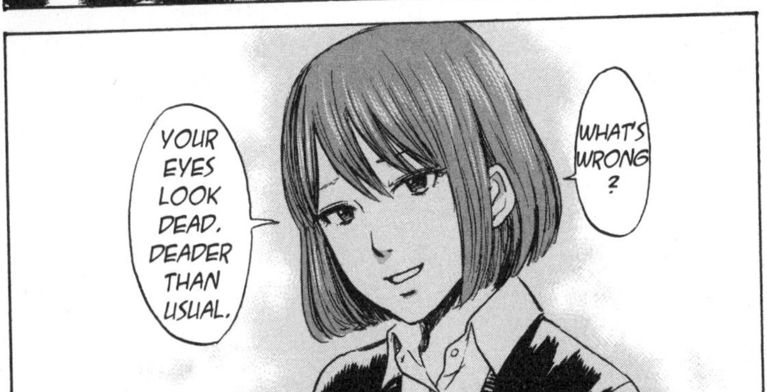
WHAT'S WRONG?
YOUR EYES LOOK DEAD. DEADER THAN USUAL.

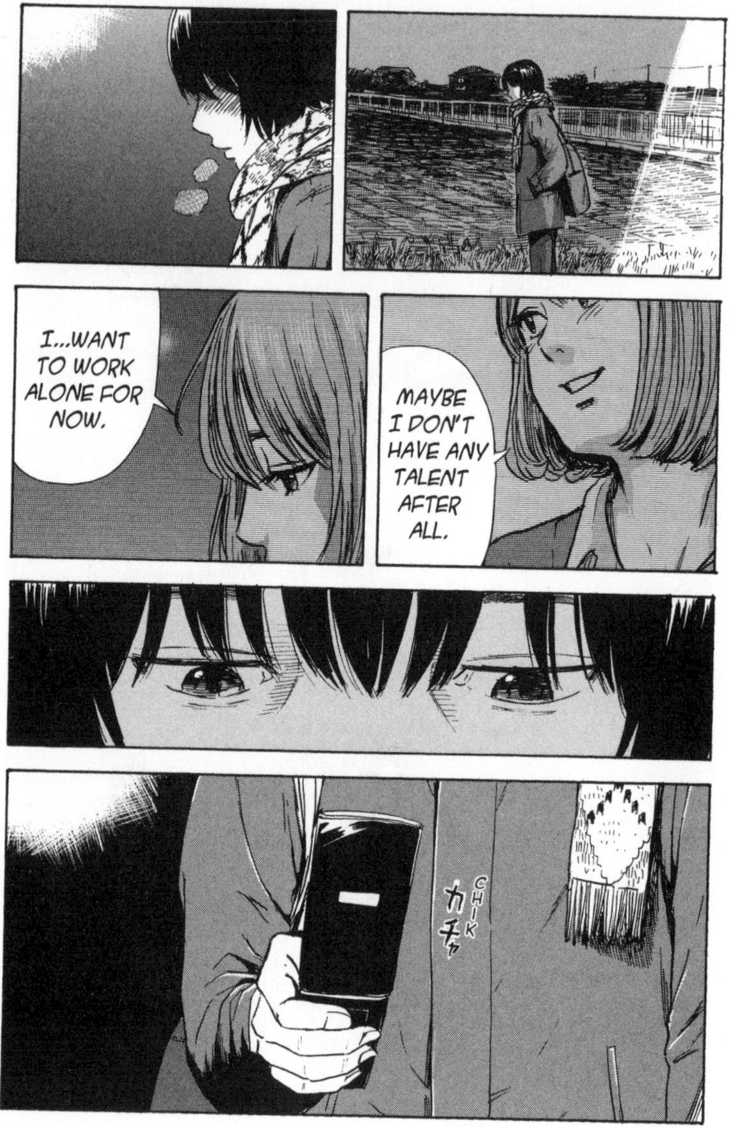
MAYBE I DON'T HAVE ANY TALENT AFTER ALL.
I...WANT TO WORK ALONE FOR NOW.
カチャ
CHIK

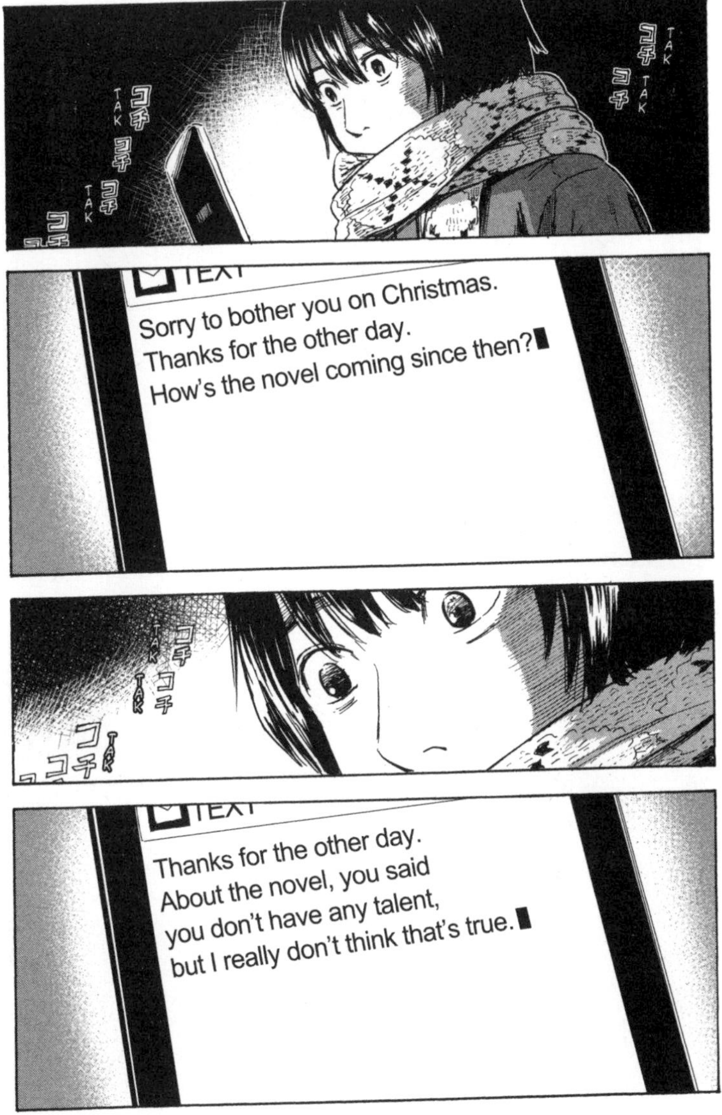
コチ TAK
コチ TAK
コチ TAK
コチ
コチ TAK
コチ
Sorry to bother you on Christmas.
Thanks for the other day.
How's the novel coming since then?
コチ TAK
コチ TAK
コチ TAK
Thanks for the other day.
About the novel, you said
you don't have any talent,
but I really don't think that's true.

WHOOOO

Thanks for the other day.
I don't have any right to say
anything about your novel,
but ■

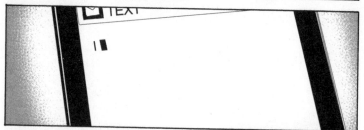

TEXT

I ■

IS SHE
STANDING
IN FOR
NAKAMURA
?

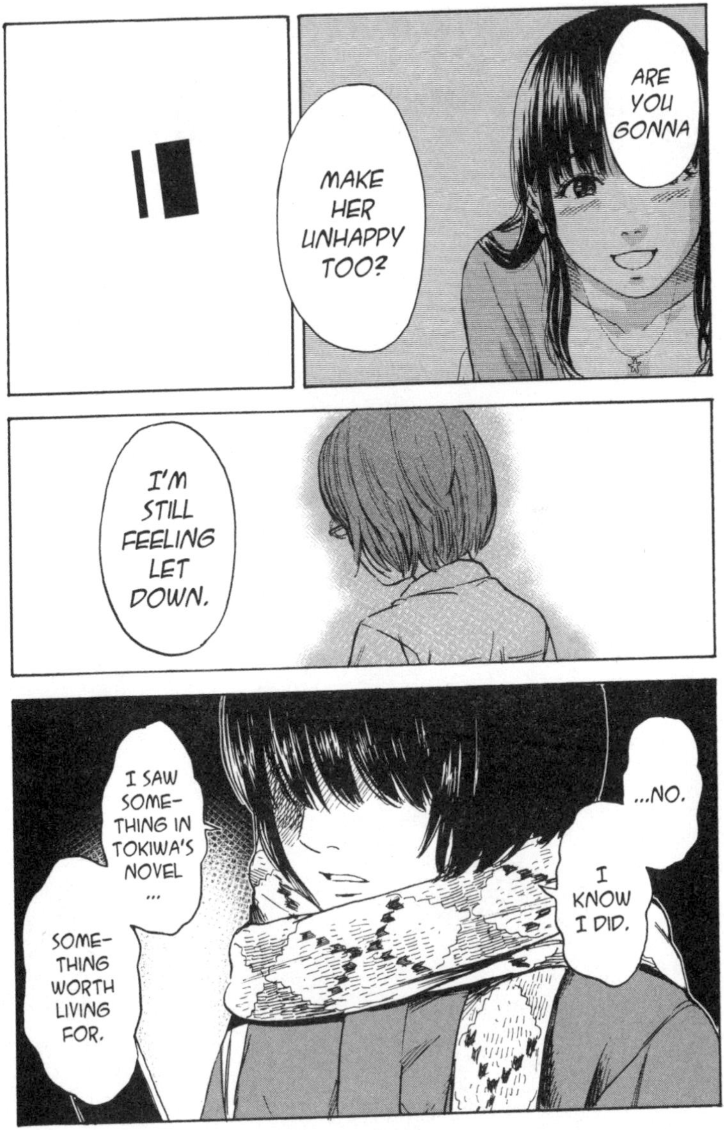
ARE YOU GONNA
MAKE HER UNHAPPY TOO?
I'M STILL FEELING LET DOWN.
...NO.
I KNOW I DID.
I SAW SOME-THING IN TOKIWA'S NOVEL ...
SOME-THING WORTH LIVING FOR.

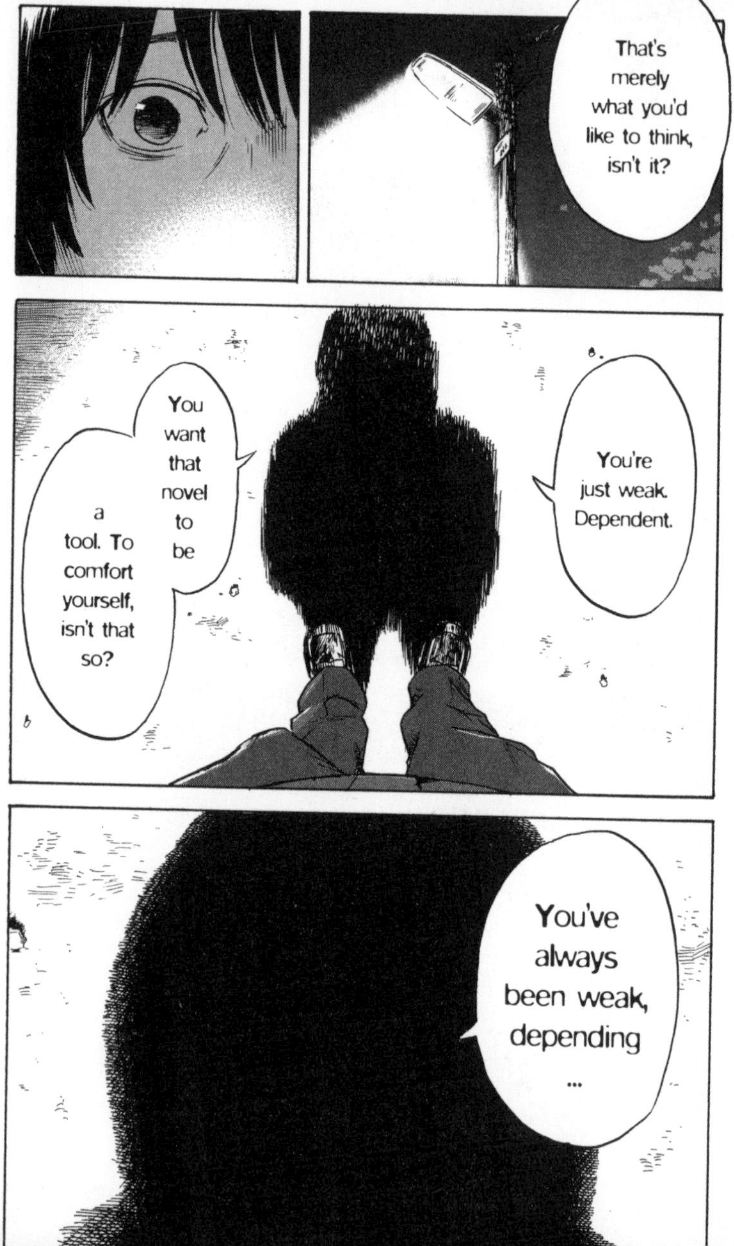
That's merely what you'd like to think, isn't it?
You're just weak. Dependent.
You want that novel to be a tool. To comfort yourself, isn't that so?
You've always been weak, depending ...

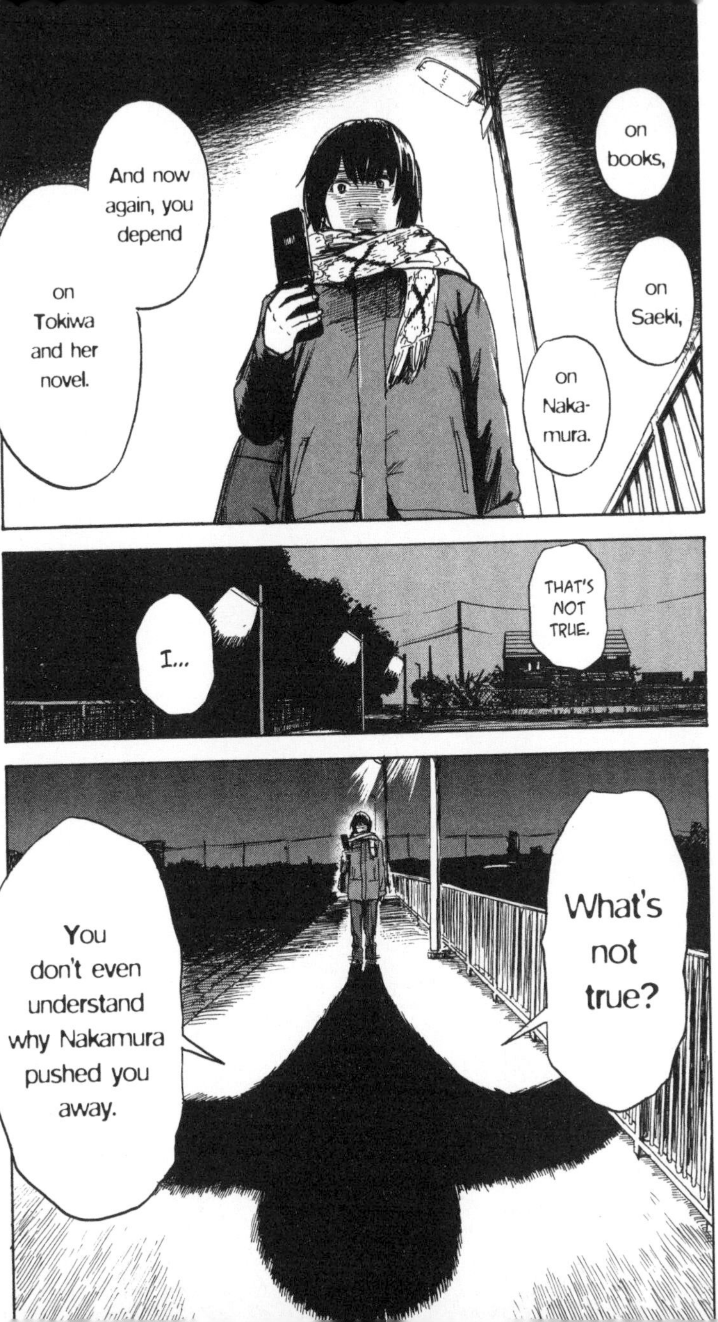
on books,
on Saeki,
on Nakamura.
And now again, you depend
on Tokiwa and her novel.
THAT'S NOT TRUE.
I...
What's not true?
You don't even understand why Nakamura pushed you away.

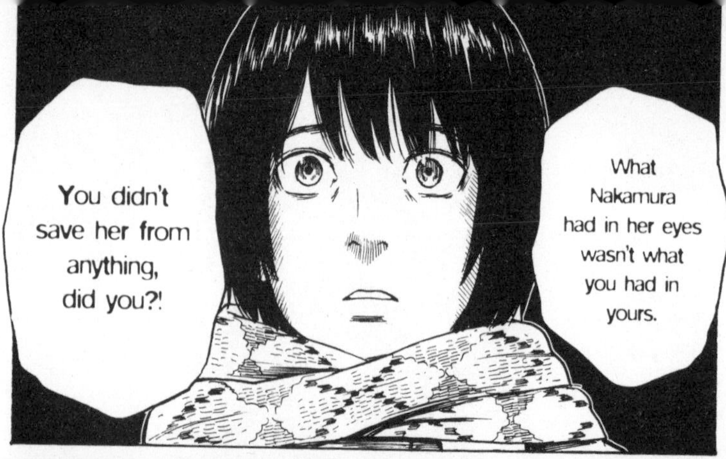
What Nakamura had in her eyes wasn't what you had in yours.
You didn't save her from anything, did you?!

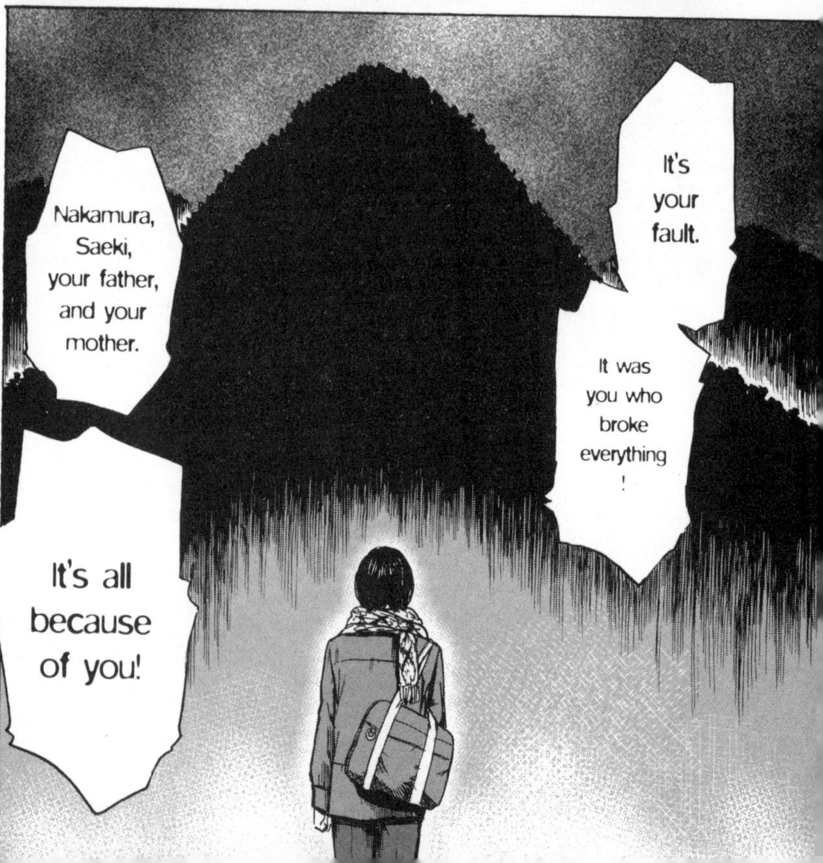
It's your fault.
Nakamura, Saeki, your father, and your mother.
It was you who broke everything!
It's all because of you!

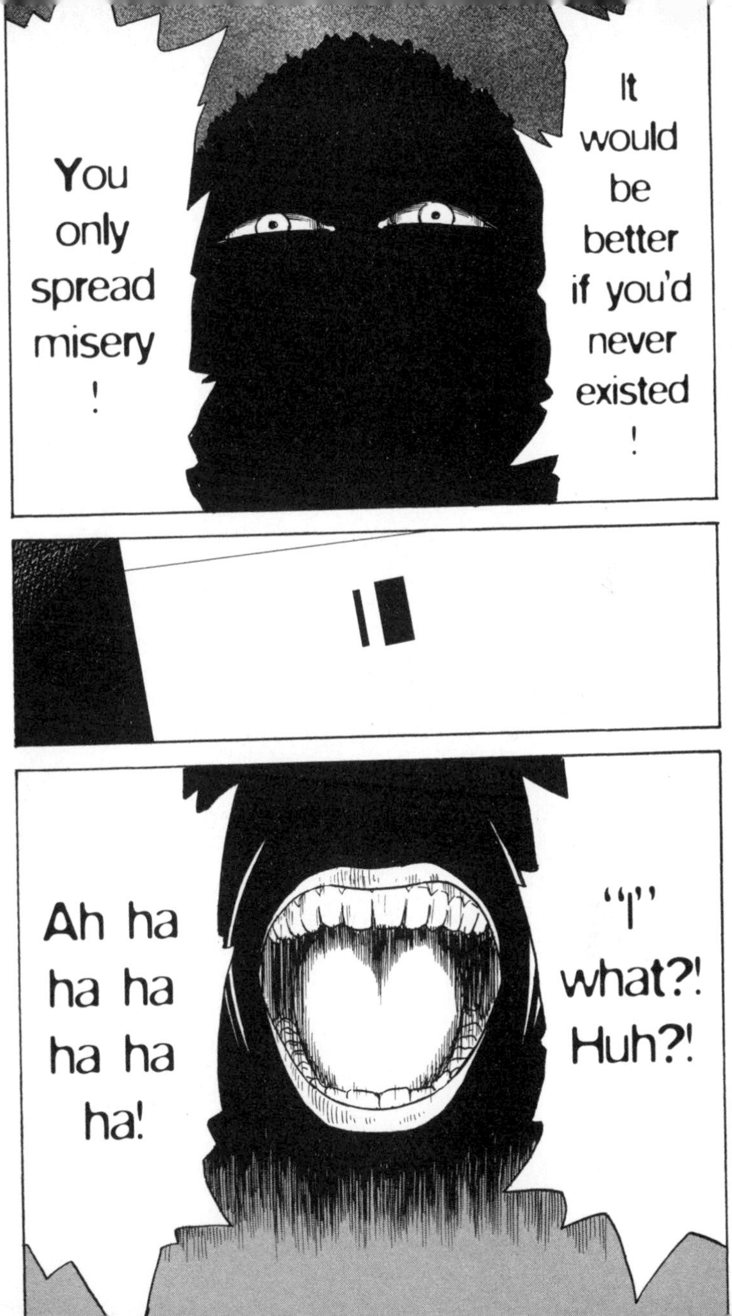

It would be better if you'd never existed!
You only spread misery!
"I" what?! Huh?!
Ah ha ha ha ha ha ha!

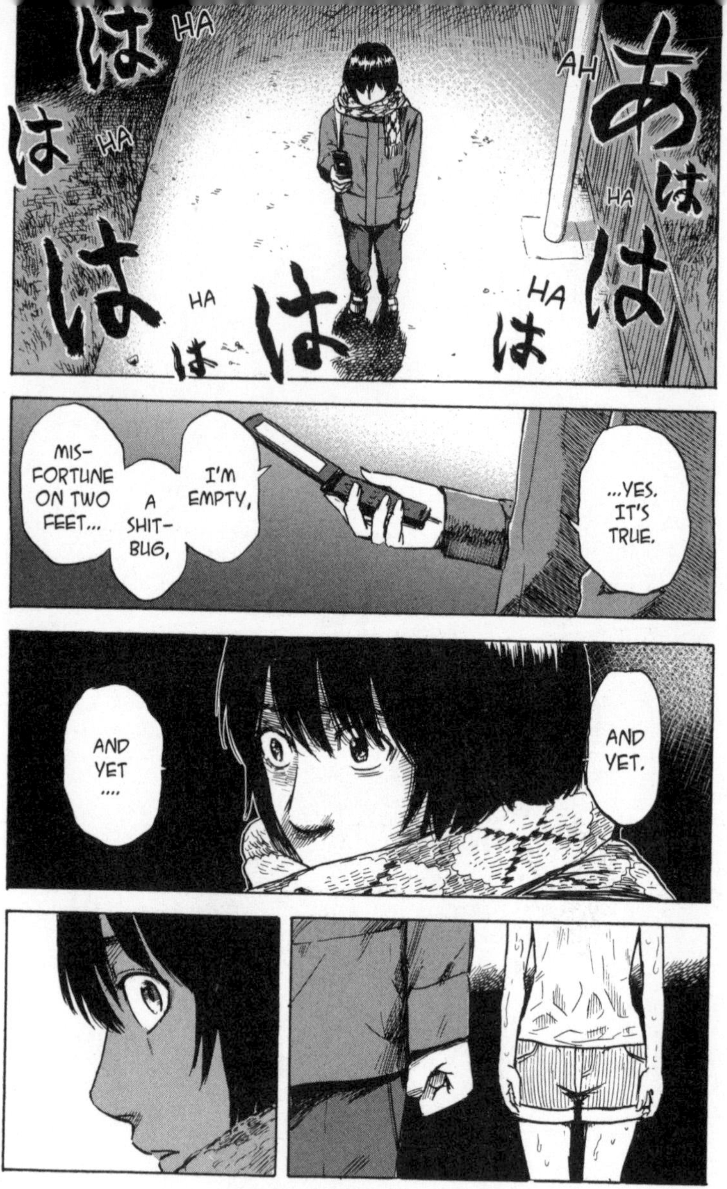

あ
AH
は
HA
は
HA
は
HA
は
HA
は
HA
は
HA
...YES. IT'S TRUE.
I'M EMPTY,
A SHIT-BUG,
MIS-FORTUNE ON TWO FEET...
AND YET.
AND YET ....

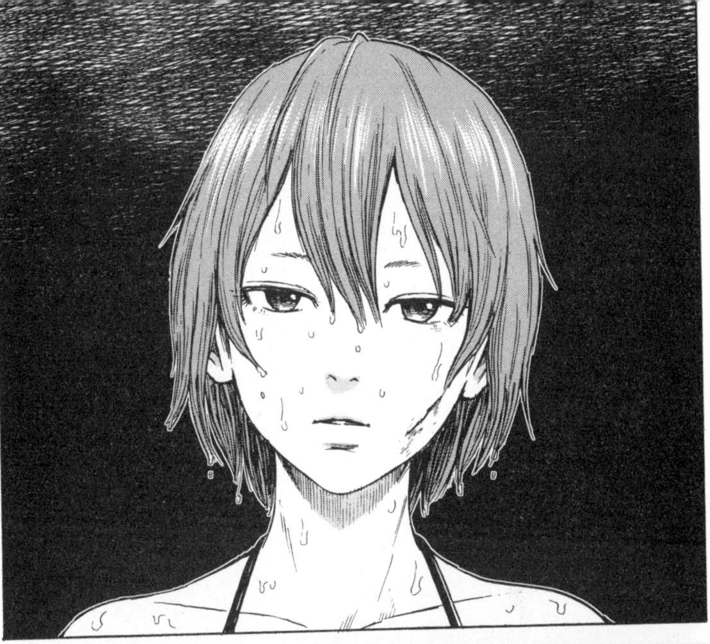

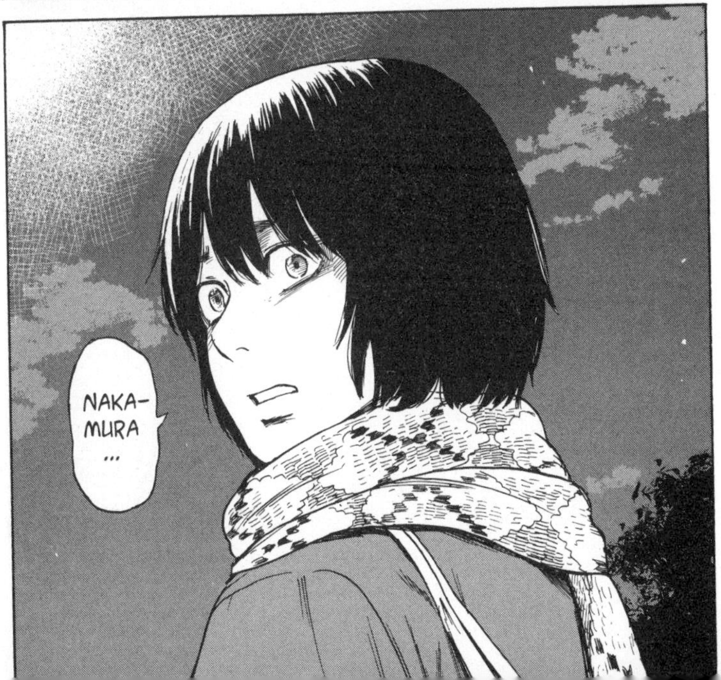
NAKA-
MURA
...

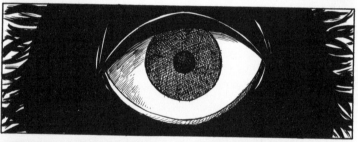

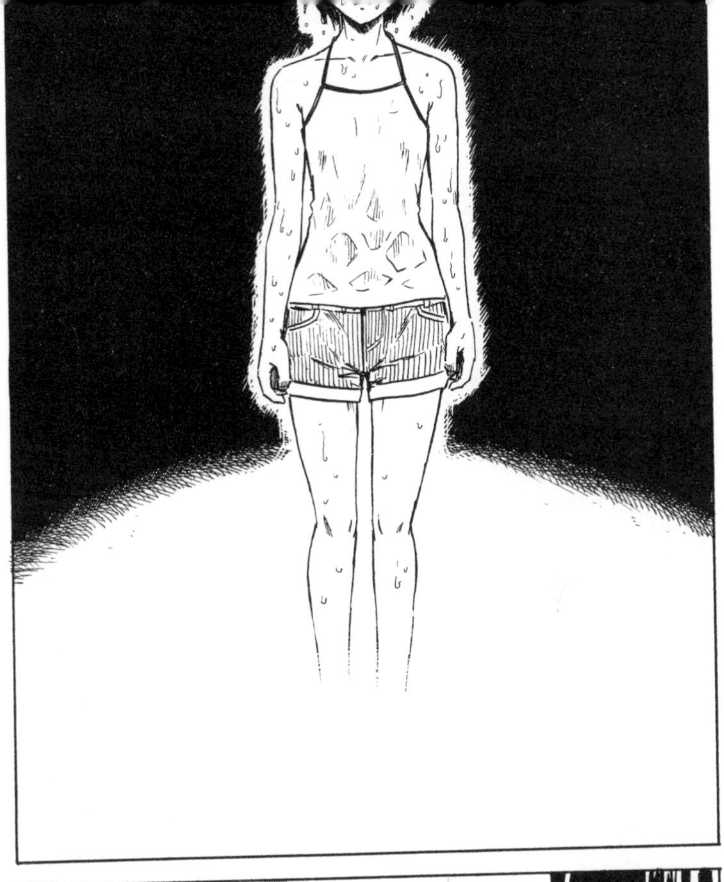

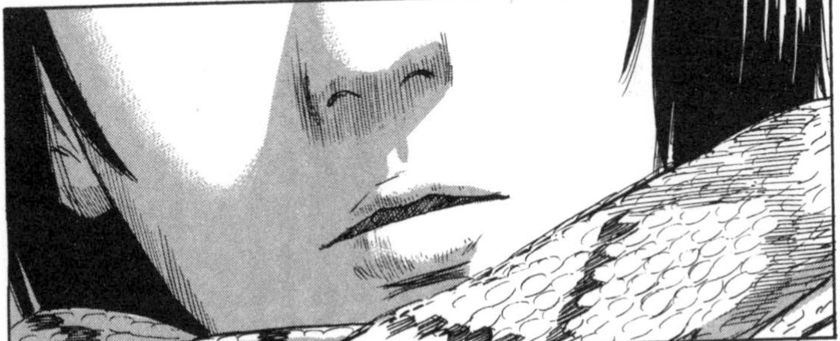

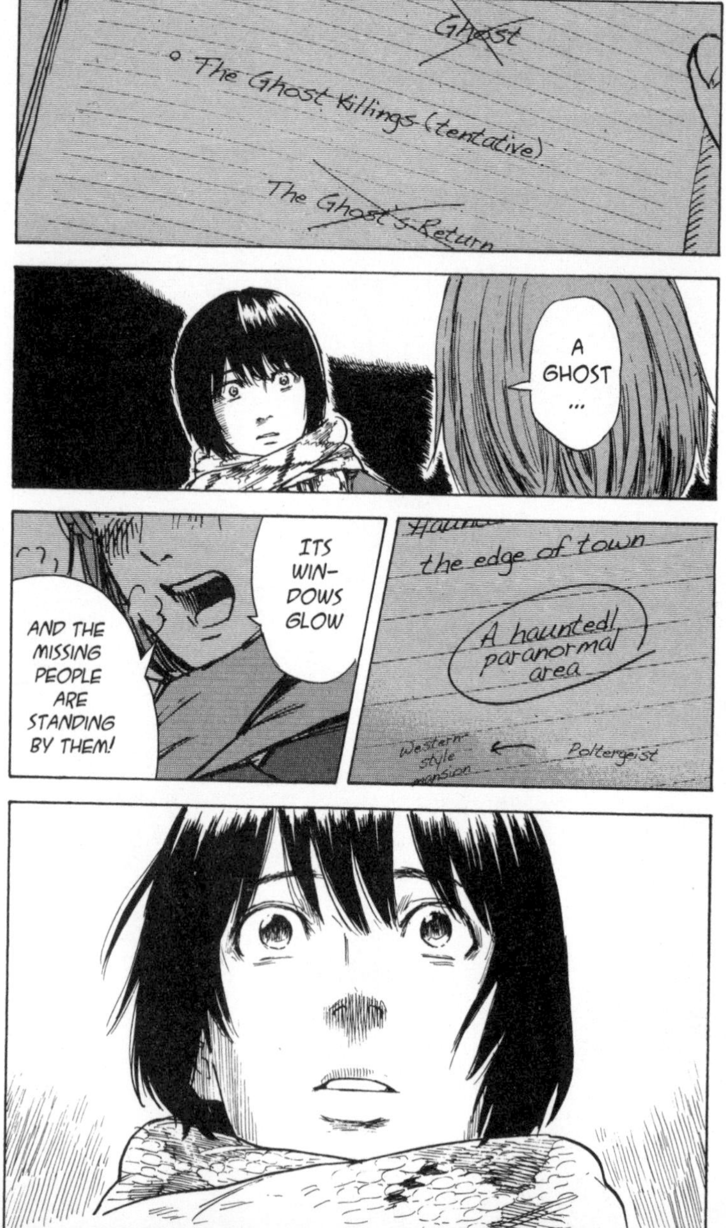
Ghost
The Ghost Killings (tentative)
The Ghost's Return
A GHOST ...
the edge of town
A haunted/paranormal area
Western-style mansion ← Poltergeist
ITS WIN-DOWS GLOW
AND THE MISSING PEOPLE ARE STANDING BY THEM!

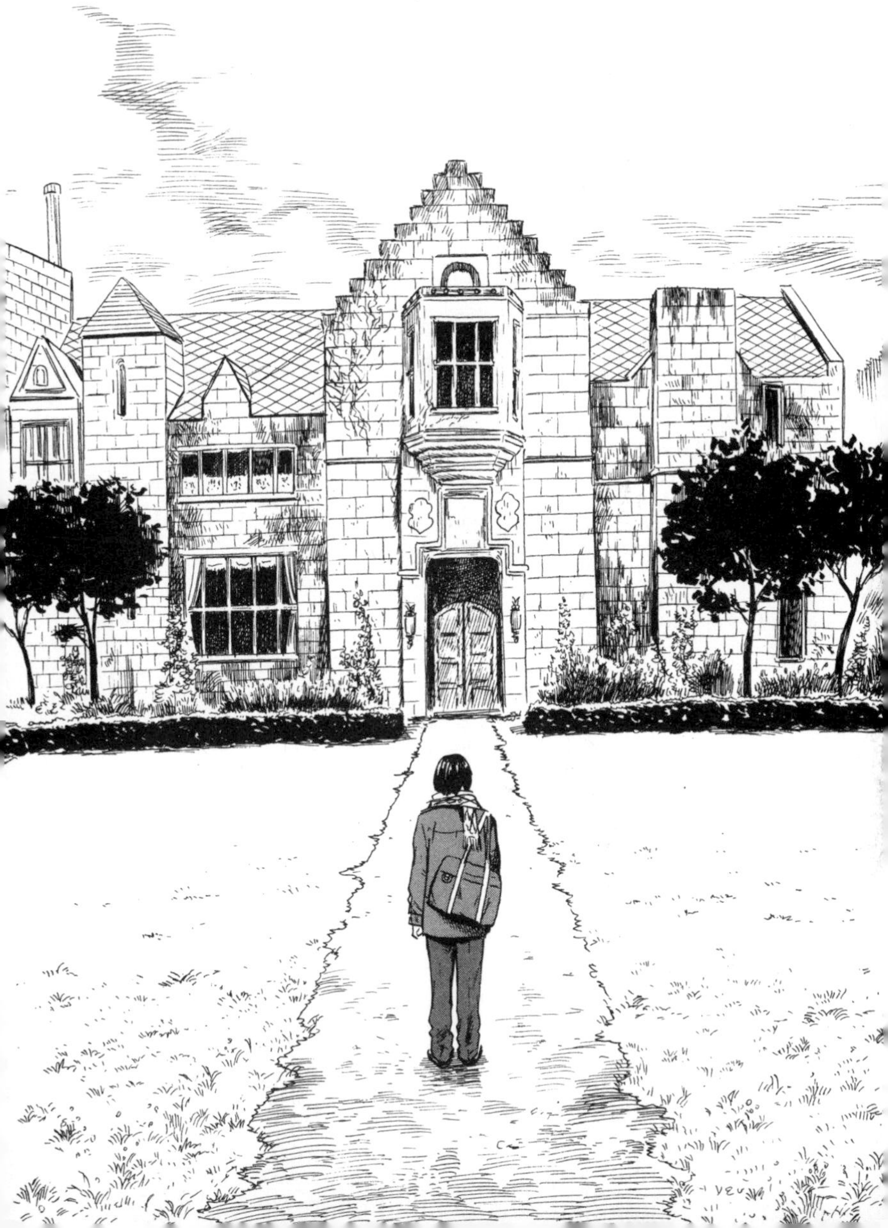

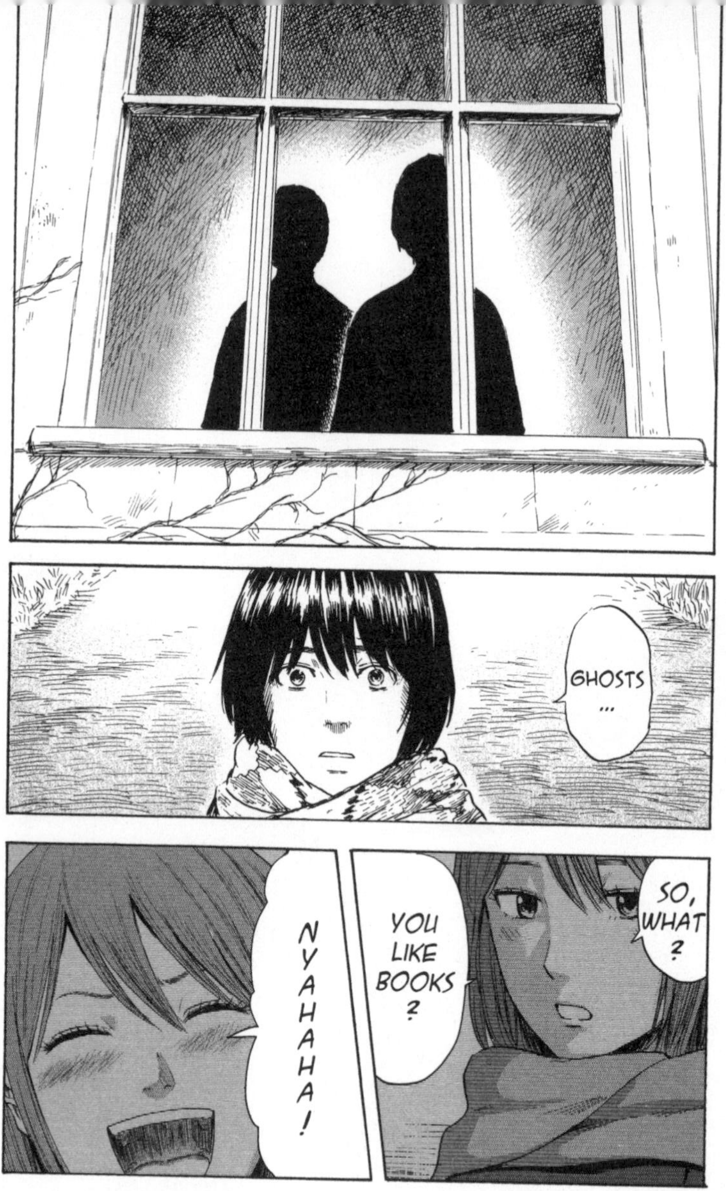
GHOSTS ...
SO, WHAT?
YOU LIKE BOOKS?
NYAHAHAHA!

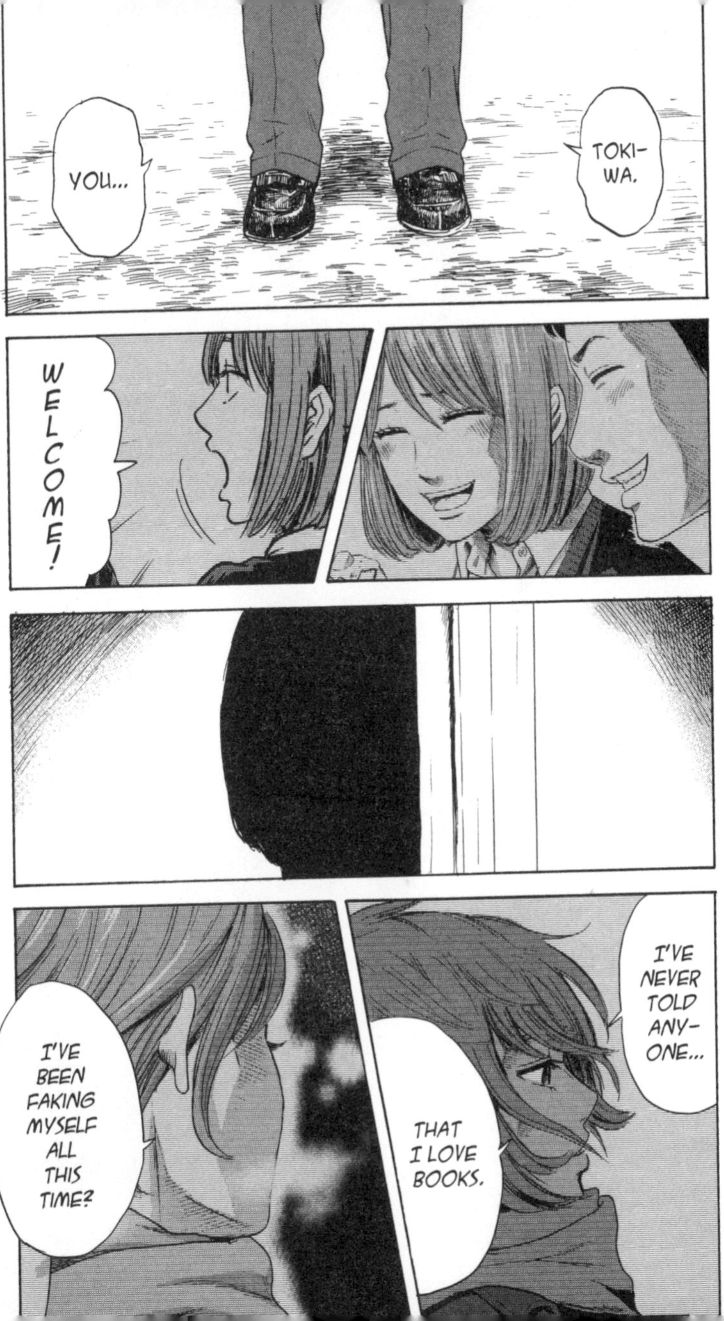
TOKI-WA.
YOU...
WELCOME!
I'VE NEVER TOLD ANY-ONE...
THAT I LOVE BOOKS.
I'VE BEEN FAKING MYSELF ALL THIS TIME?

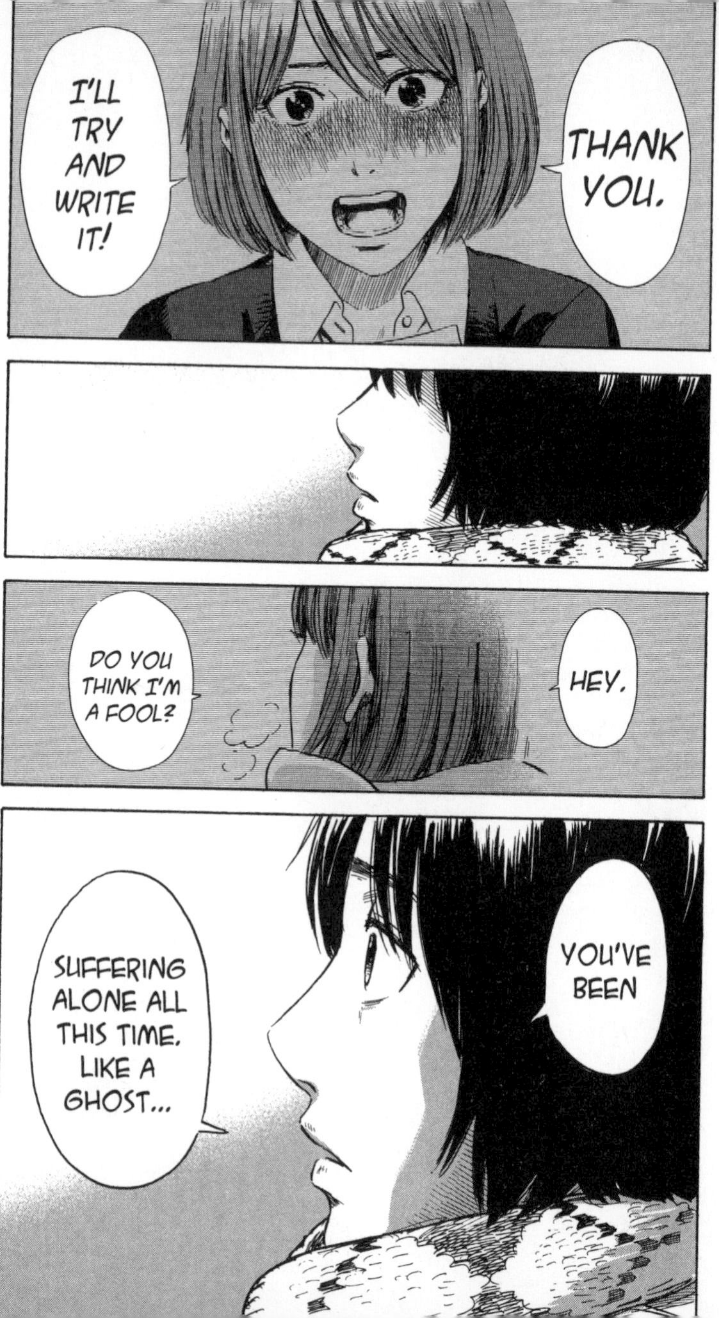
THANK YOU.
I'LL TRY AND WRITE IT!
HEY.
DO YOU THINK I'M A FOOL?
YOU'VE BEEN
SUFFERING ALONE ALL THIS TIME, LIKE A GHOST...

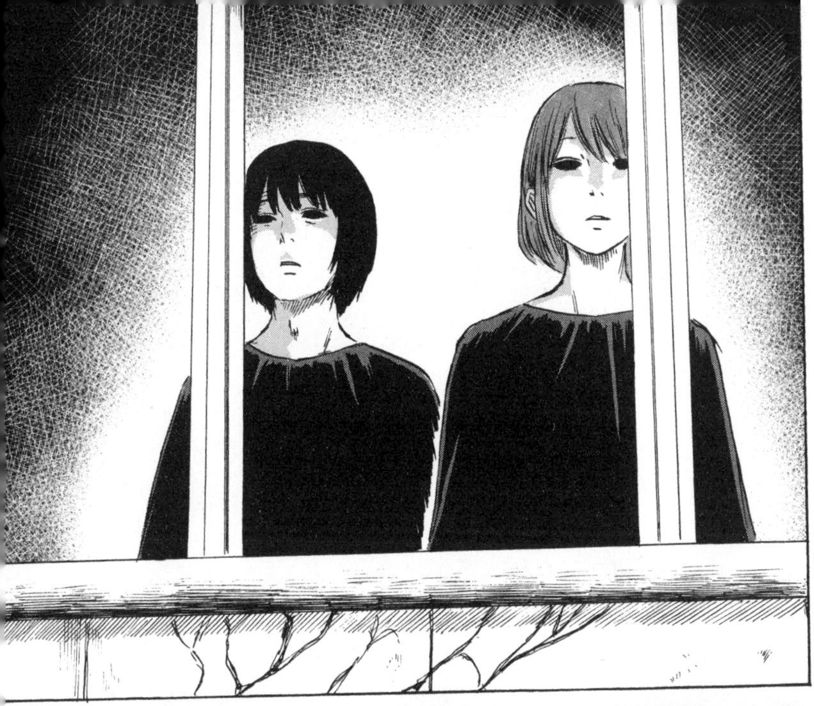
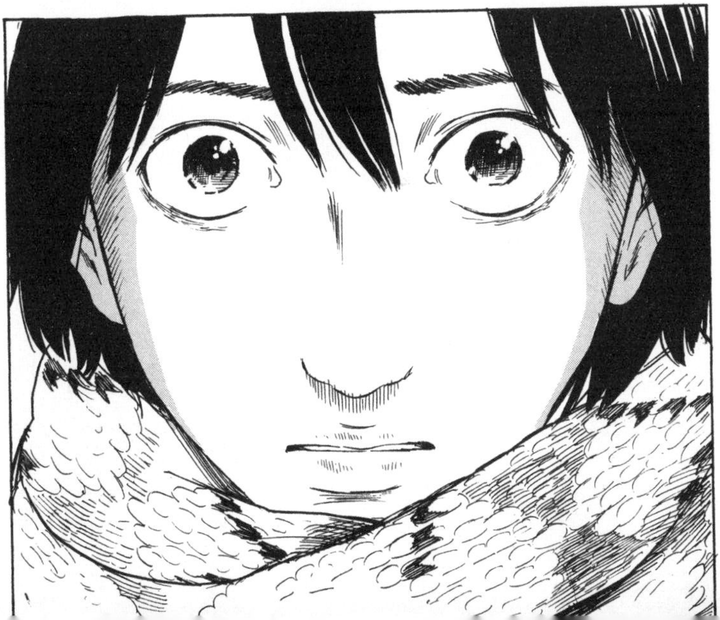

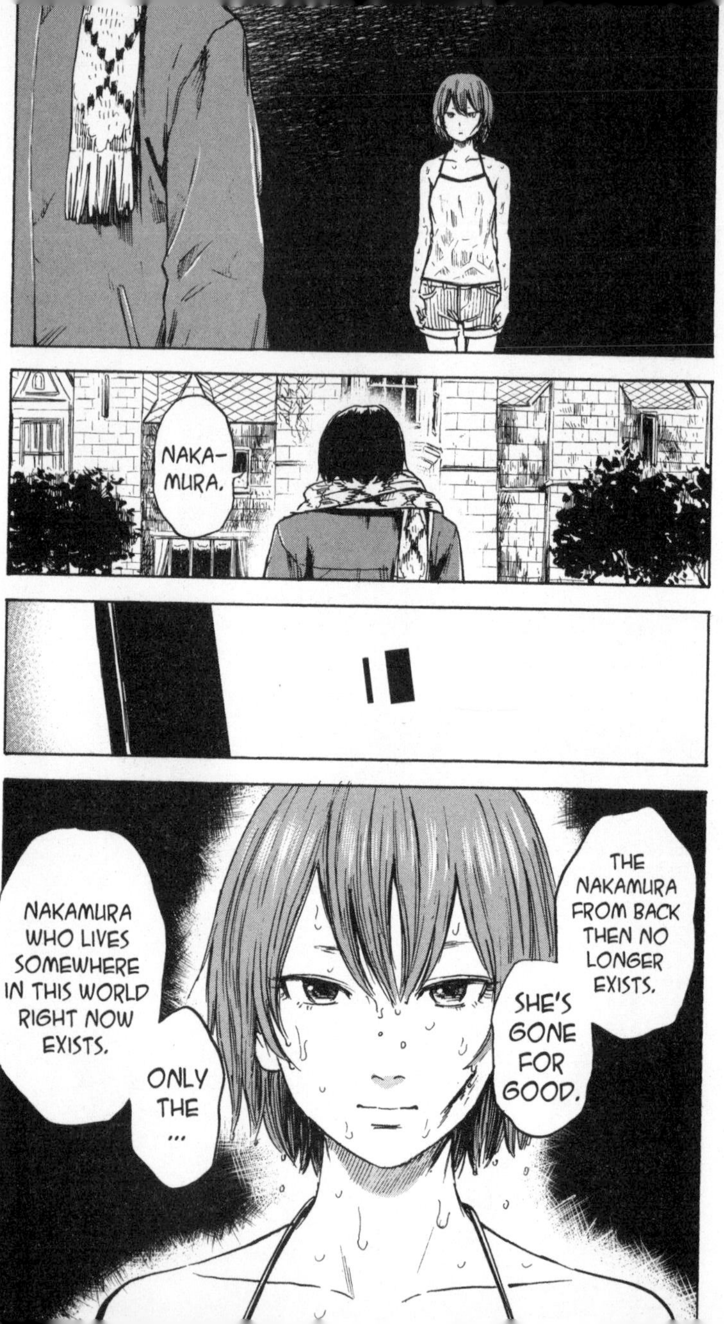
NAKA-MURA.
THE NAKAMURA FROM BACK THEN NO LONGER EXISTS.
SHE'S GONE FOR GOOD.
ONLY THE ...
NAKAMURA WHO LIVES SOMEWHERE IN THIS WORLD RIGHT NOW EXISTS.

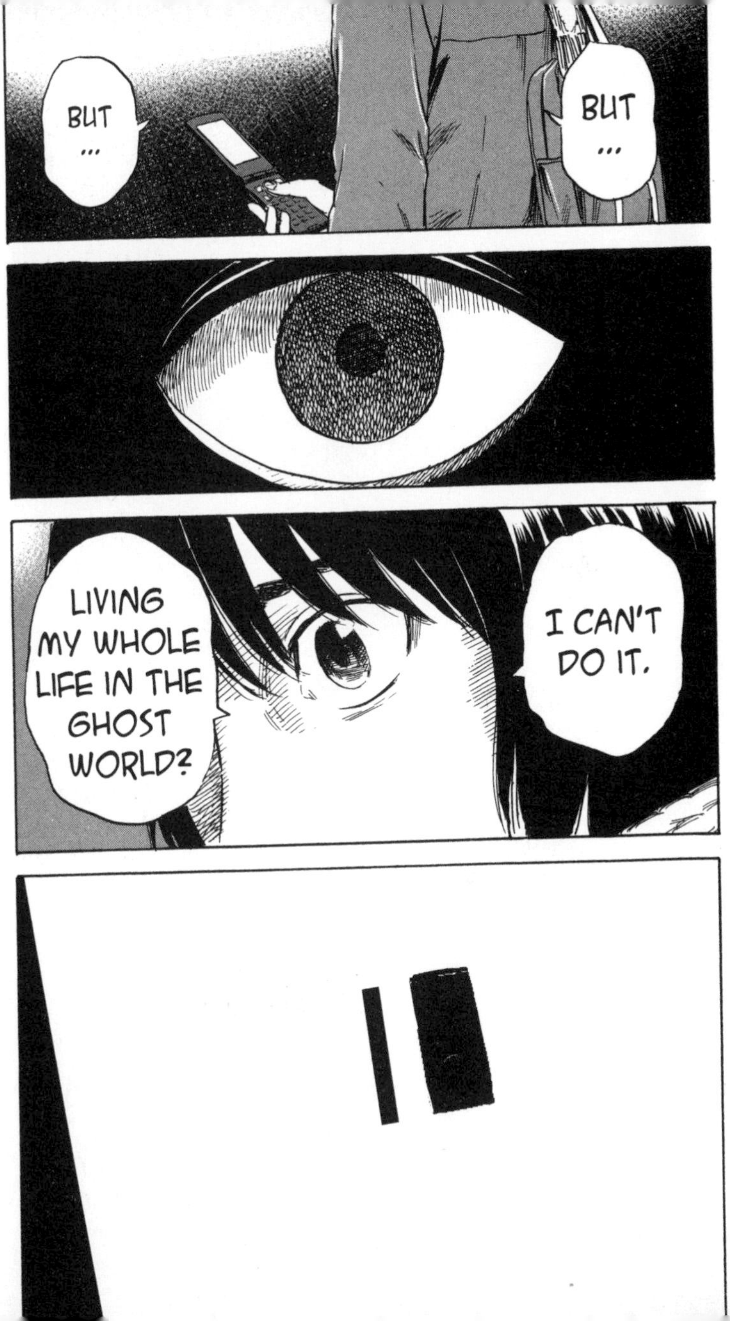
BUT ...
BUT ...
LIVING MY WHOLE LIFE IN THE GHOST WORLD?
I CAN'T DO IT.

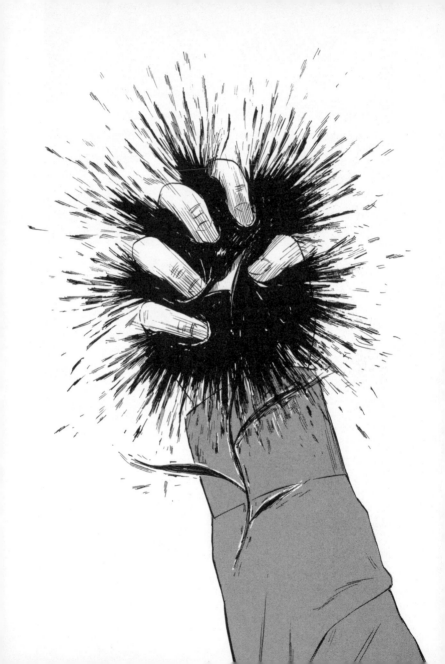

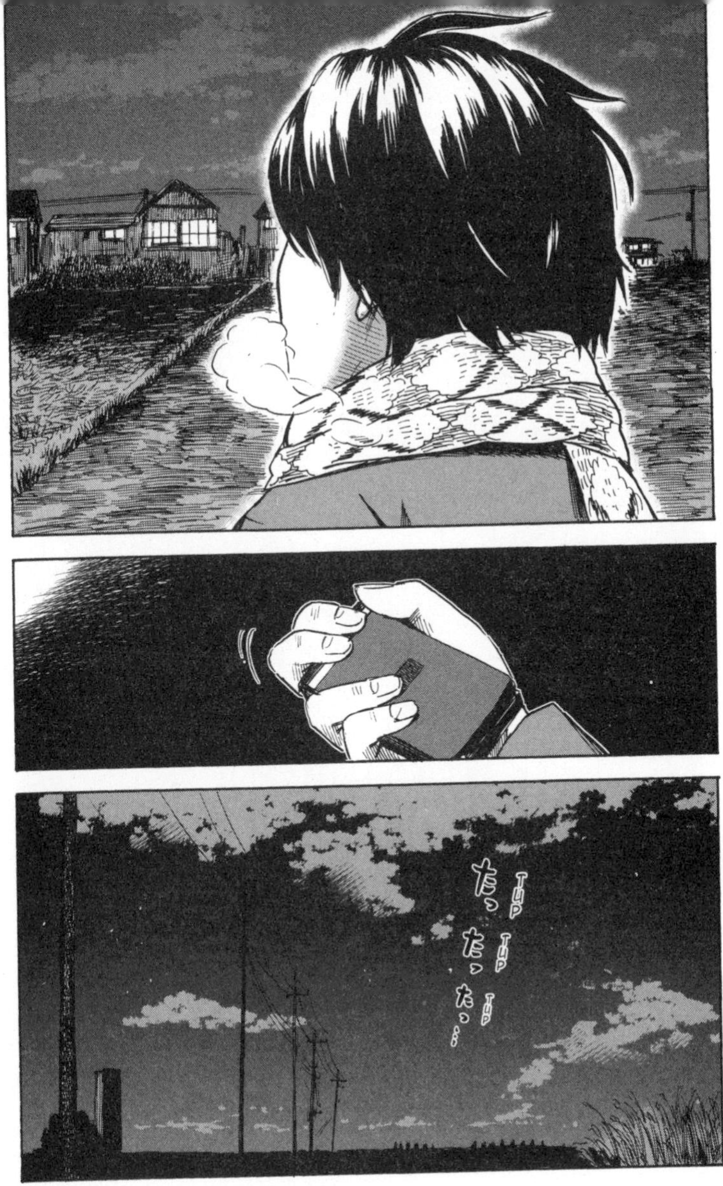
たっ たっ たっ…
TUP TUP TUP

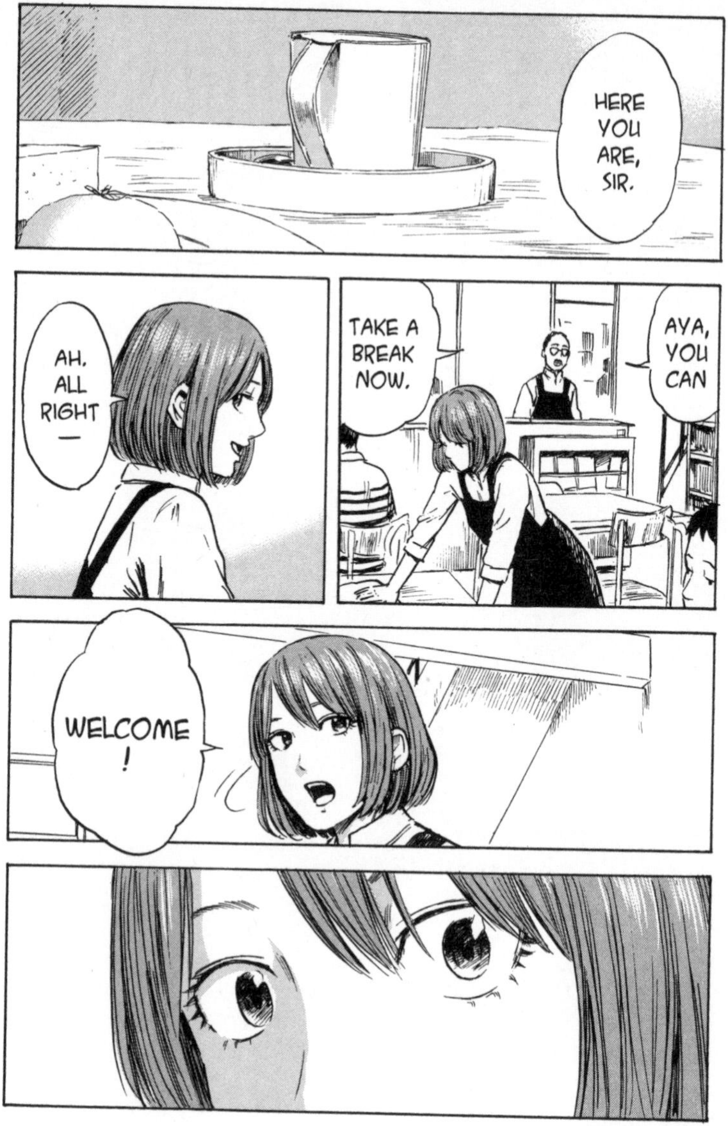
HERE YOU ARE, SIR.
AYA, YOU CAN
TAKE A BREAK NOW.
AH, ALL RIGHT —
WELCOME !

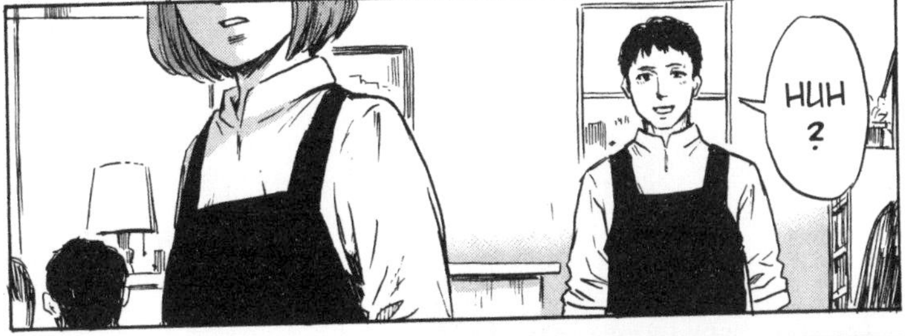
HUH?

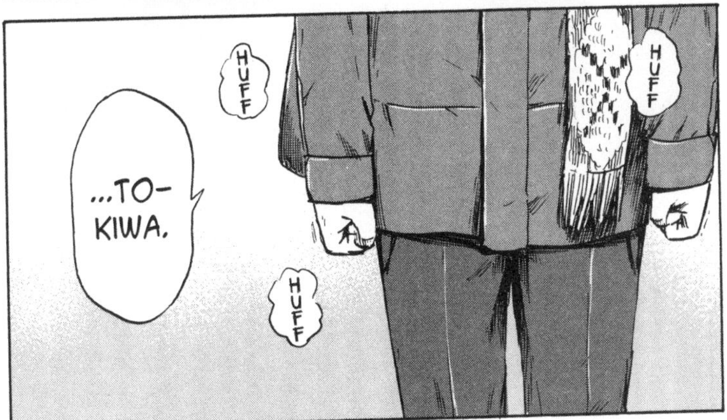
HUFF
HUFF
...TO-KIWA.
HUFF

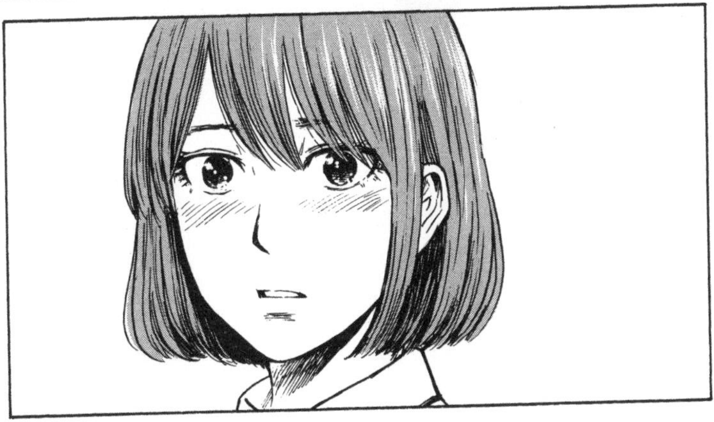

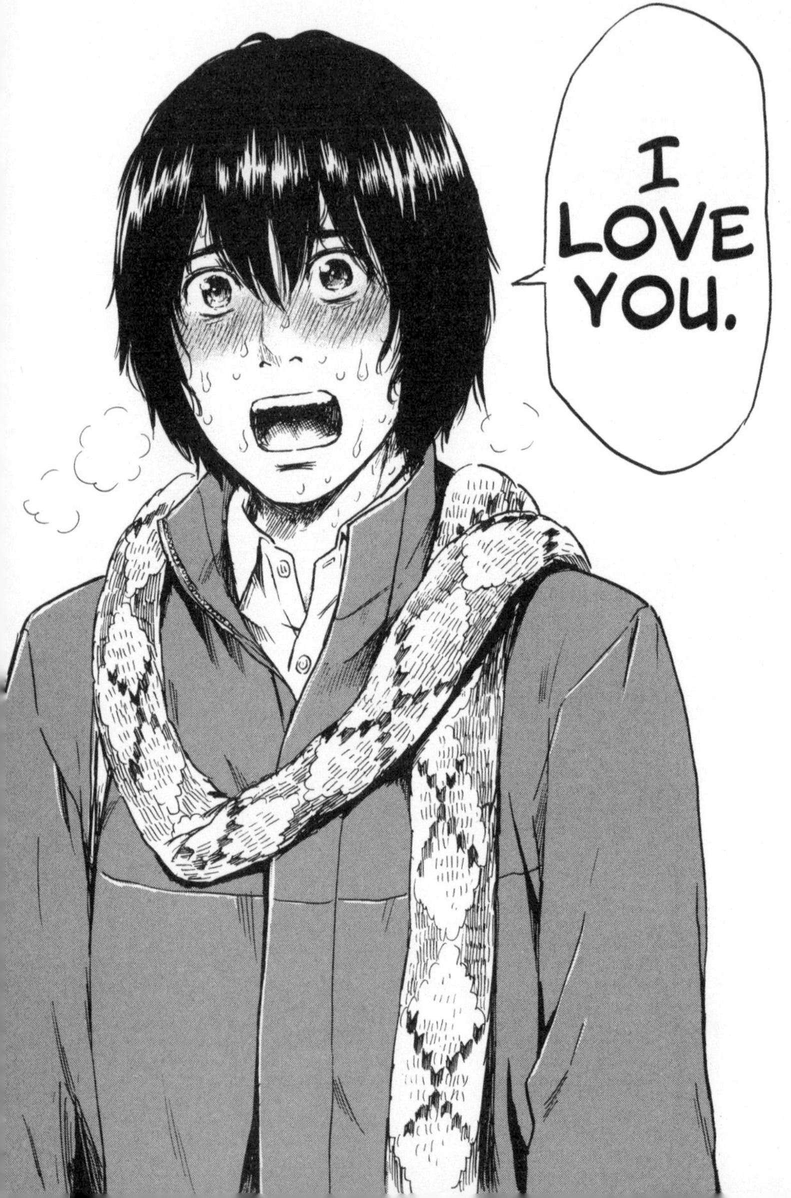
I LOVE YOU.

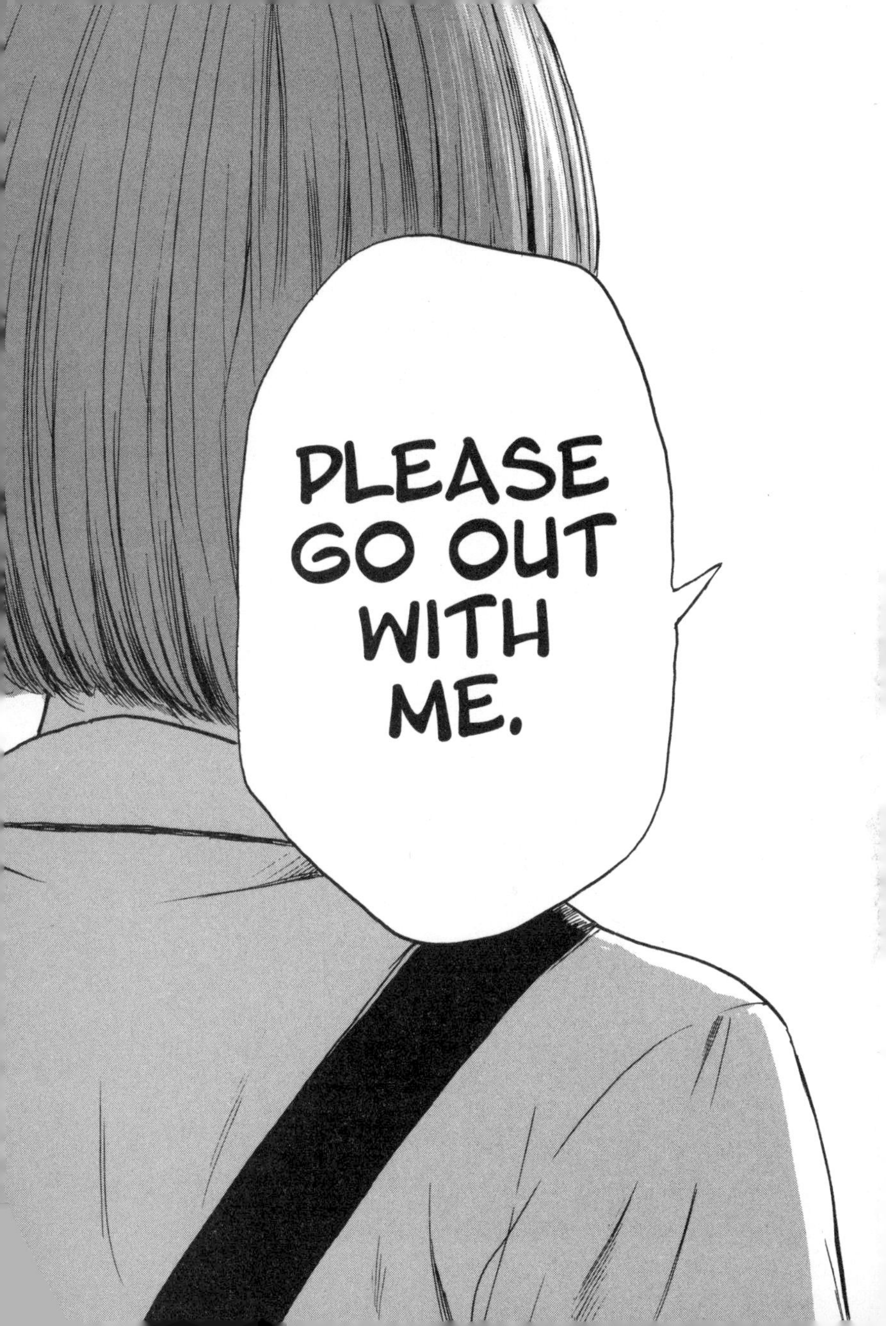
PLEASE GO OUT WITH ME.

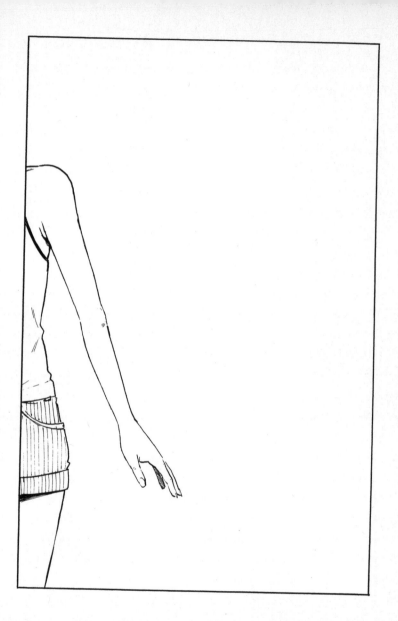

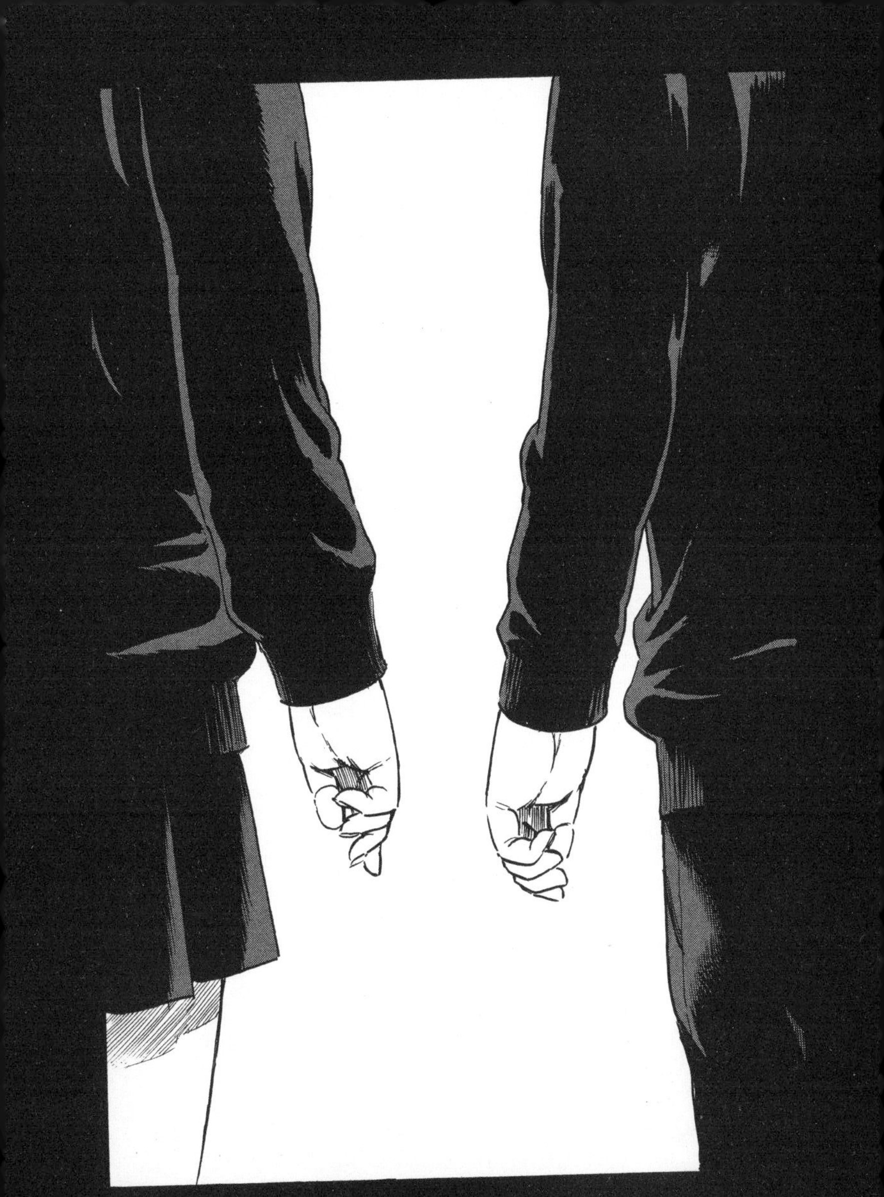

Chapter 45: You as Dear as the Night Sky

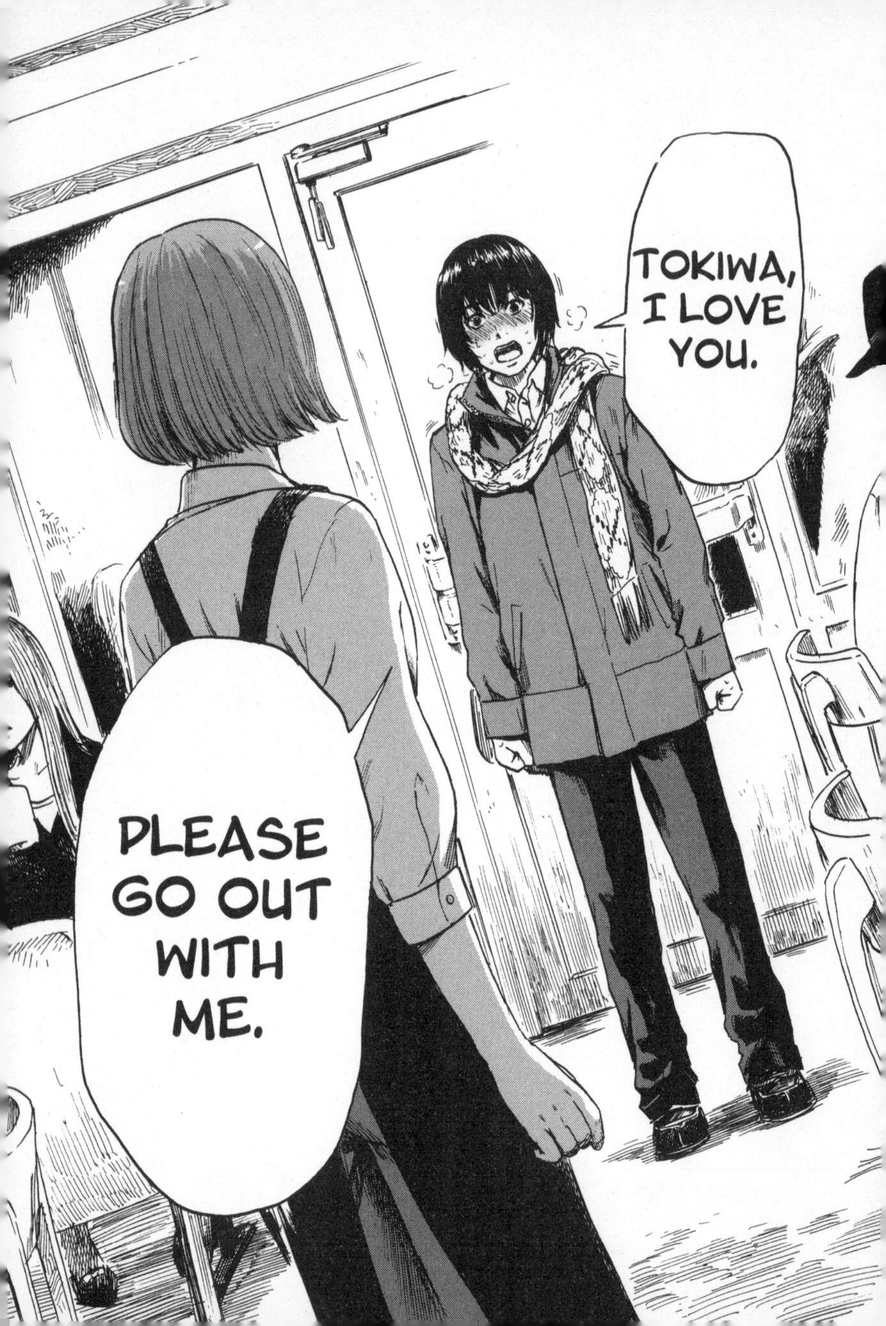
TOKIWA, I LOVE YOU.
PLEASE GO OUT WITH ME.

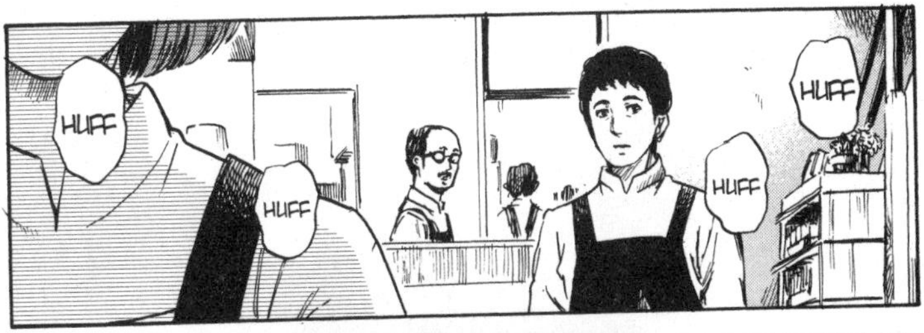
HUFF
HUFF
HUFF
HUFF
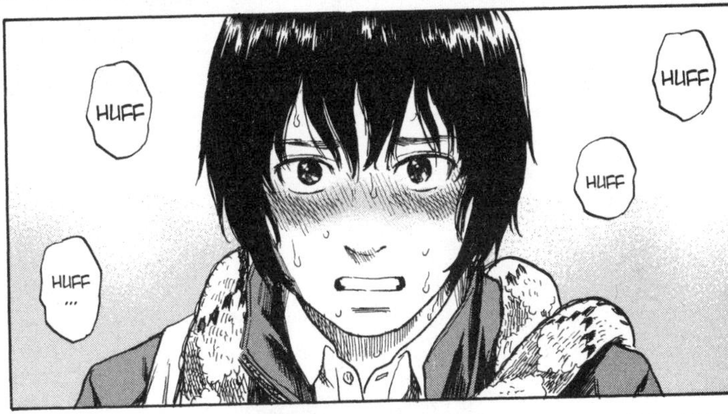
HUFF
HUFF
HUFF
HUFF ...
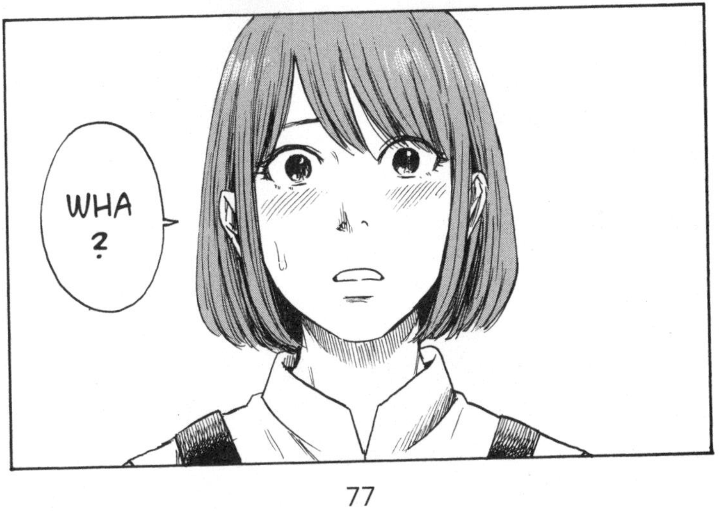
WHA ?

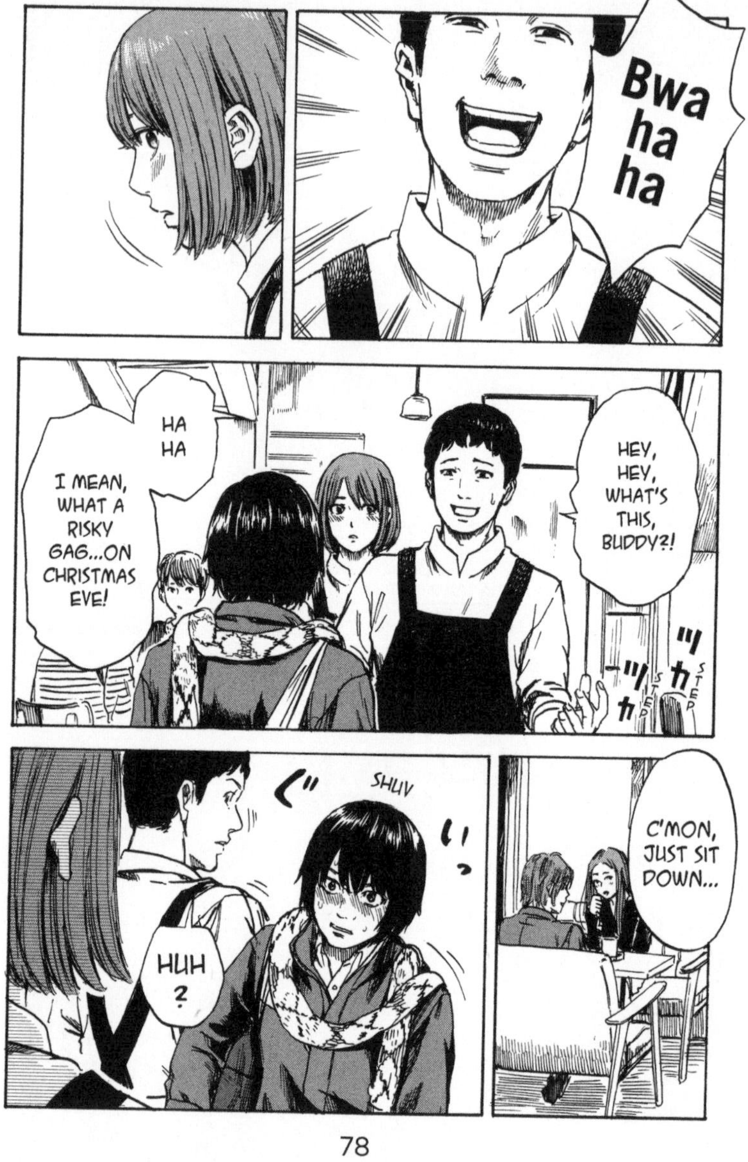
Bwa ha ha
HEY, HEY, WHAT'S THIS, BUDDY?!
ツカツカ
STEP STEP
HA HA
I MEAN, WHAT A RISKY GAG...ON CHRISTMAS EVE!
C'MON, JUST SIT DOWN...
ぐ
SHUV
いっ
HUH?

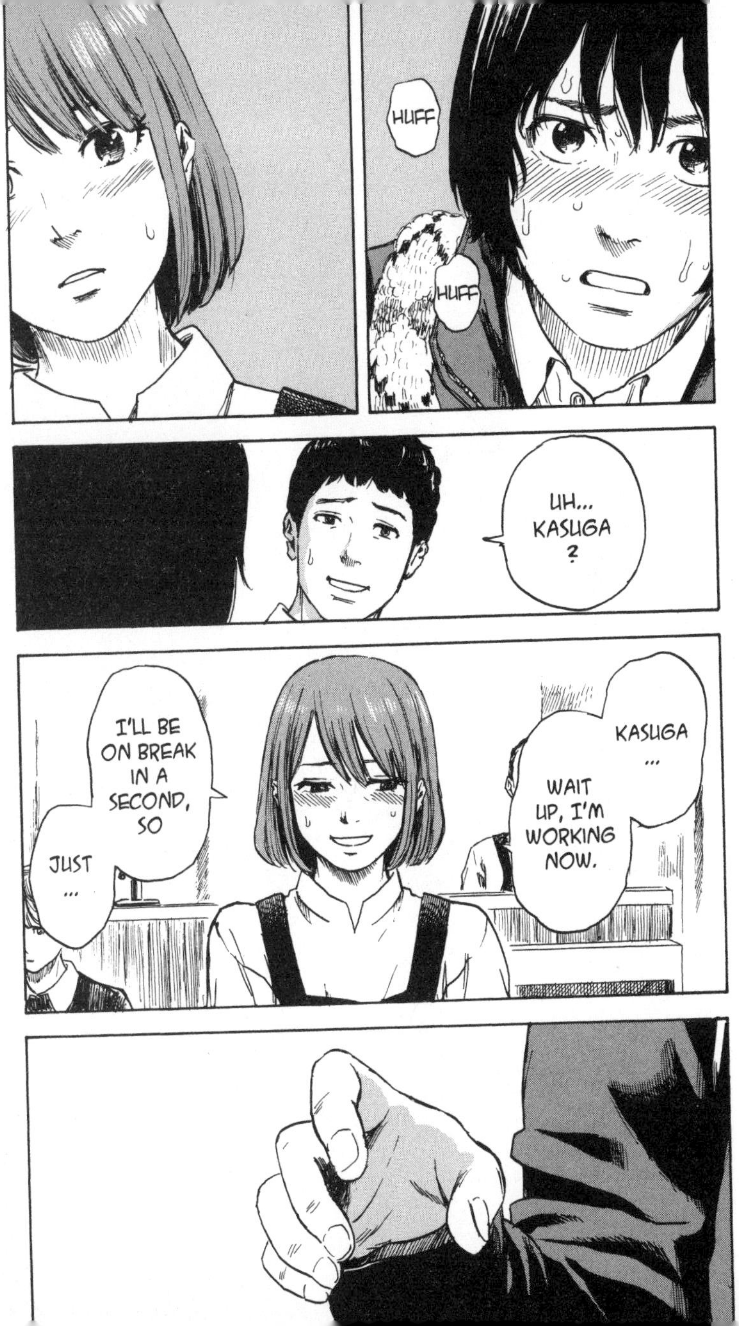
HUFF
HUFF
UH... KASUGA ?
KASUGA ...
WAIT UP, I'M WORKING NOW.
I'LL BE ON BREAK IN A SECOND, SO
JUST ...

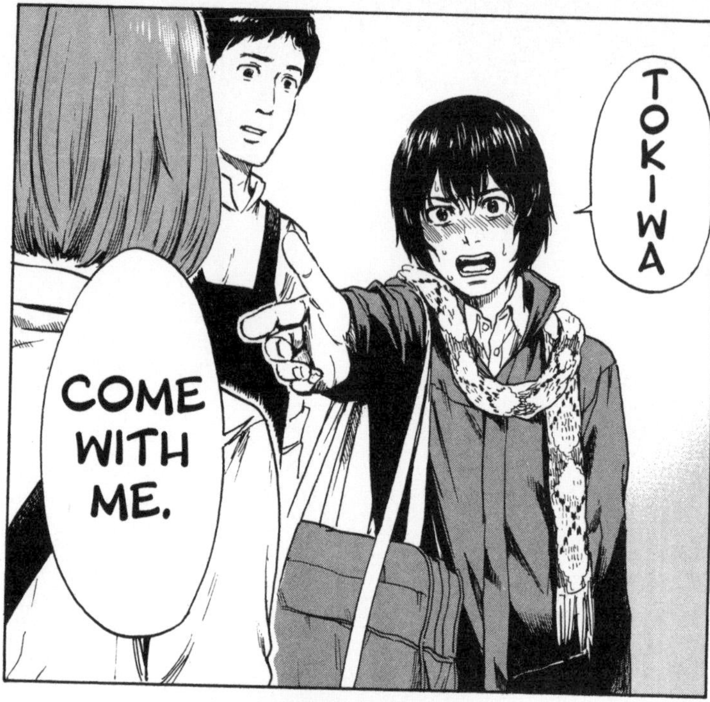
TOKIWA
COME WITH ME.

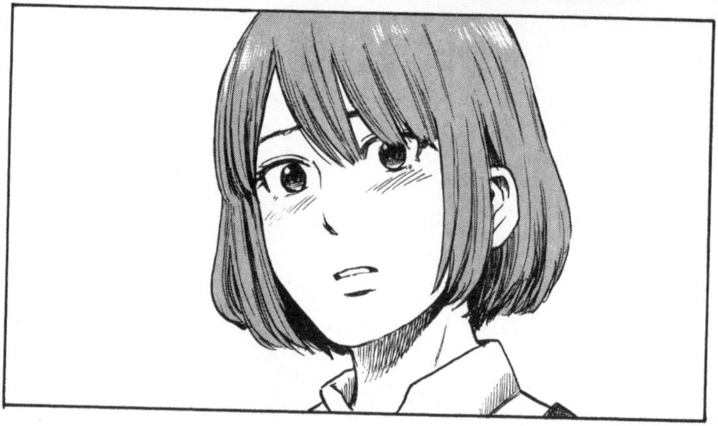

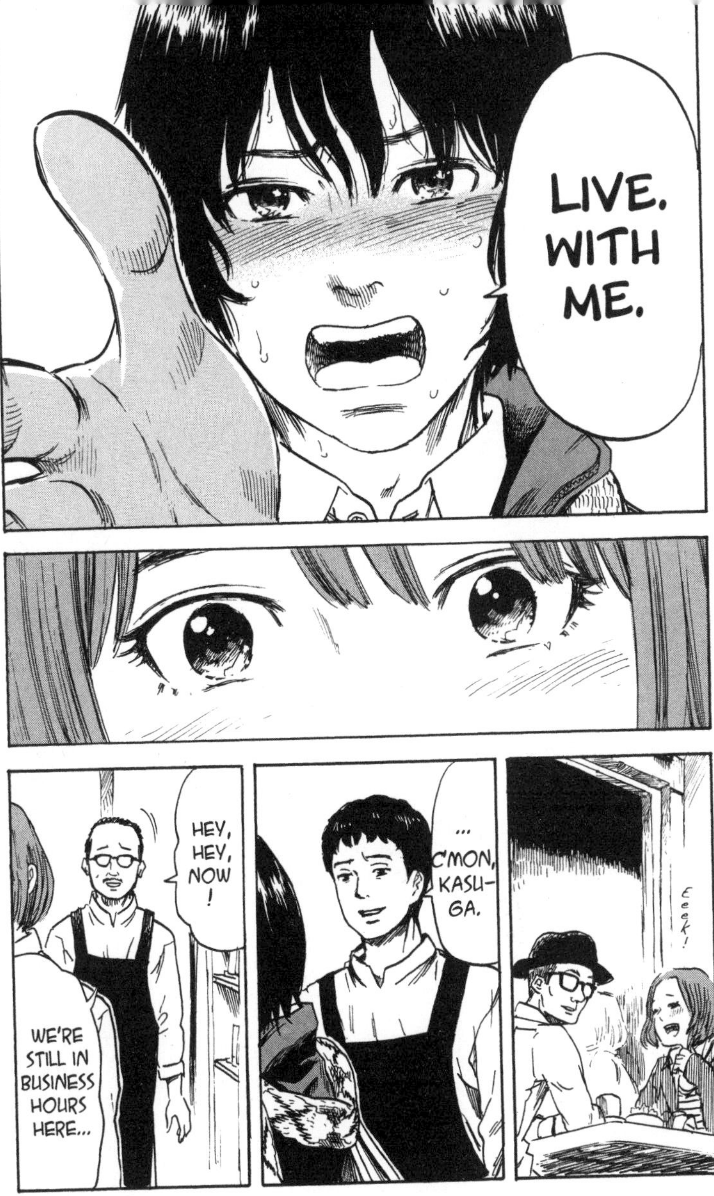
LIVE. WITH ME.
Eeek!
... C'MON, KASU-GA.
HEY, HEY, NOW!
WE'RE STILL IN BUSINESS HOURS HERE...

I'LL BE THE ONE TO KILL YOUR GHOST.

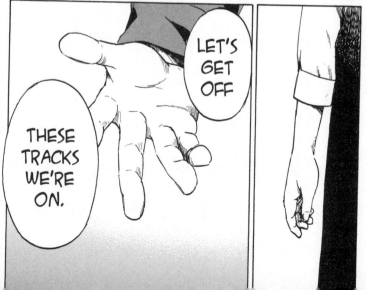

LET'S GET OFF

THESE TRACKS WE'RE ON.

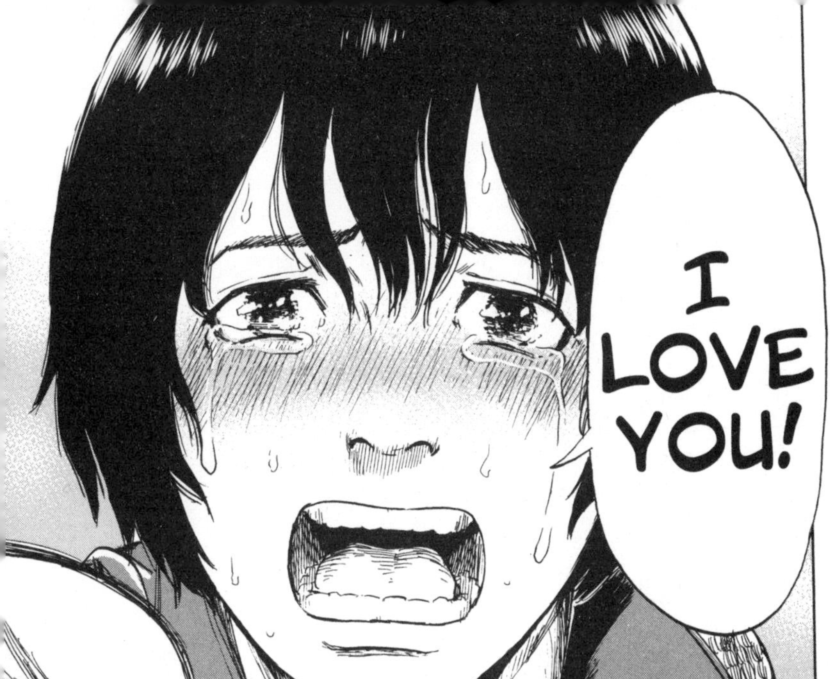
I LOVE YOU!
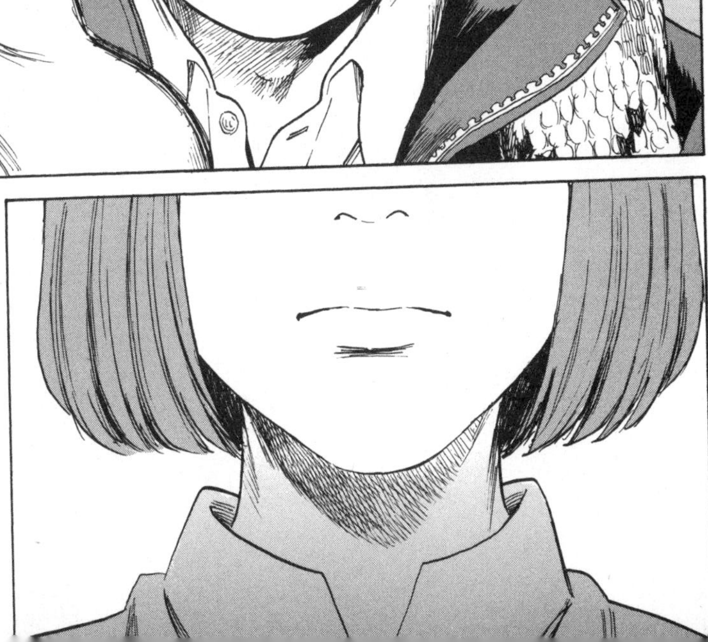

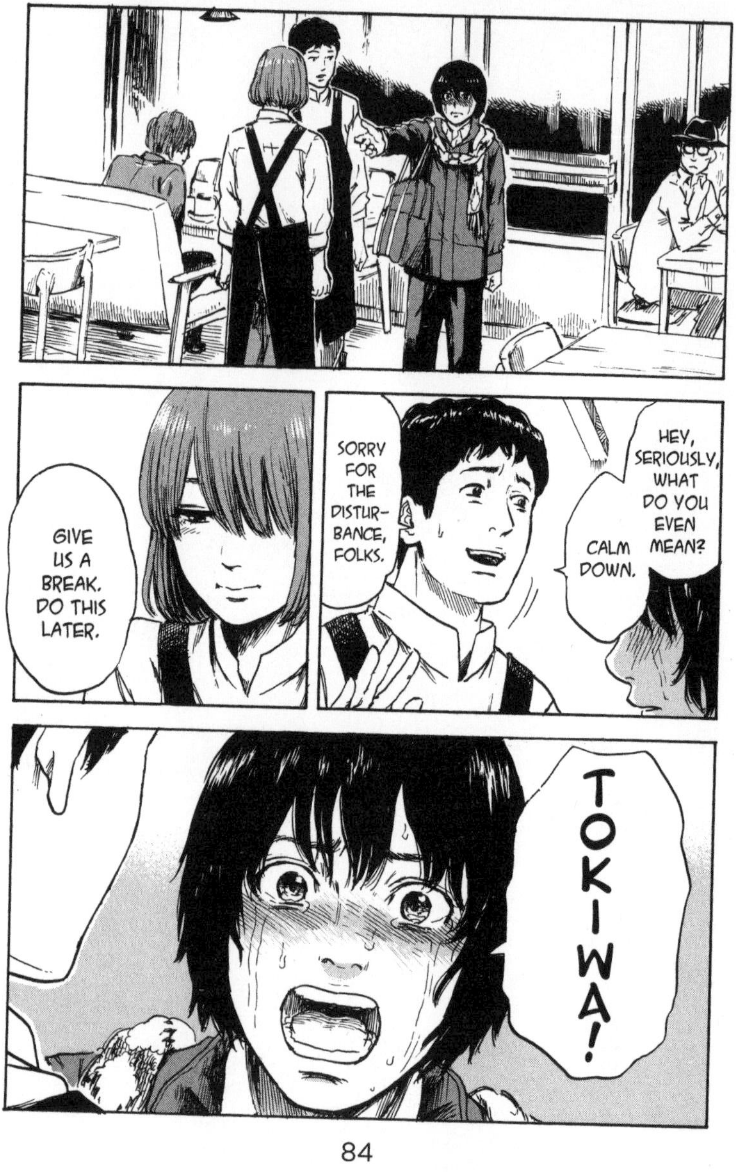
HEY, SERIOUSLY, WHAT DO YOU EVEN MEAN?
CALM DOWN.
SORRY FOR THE DISTURBANCE, FOLKS.
GIVE US A BREAK. DO THIS LATER.
TOKIWA!

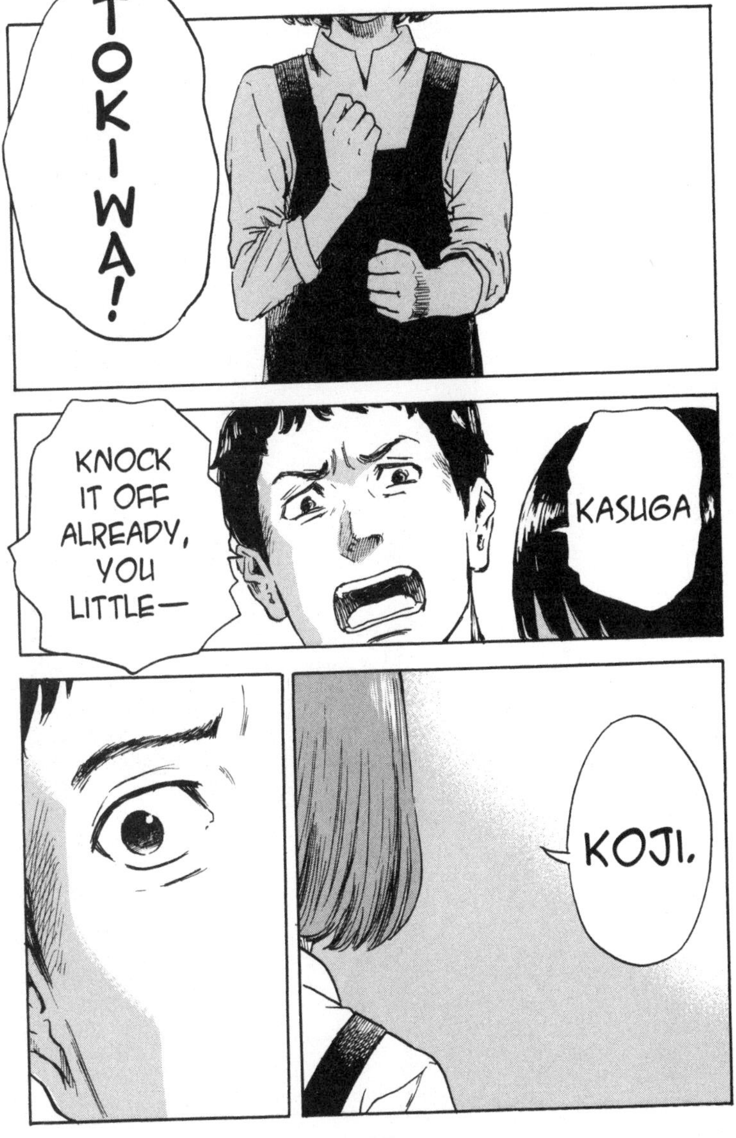
TOKIWA!
KASUGA
KNOCK IT OFF ALREADY, YOU LITTLE—
KOJI.

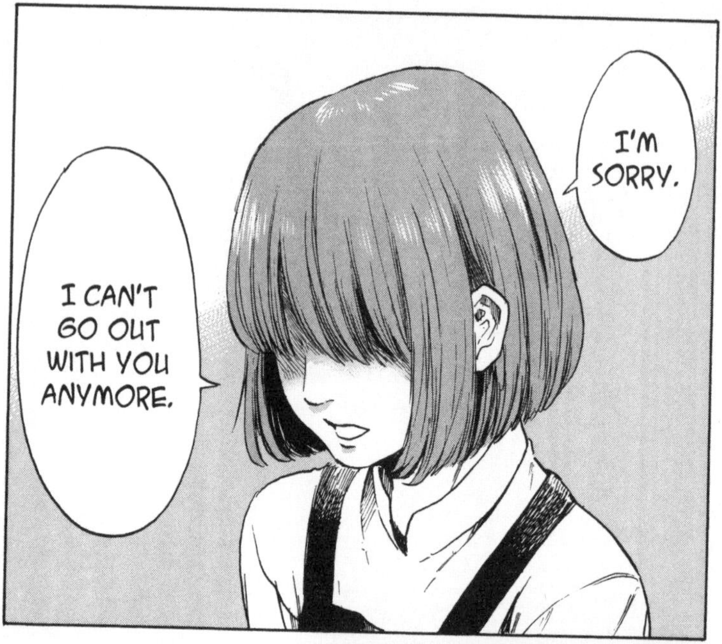
I'M SORRY.
I CAN'T GO OUT WITH YOU ANYMORE.
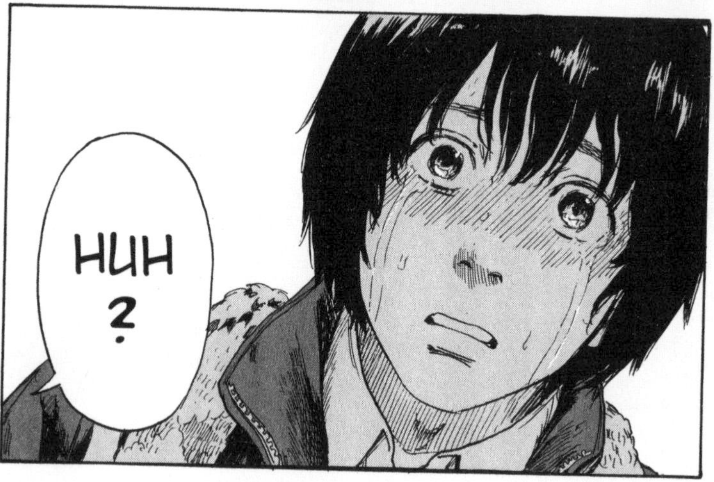
HUH?

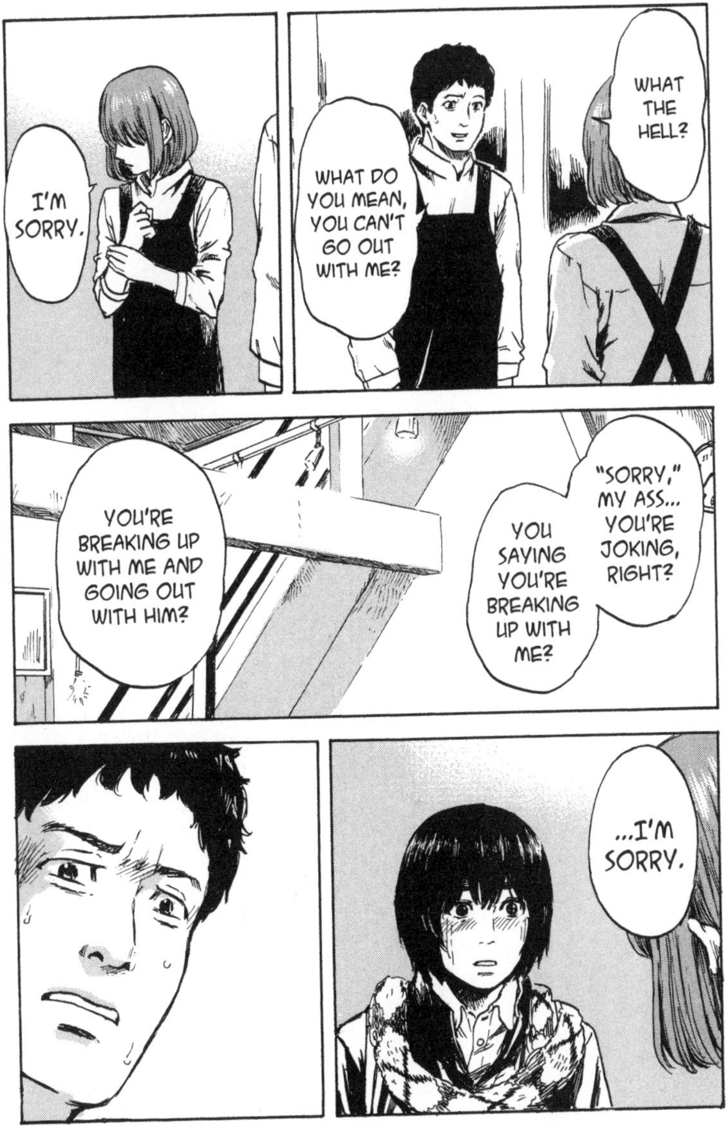
WHAT THE HELL?
WHAT DO YOU MEAN, YOU CAN'T GO OUT WITH ME?
I'M SORRY.
"SORRY," MY ASS... YOU'RE JOKING, RIGHT?
YOU SAYING YOU'RE BREAKING UP WITH ME?
YOU'RE BREAKING UP WITH ME AND GOING OUT WITH HIM?
...I'M SORRY.

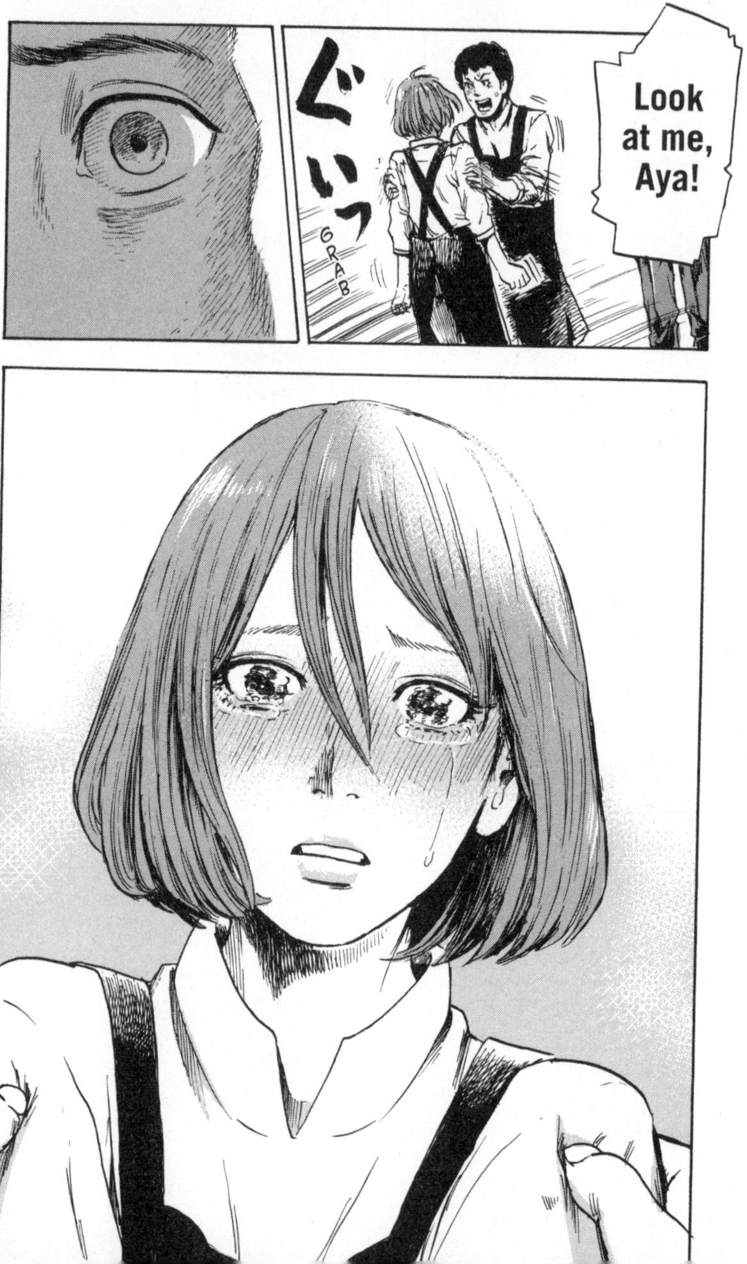
Look at me, Aya!
ぐいっ
GRAB

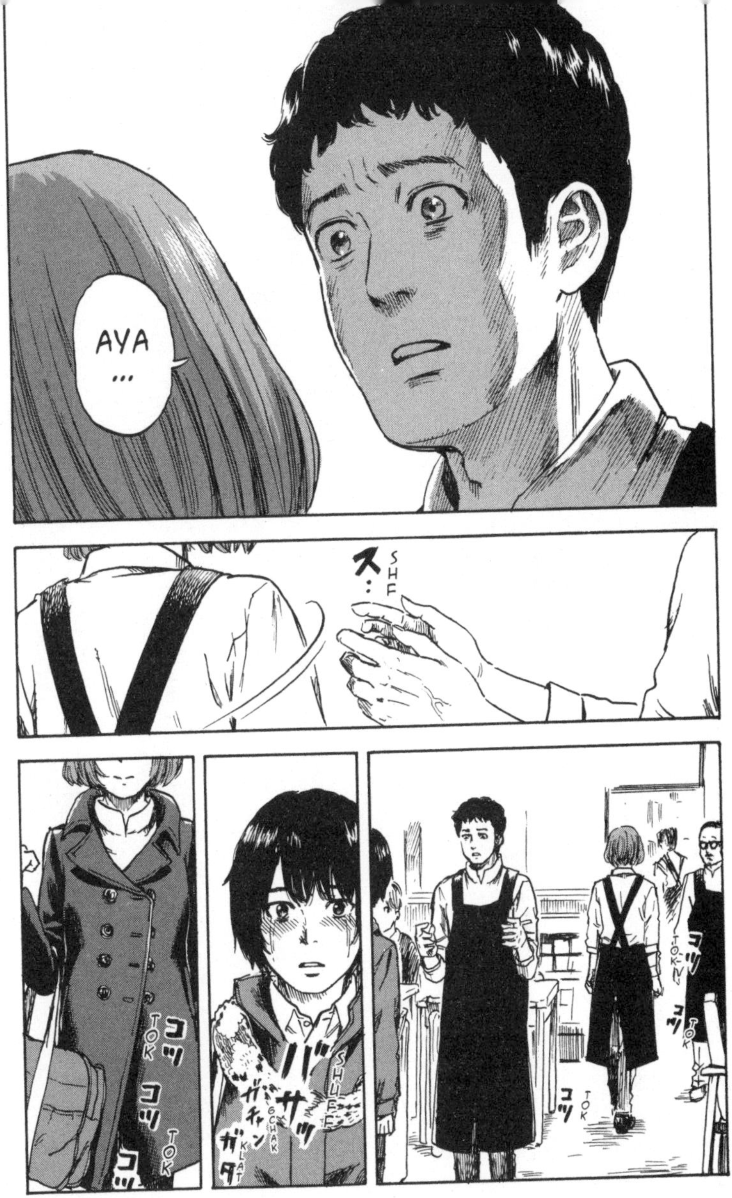
AYA
...
ス...
SHF
コツ
TOK
コツ
TOK
コツ
TOK
バサッ
SHUFF
ガチャン
GCHAK
ガタ
KLAT
コツ
TOK
コツ
TOK
コッ

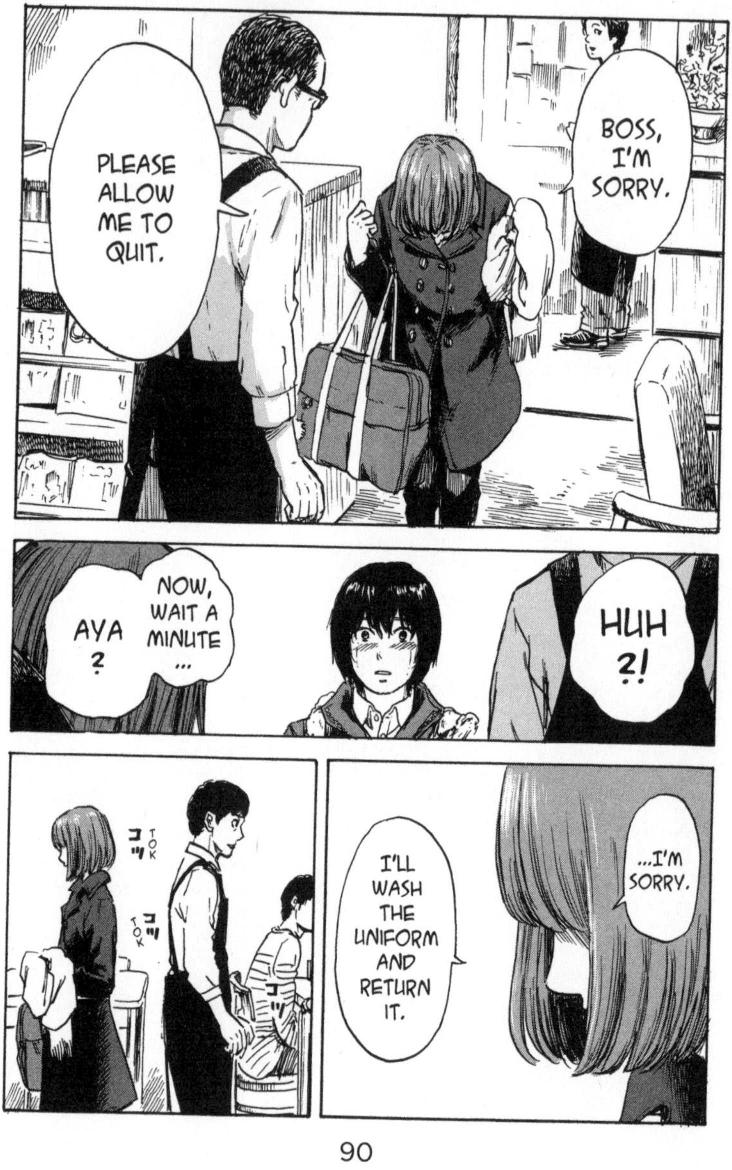
BOSS, I'M SORRY.
PLEASE ALLOW ME TO QUIT.
HUH ?!
NOW, WAIT A MINUTE ...
AYA ?
...I'M SORRY.
I'LL WASH THE UNIFORM AND RETURN IT.
コツ TOK
コツ TOK
コツ

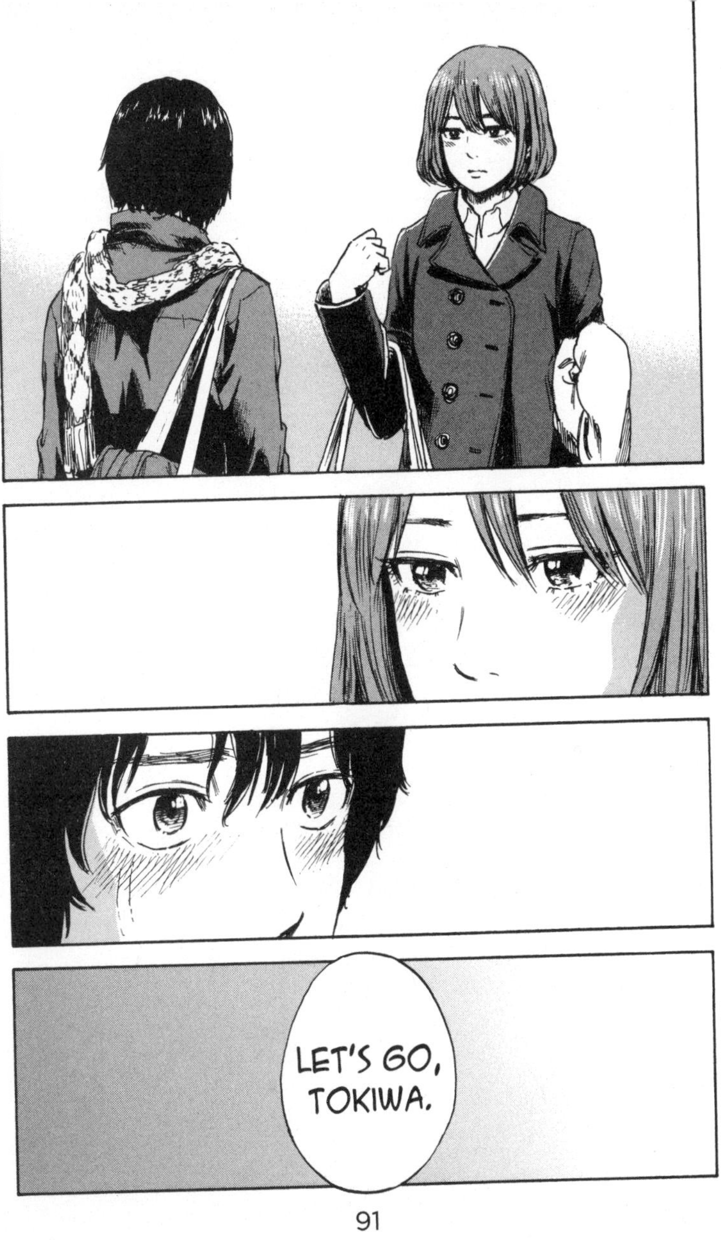
LET'S GO, TOKIWA.

ギ…
SQUEE

カラン
DINGLE
コロン
DANGLE
カラン
DINGLE

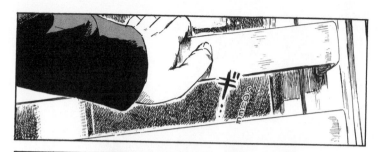

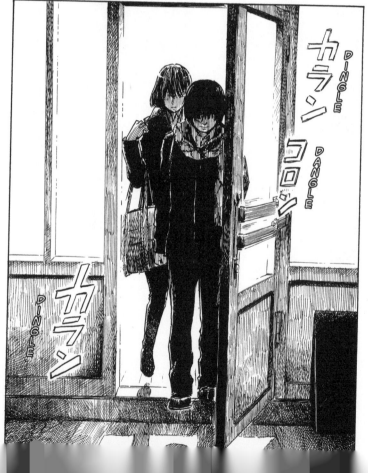

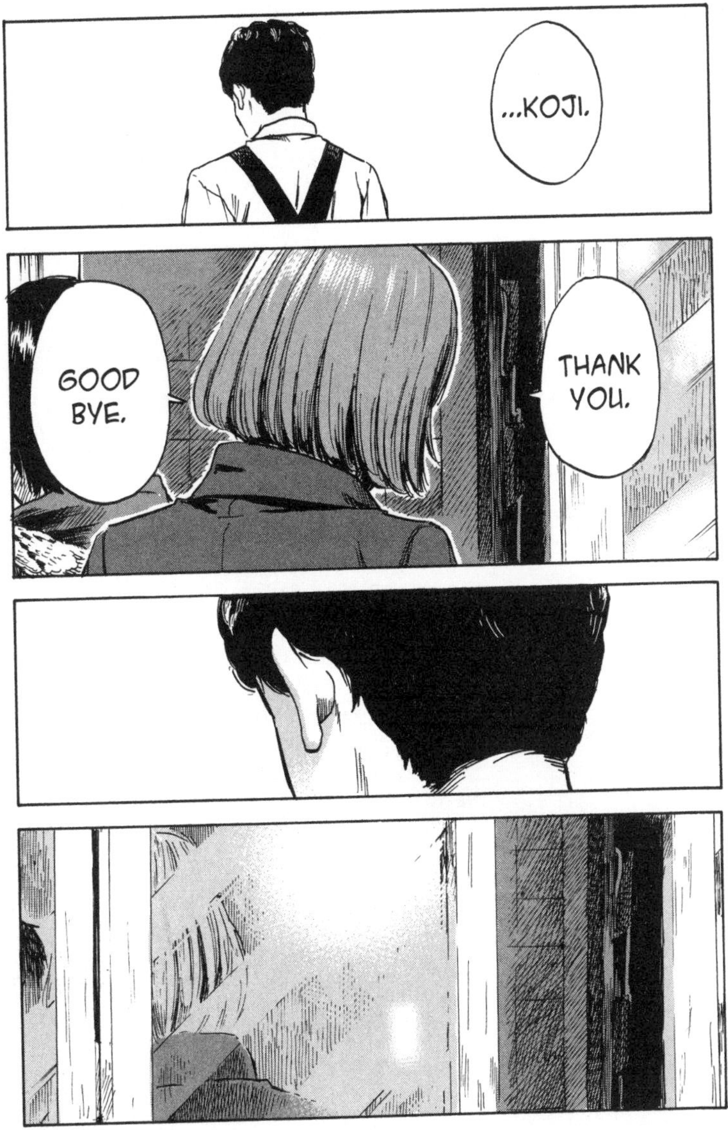
...KOJI.
THANK YOU.
GOOD BYE.

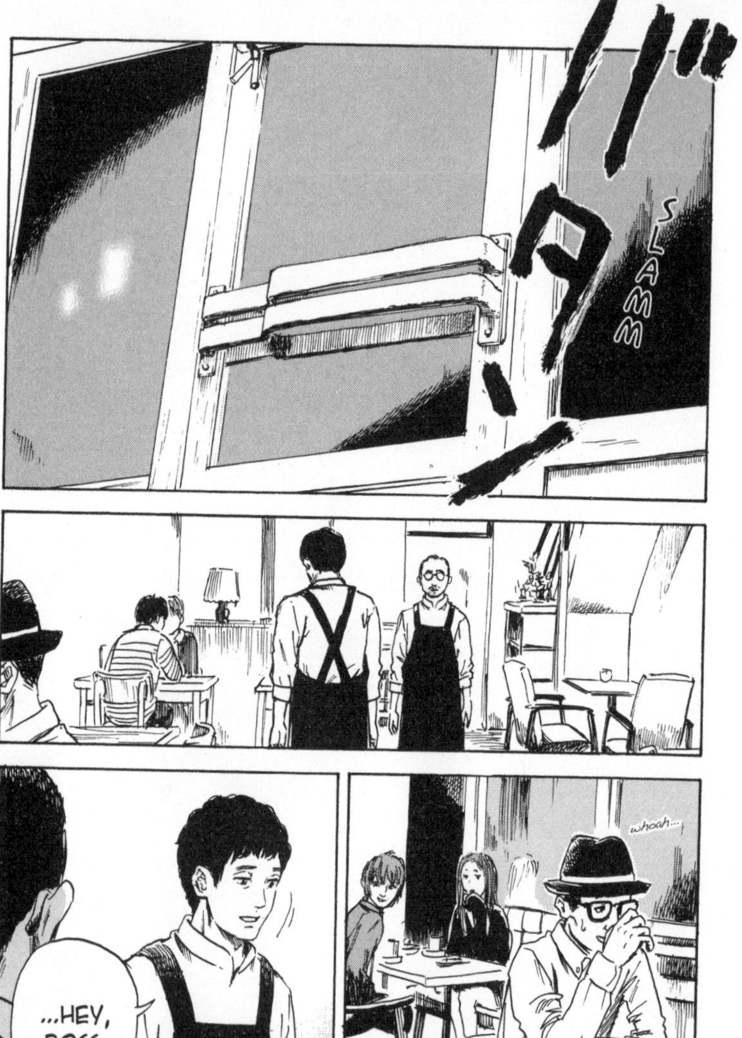
バタン
SLAMM
whoah...
...HEY, BOSS.

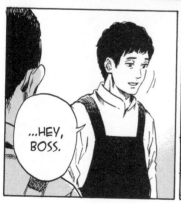

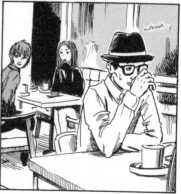

...

SURE ...

CAN I GO ON MY BREAK, NOW?

I'VE NEVER SEEN AYA

LOOK LIKE THAT BEFORE. HA HA...

HA HA

I'VE...

PAT ポン

HA HA HA

95

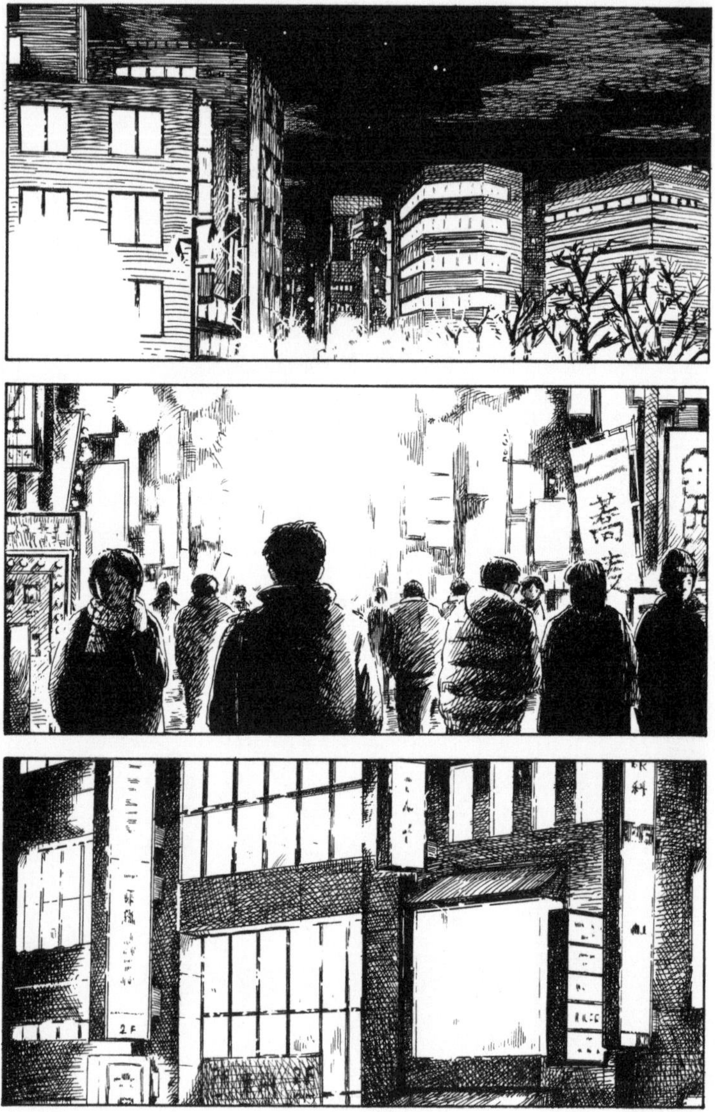
蕎麦
2F

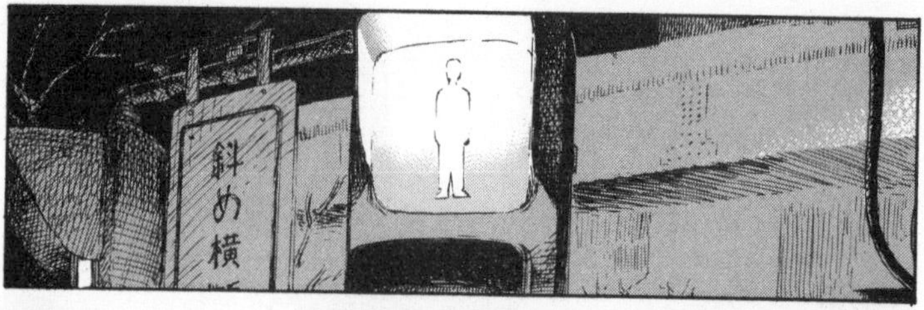
斜め横
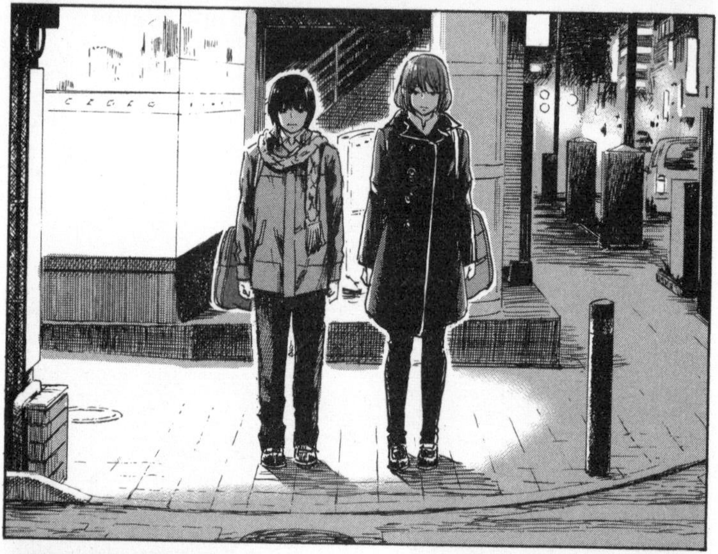
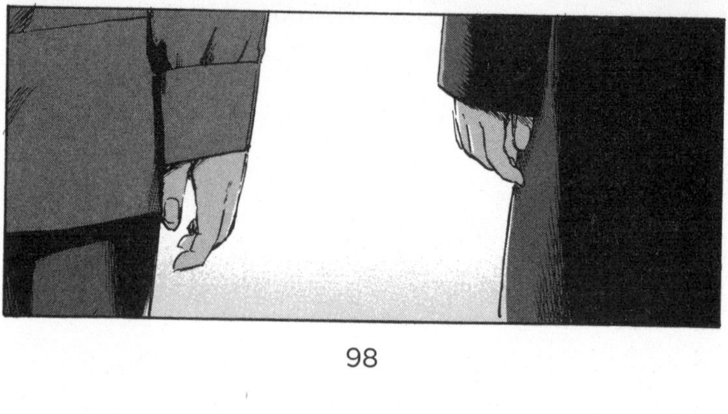

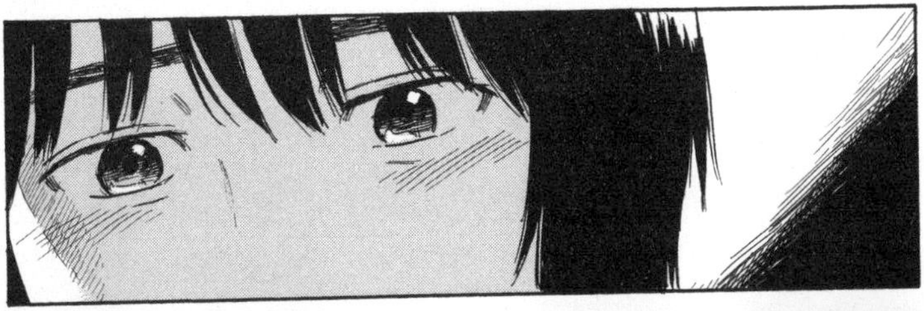
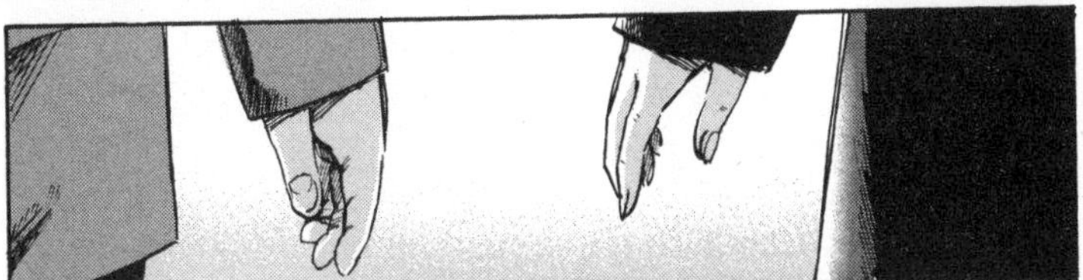
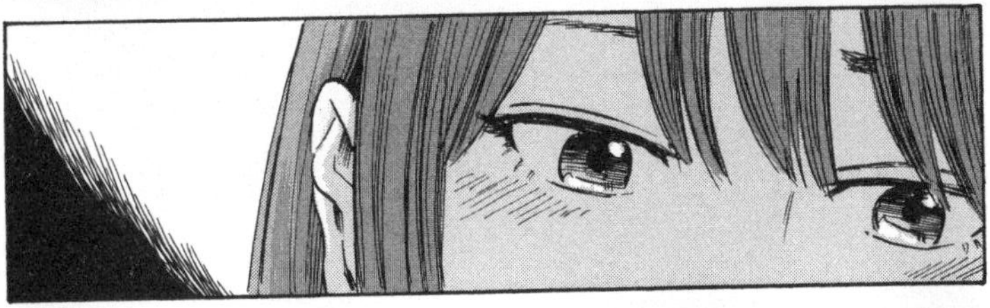
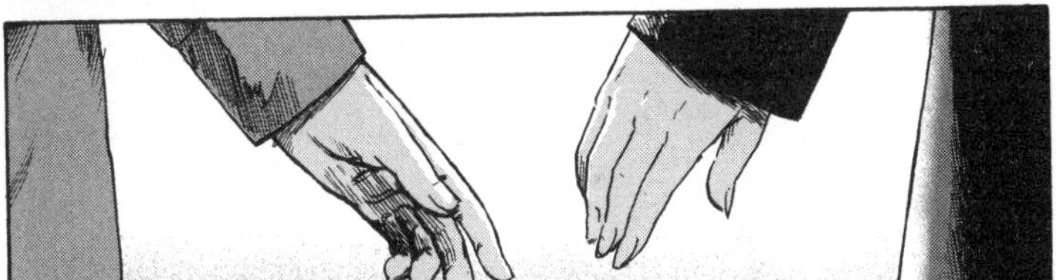
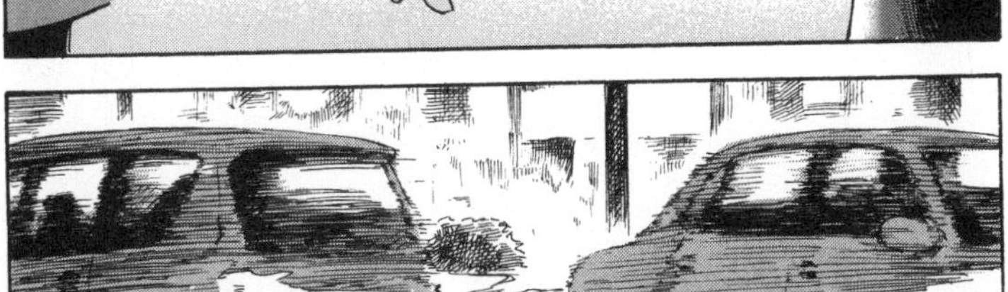

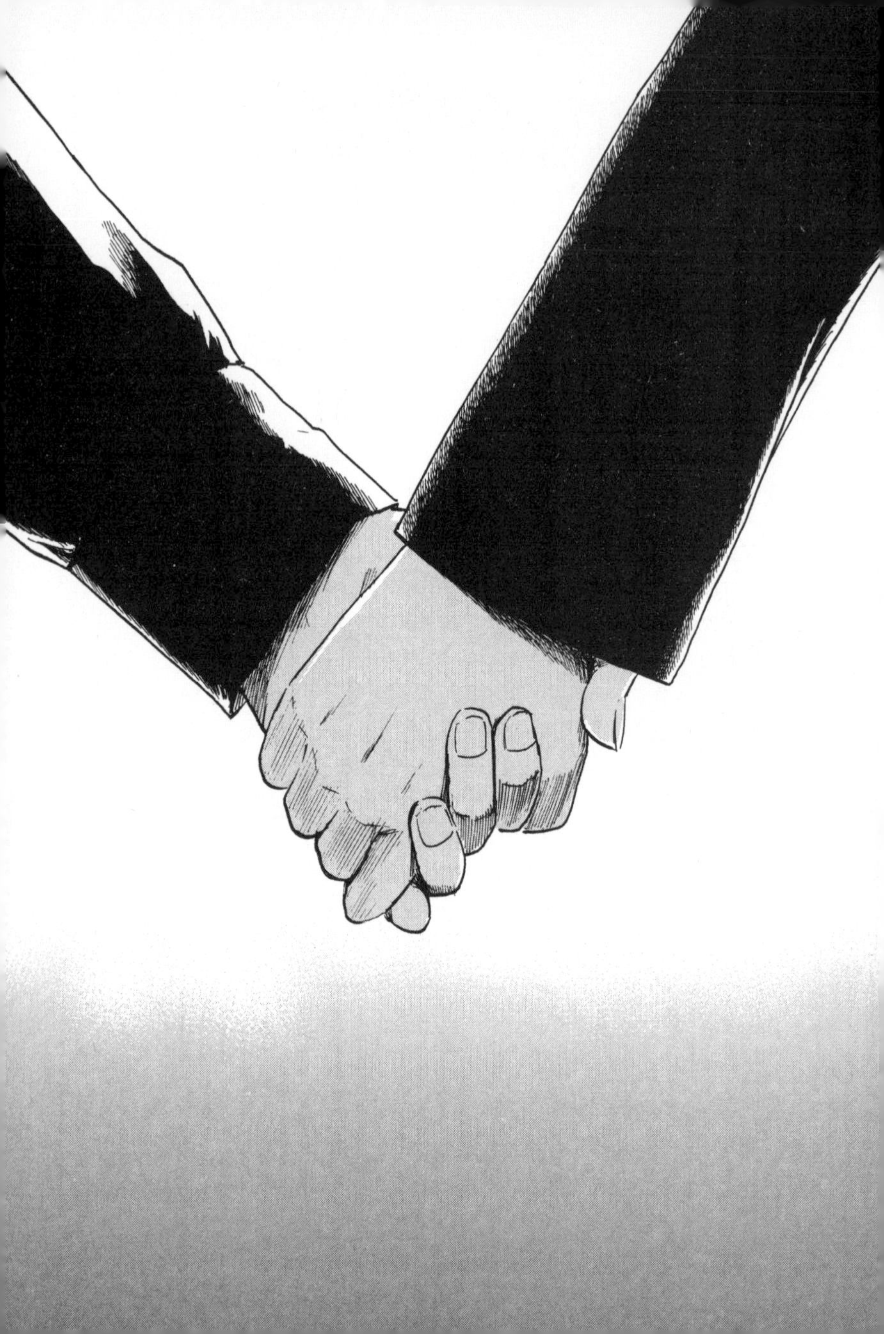

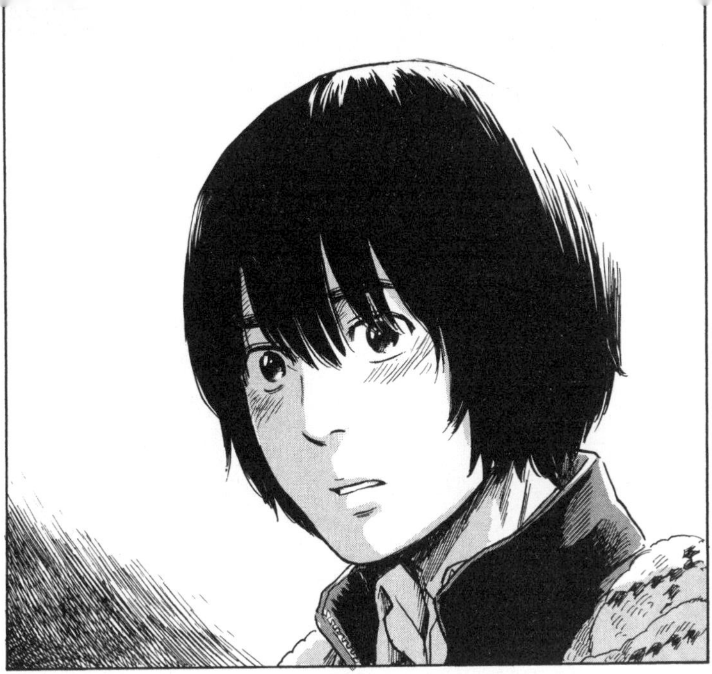
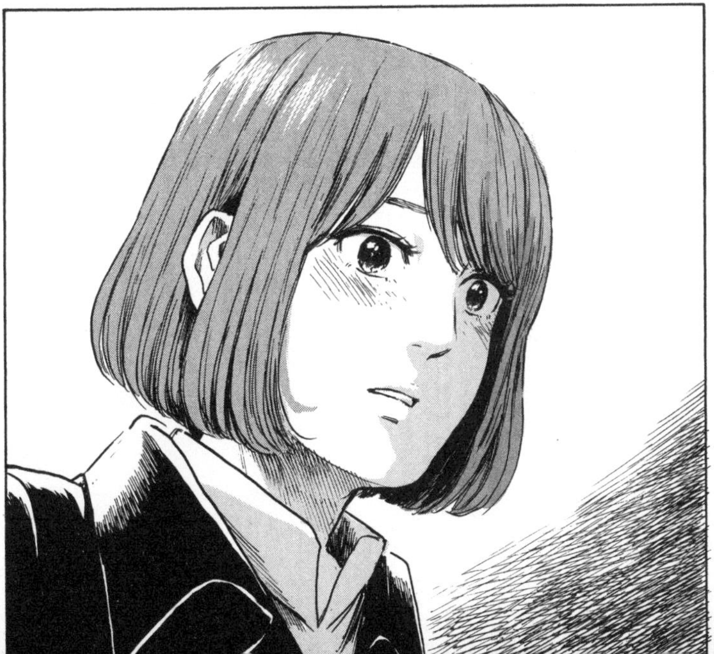

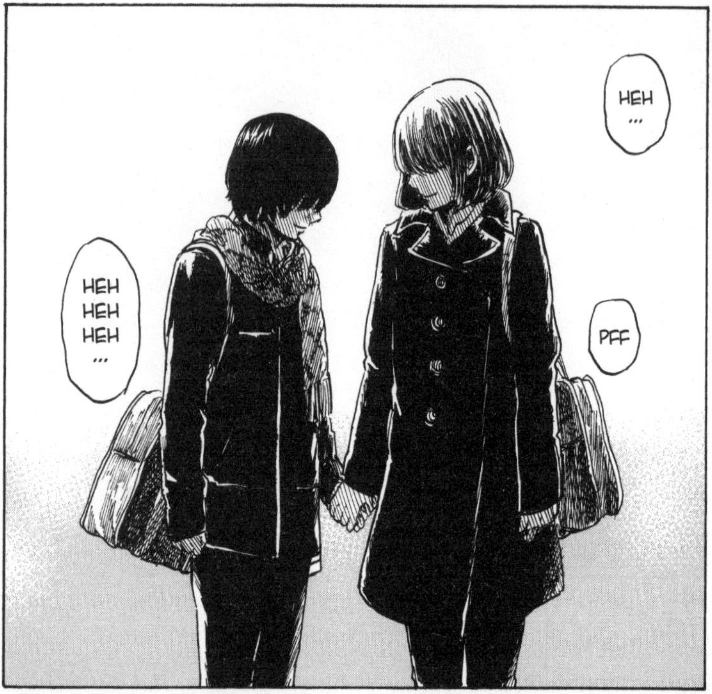
HEH ...
PFF
HEH HEH HEH ...

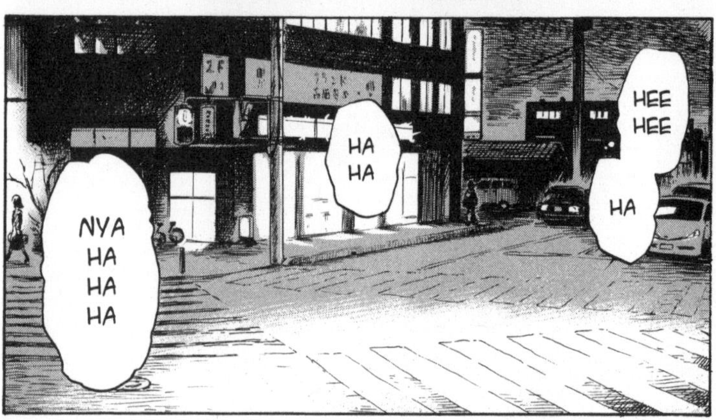
HEE HEE
HA
HA HA
NYA HA HA HA

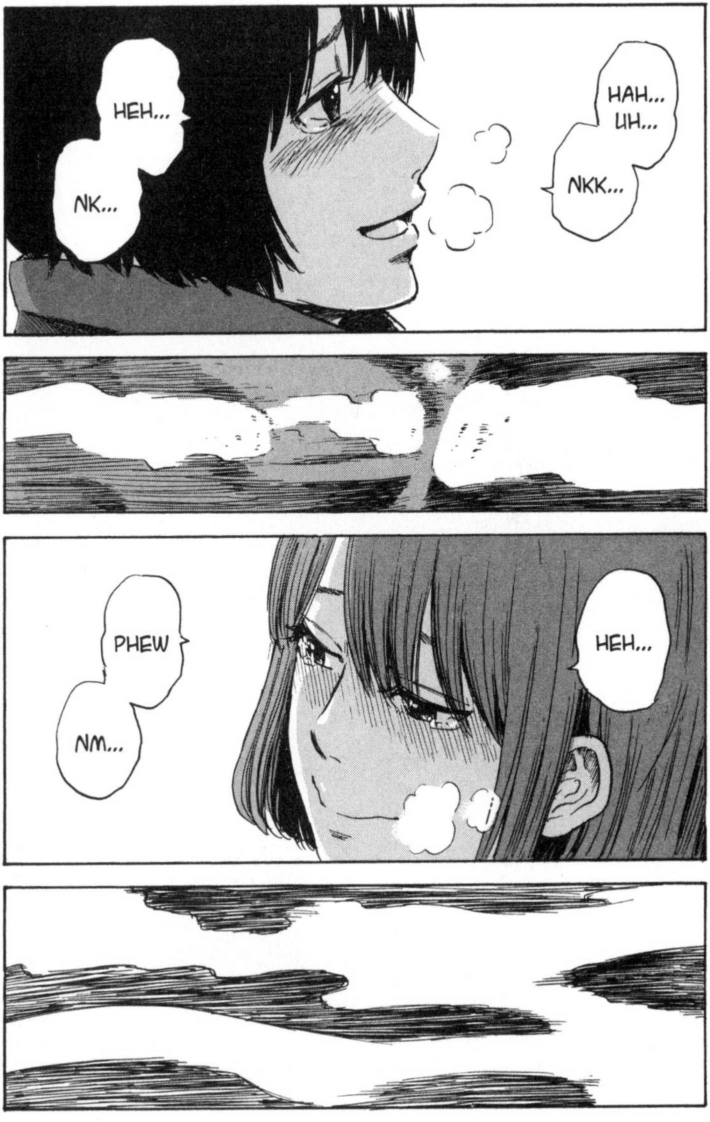
HAH... UH...
NKK...
HEH...
NK...
HEH...
PHEW
NM...

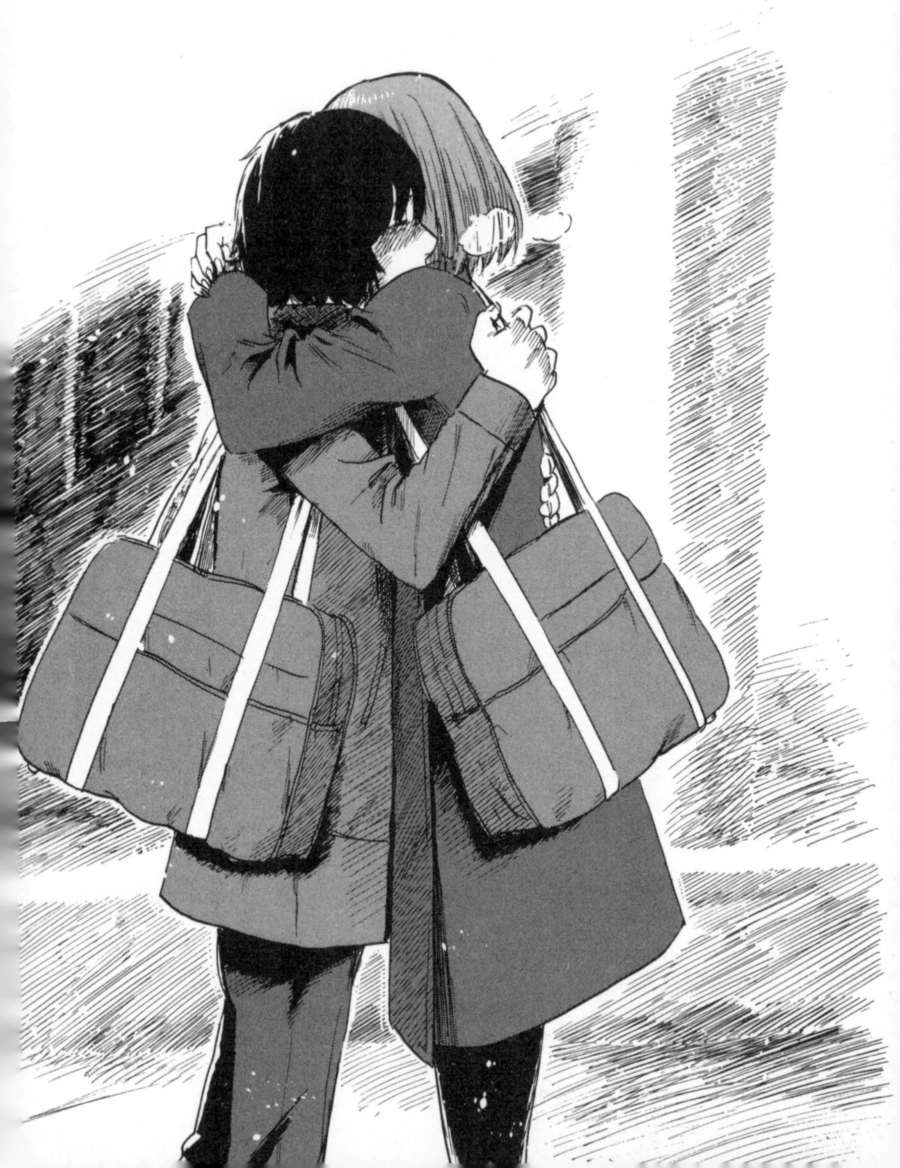

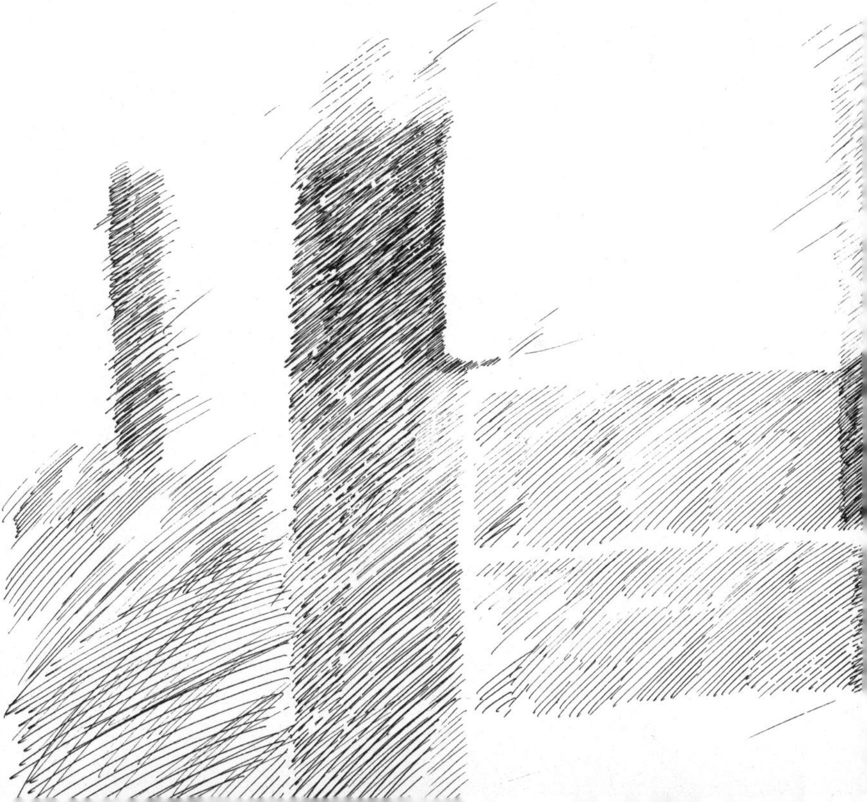

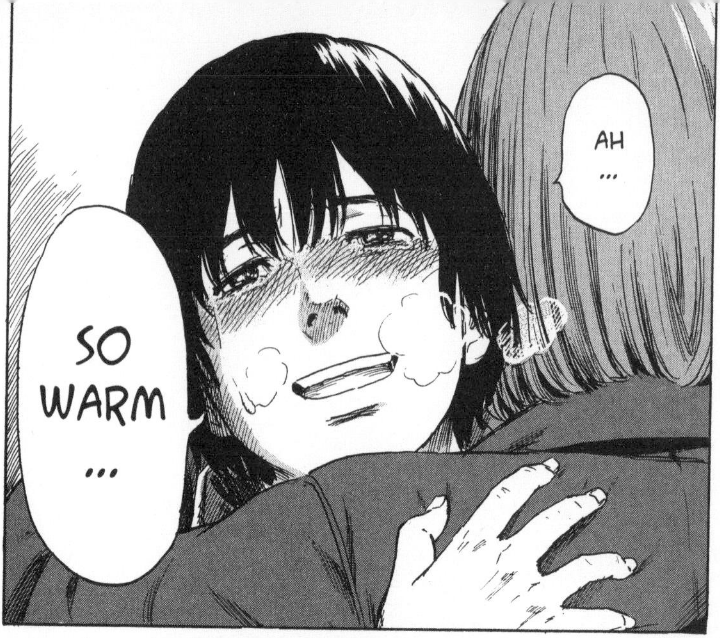
AH ...
SO WARM ...
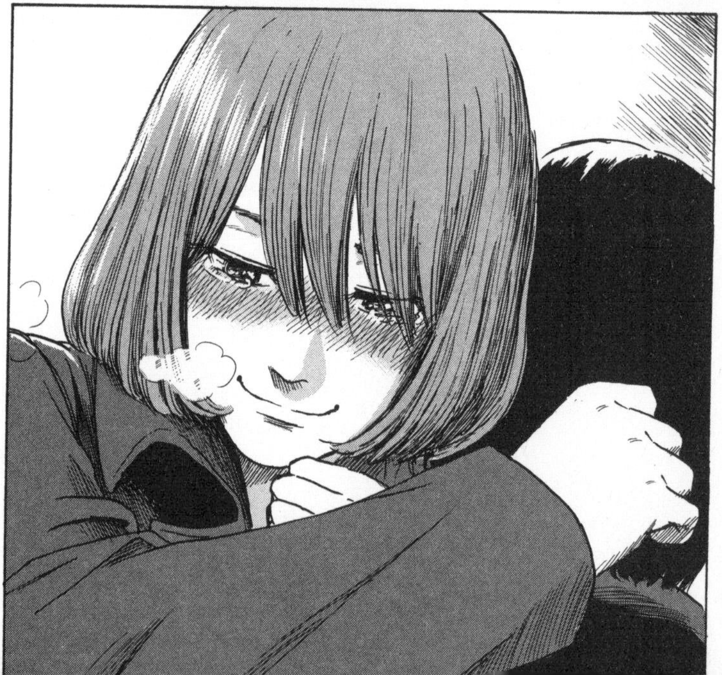

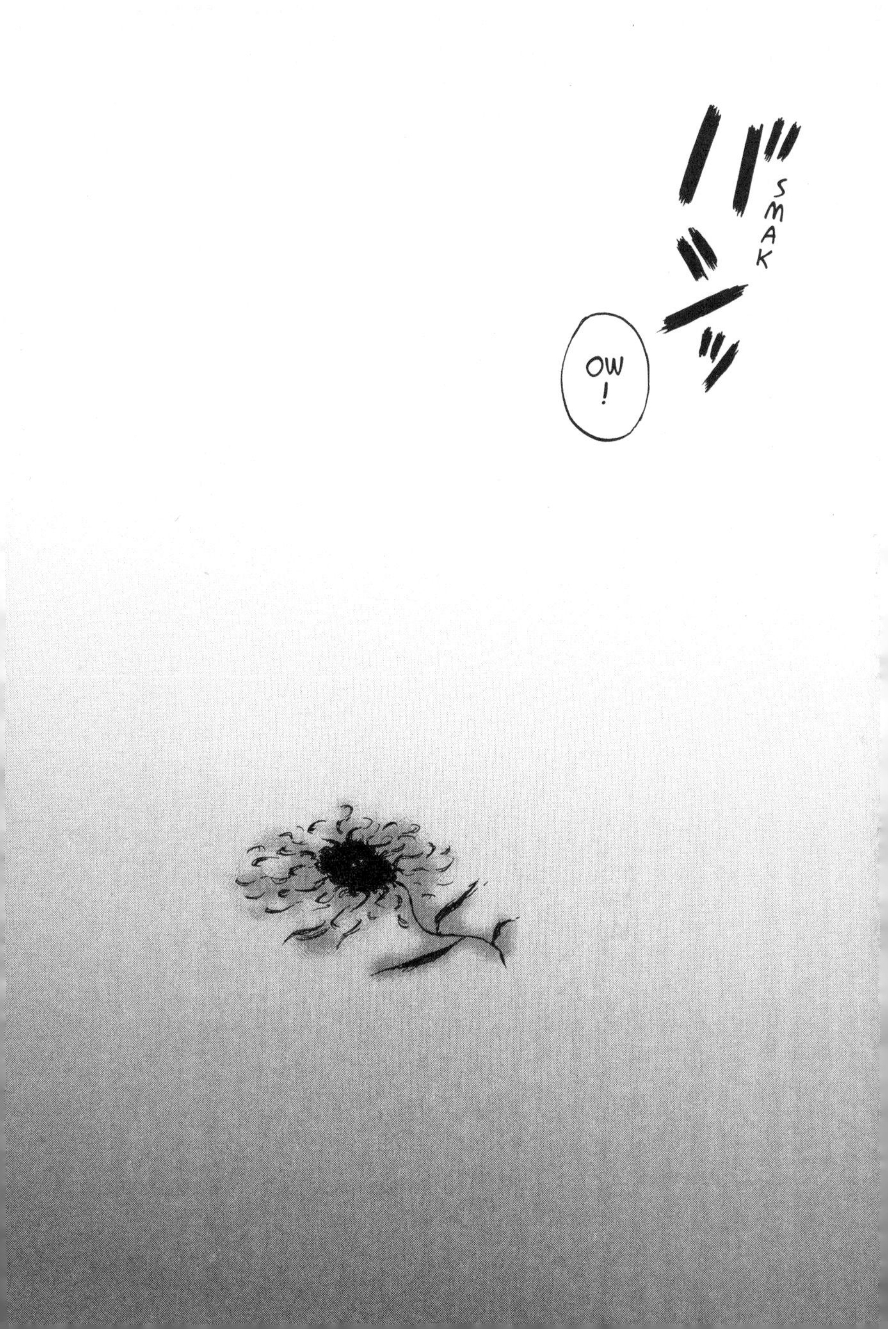
SMAK
OW!

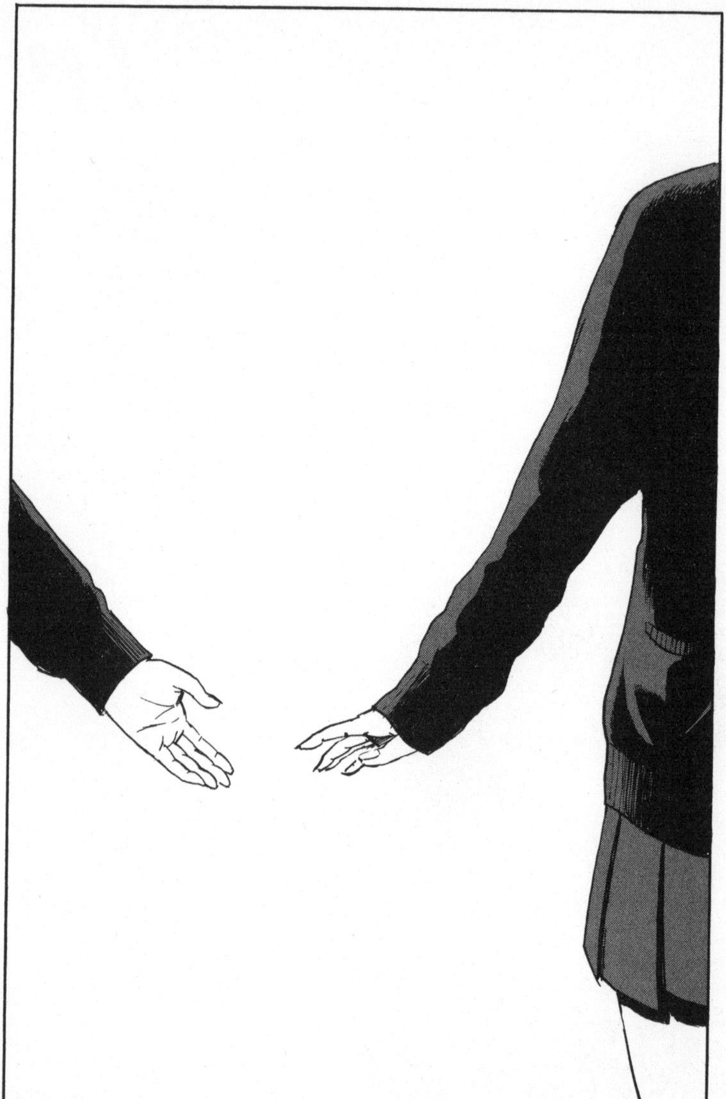

Chapter 46: O Fountain of Eternal Youth

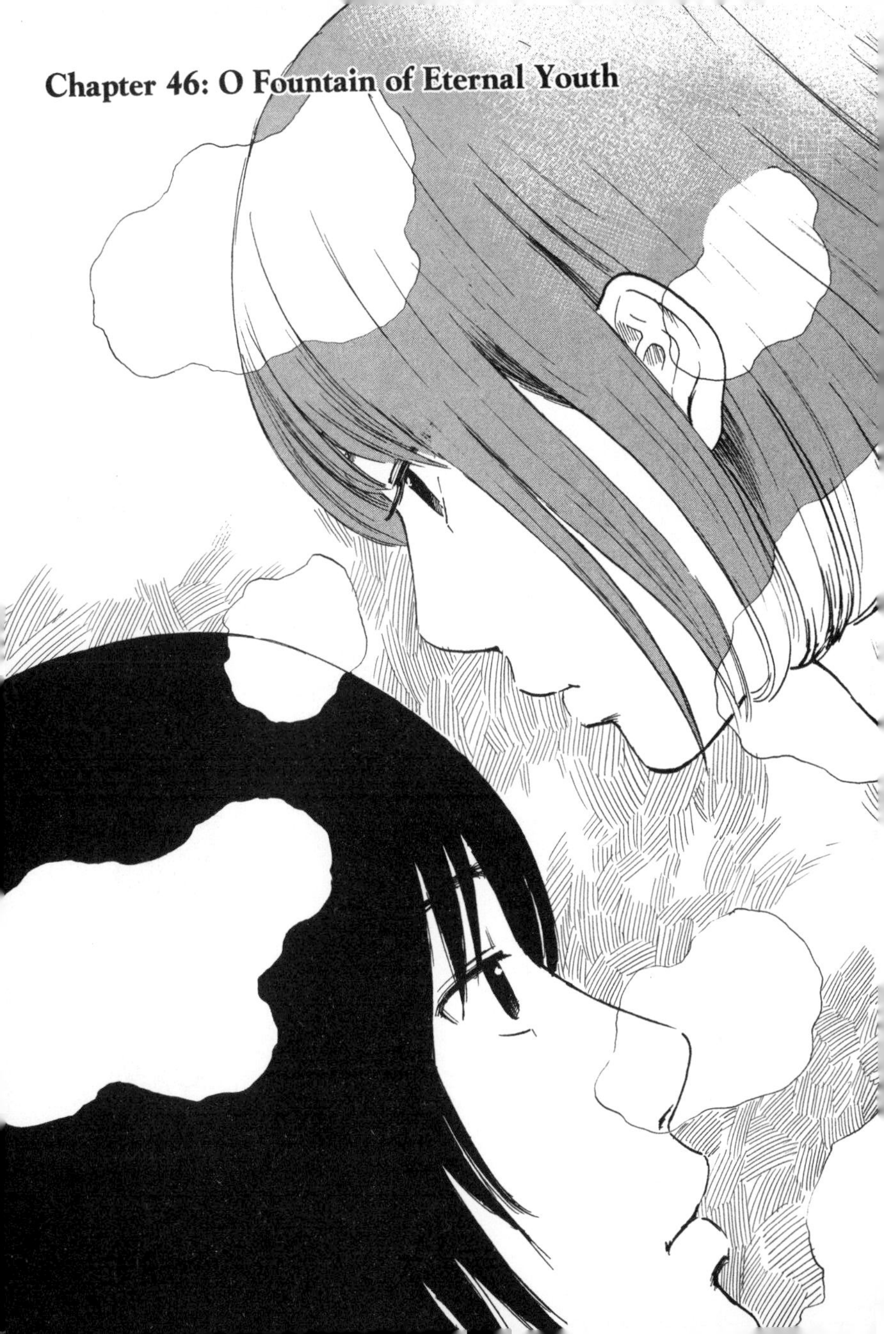

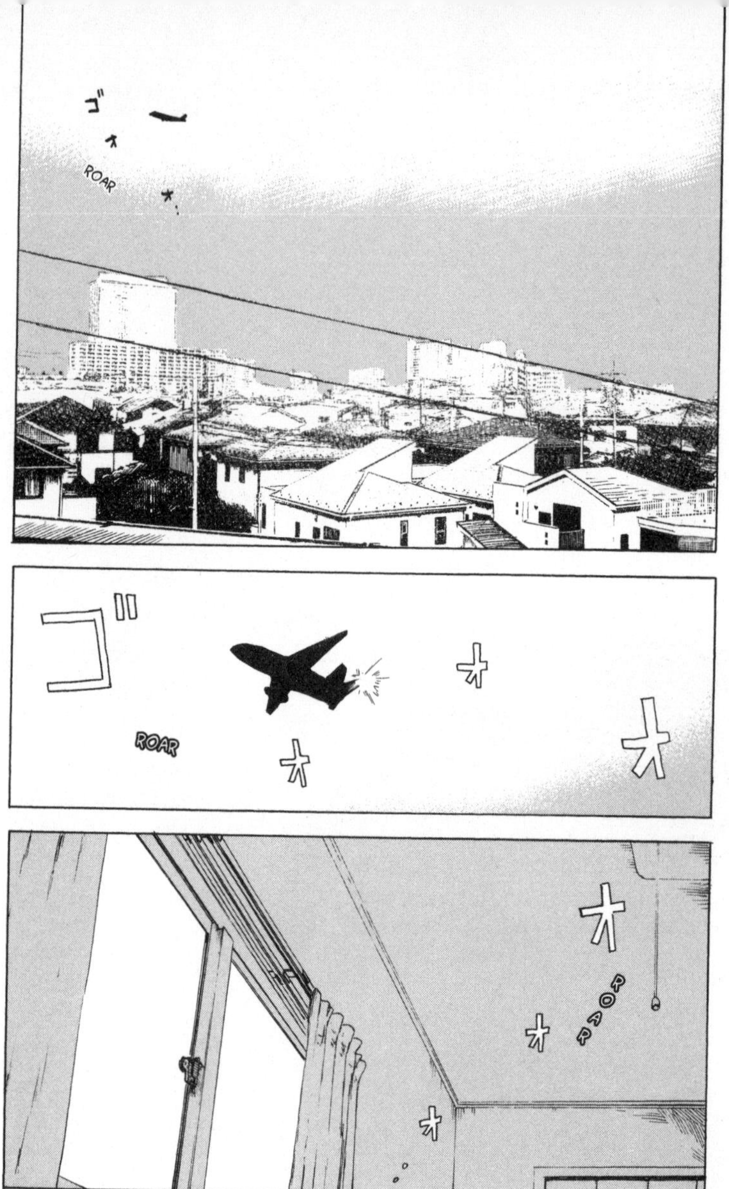
ゴォォ…
ROAR
ゴオオオ
ROAR
オオオ
ROAR

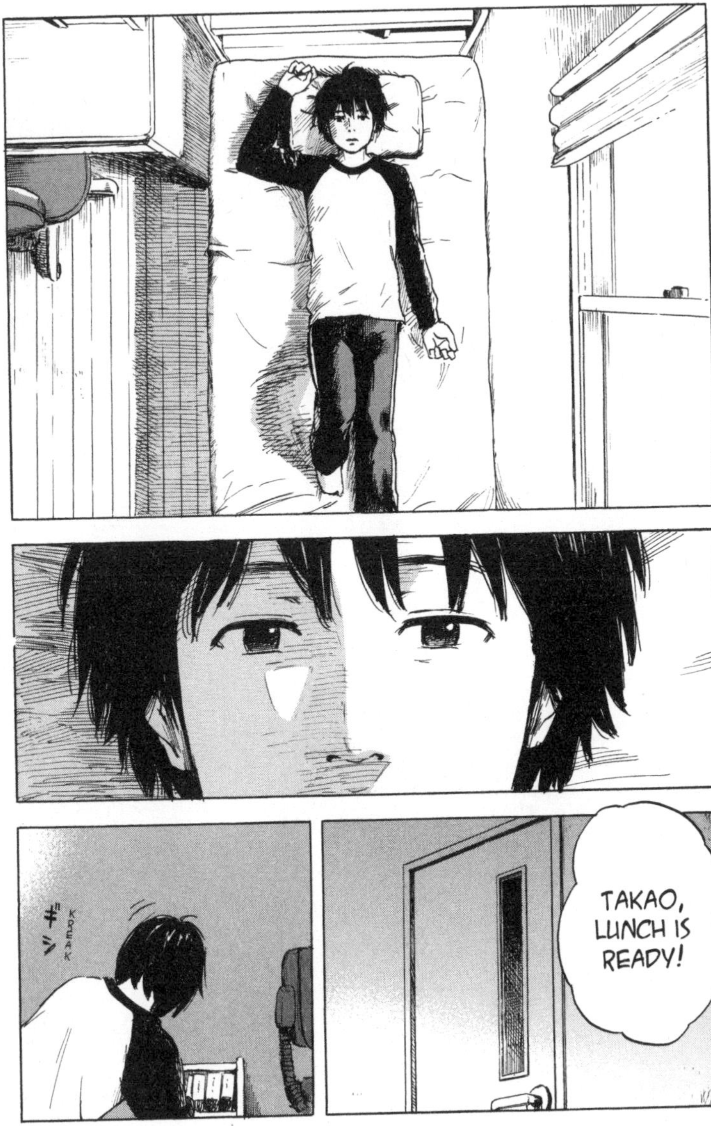
TAKAO, LUNCH IS READY!
ギシ
KREAK

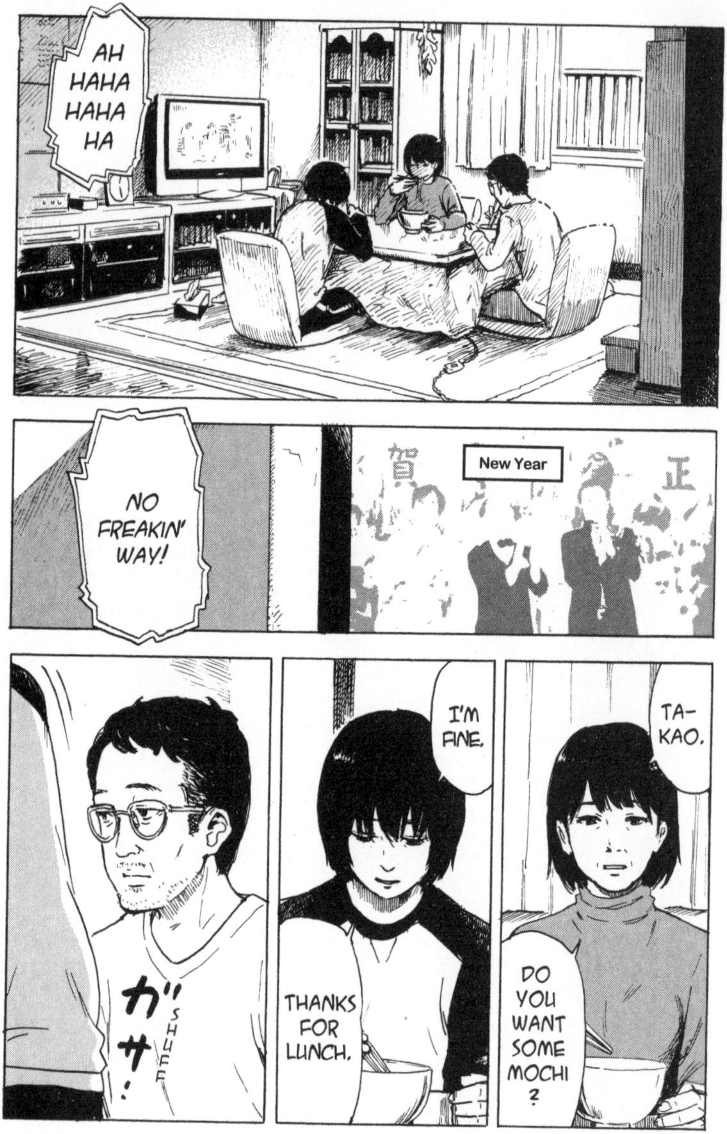
AH HAHA HAHA HA
New Year
NO FREAKIN' WAY!
TA-KAO.
DO YOU WANT SOME MOCHI?
I'M FINE.
THANKS FOR LUNCH.
ガサ!
SHUFF

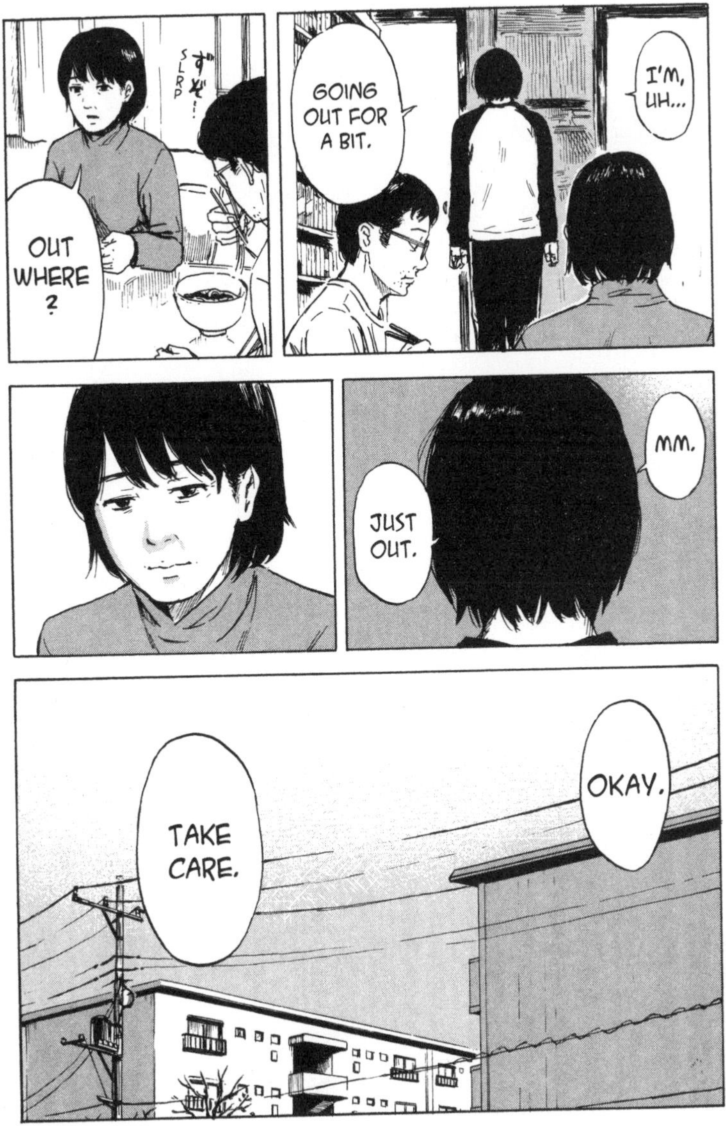
I'M, UH...
GOING OUT FOR A BIT.
ずぞ
SLRP
OUT WHERE?
MM.
JUST OUT.
OKAY.
TAKE CARE.

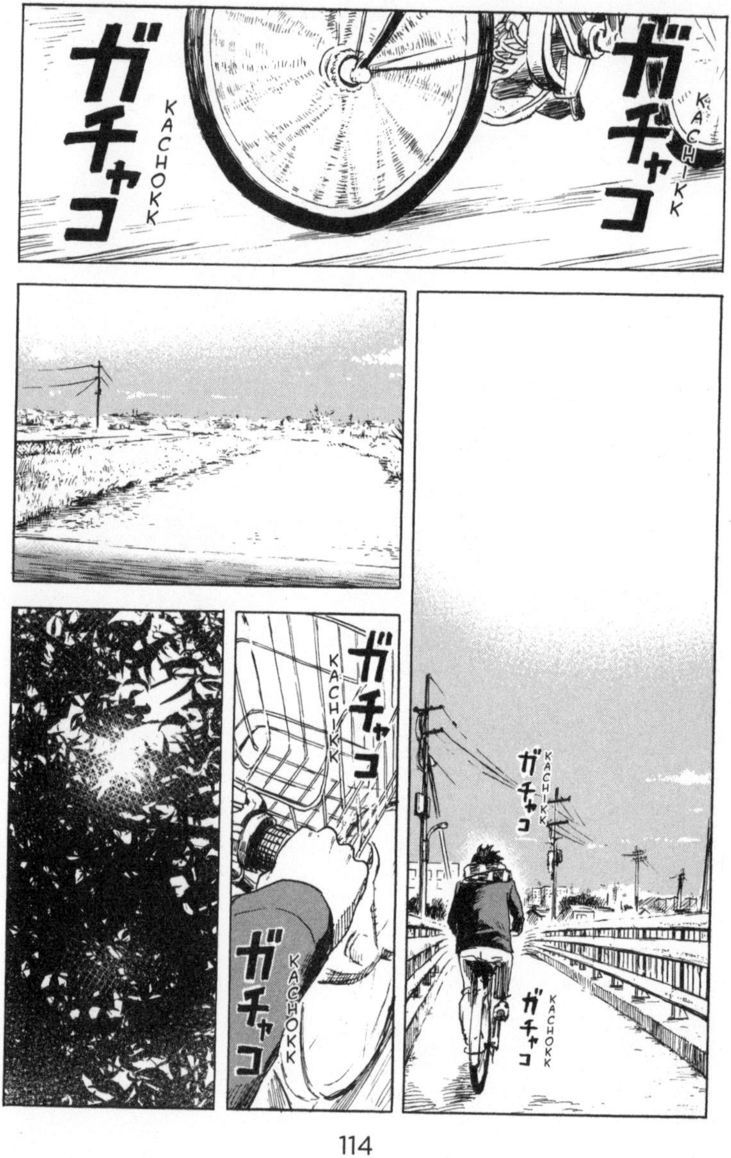
ガチャコ
KACHIKK
ガチャコ
KACHOKK
ガチャコ
KACHIKK
ガチャコ
KACHOKK
ガチャコ
KACHIKK
ガチャコ
KACHOKK

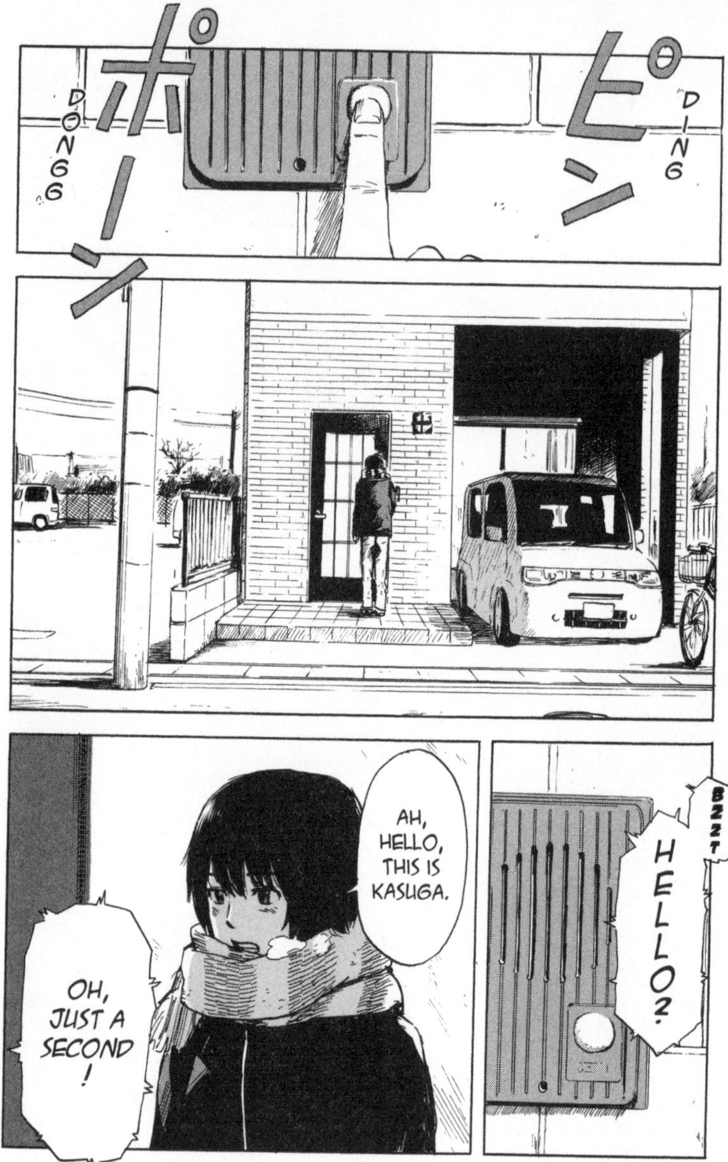
ピン
DING
ポーン
DONGG
BZZT
HELLO?
AH, HELLO, THIS IS KASUGA.
OH, JUST A SECOND!

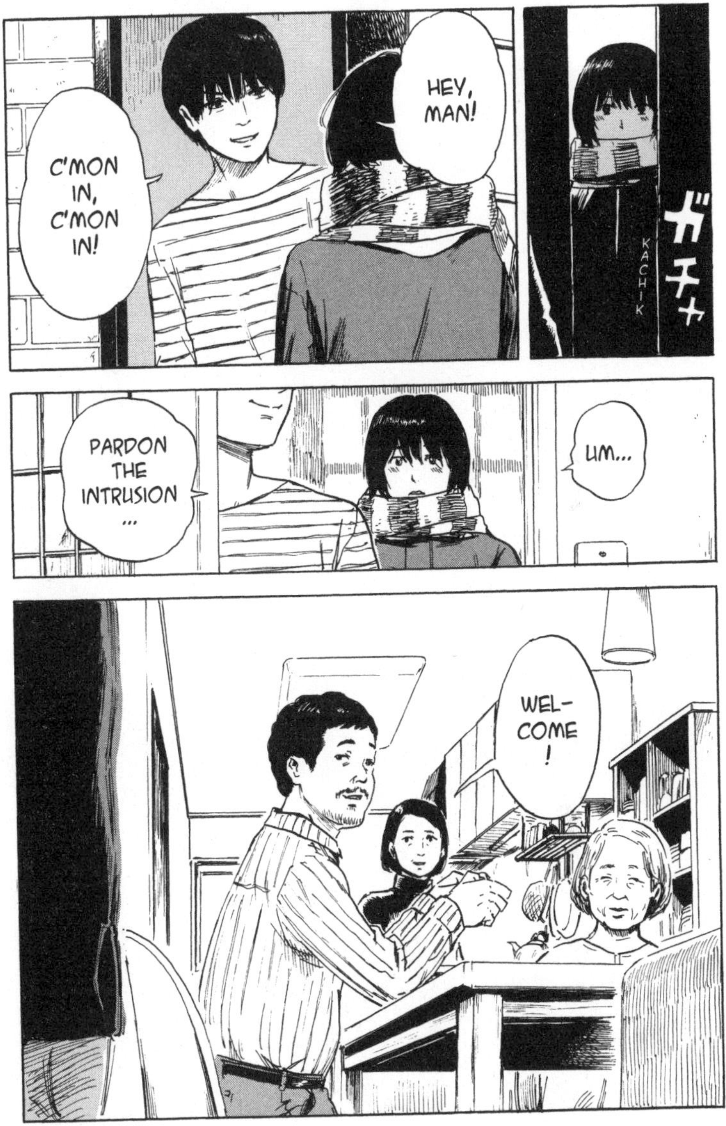
ガチャ
KACHIK
HEY, MAN!
C'MON IN, C'MON IN!
UM...
PARDON THE INTRUSION ...
WEL-COME!

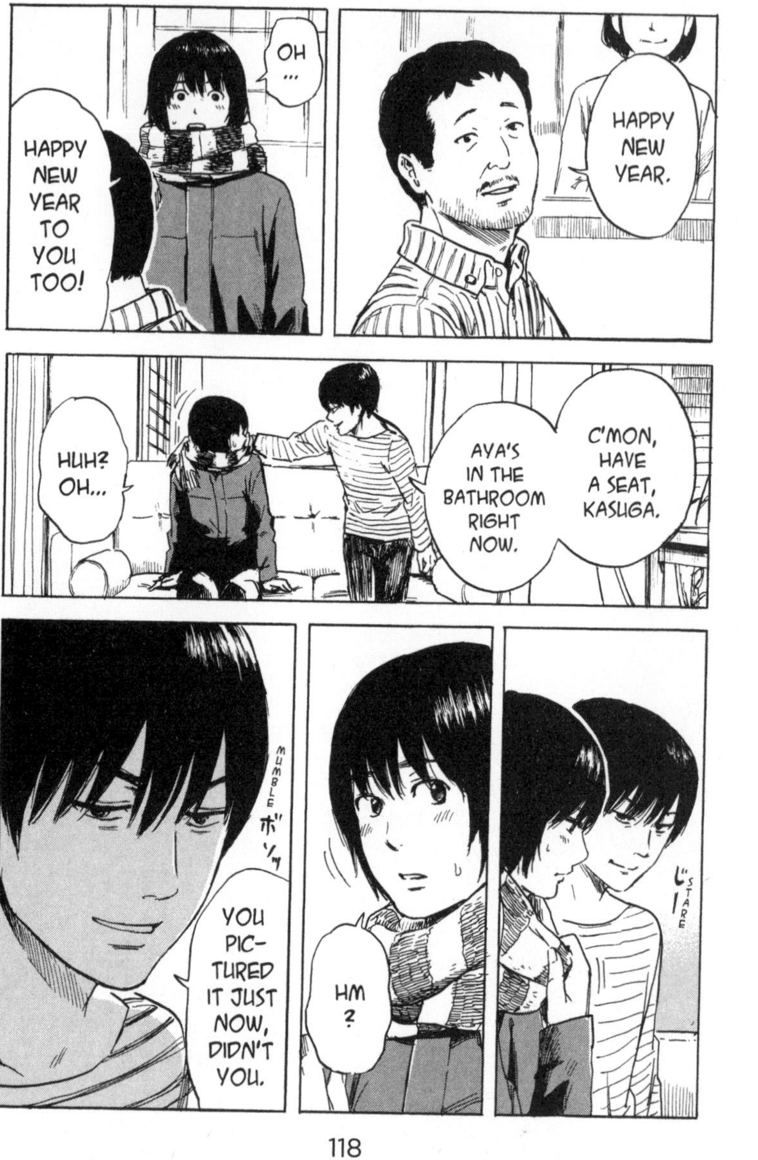
HAPPY NEW YEAR.
OH ...
HAPPY NEW YEAR TO YOU TOO!
C'MON, HAVE A SEAT, KASUGA.
AYA'S IN THE BATHROOM RIGHT NOW.
HUH? OH...
じー
STARE
HM ?
MUMBLE
ボソッ
YOU PIC-TURED IT JUST NOW, DIDN'T YOU.

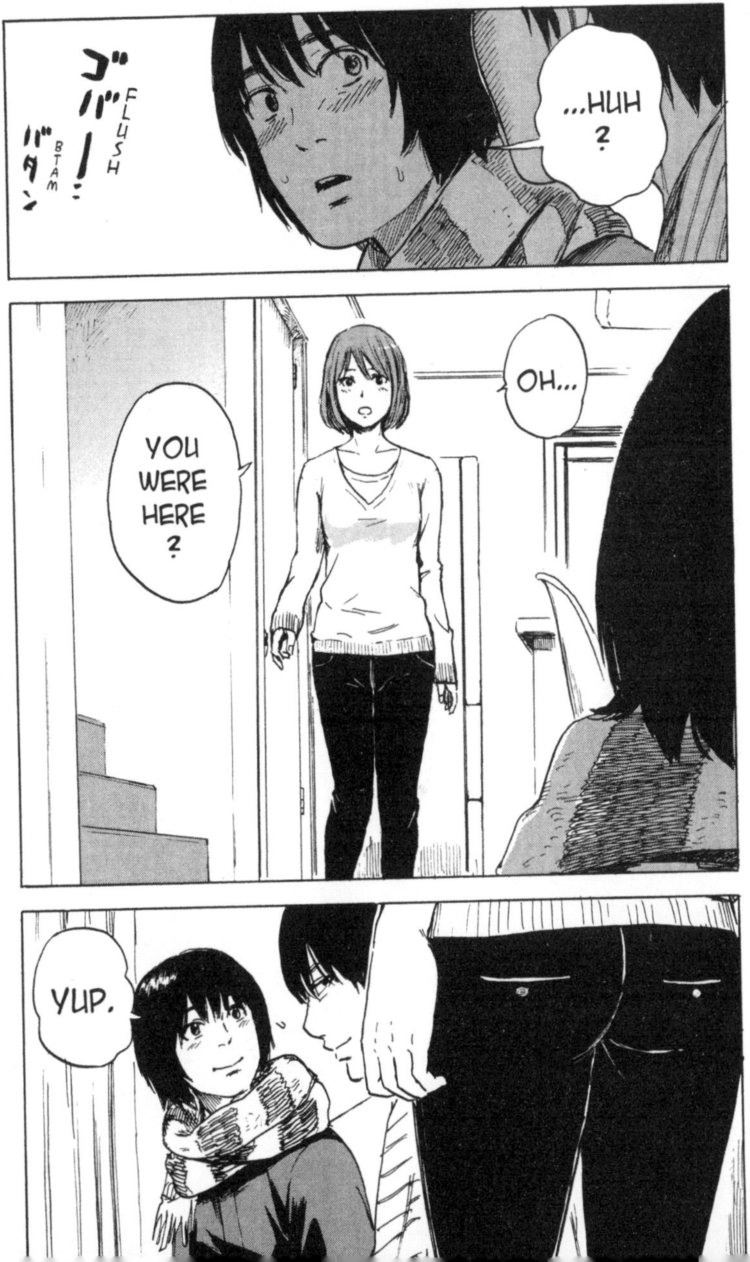
...HUH?
ゴバー!!
FLUSH
バタン
BTAM
OH...
YOU WERE HERE?
YUP.

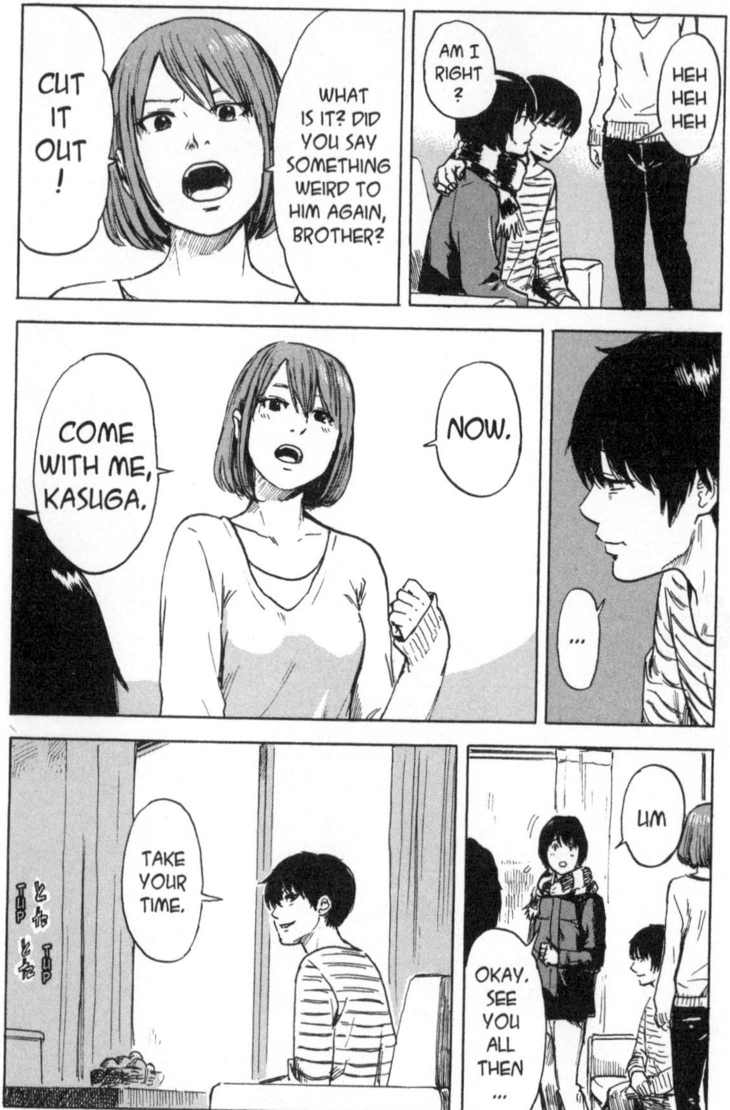
AM I RIGHT ?
HEH HEH HEH
WHAT IS IT? DID YOU SAY SOMETHING WEIRD TO HIM AGAIN, BROTHER?
CUT IT OUT !
...
COME WITH ME, KASUGA.
NOW.
UM
OKAY. SEE YOU ALL THEN ...
TAKE YOUR TIME.
とた TUP
とた TUP

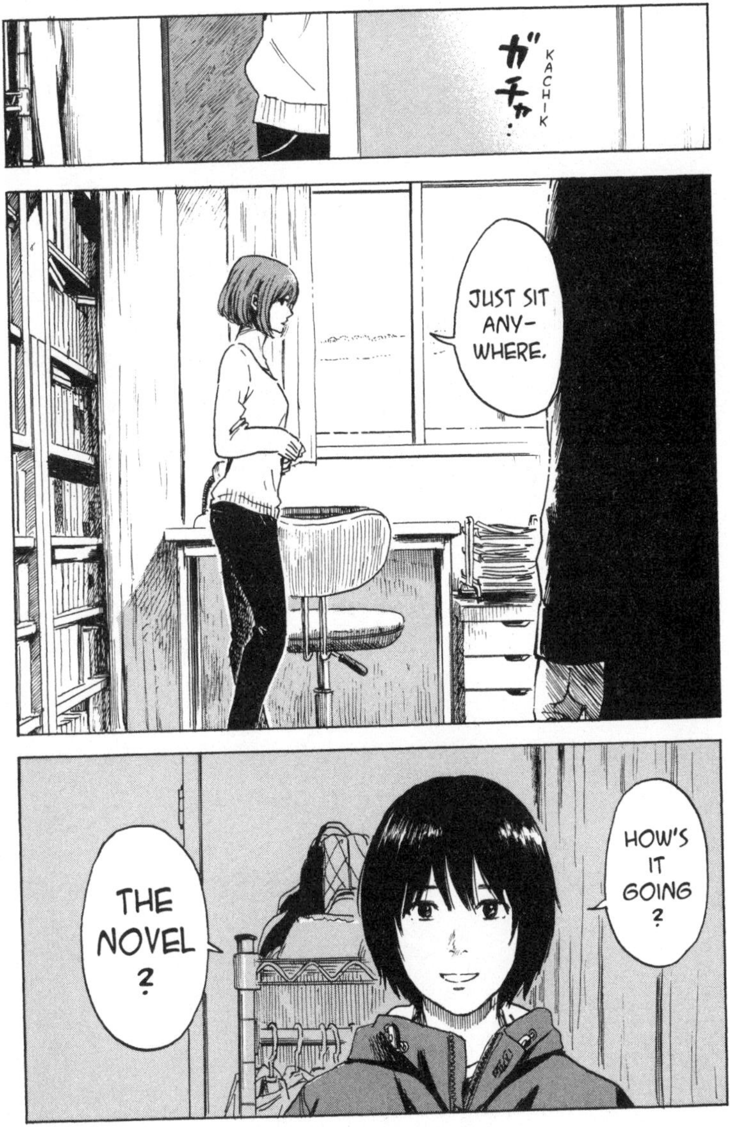
ガチャ
KACHIK
JUST SIT ANY-WHERE.
HOW'S IT GOING?
THE NOVEL?

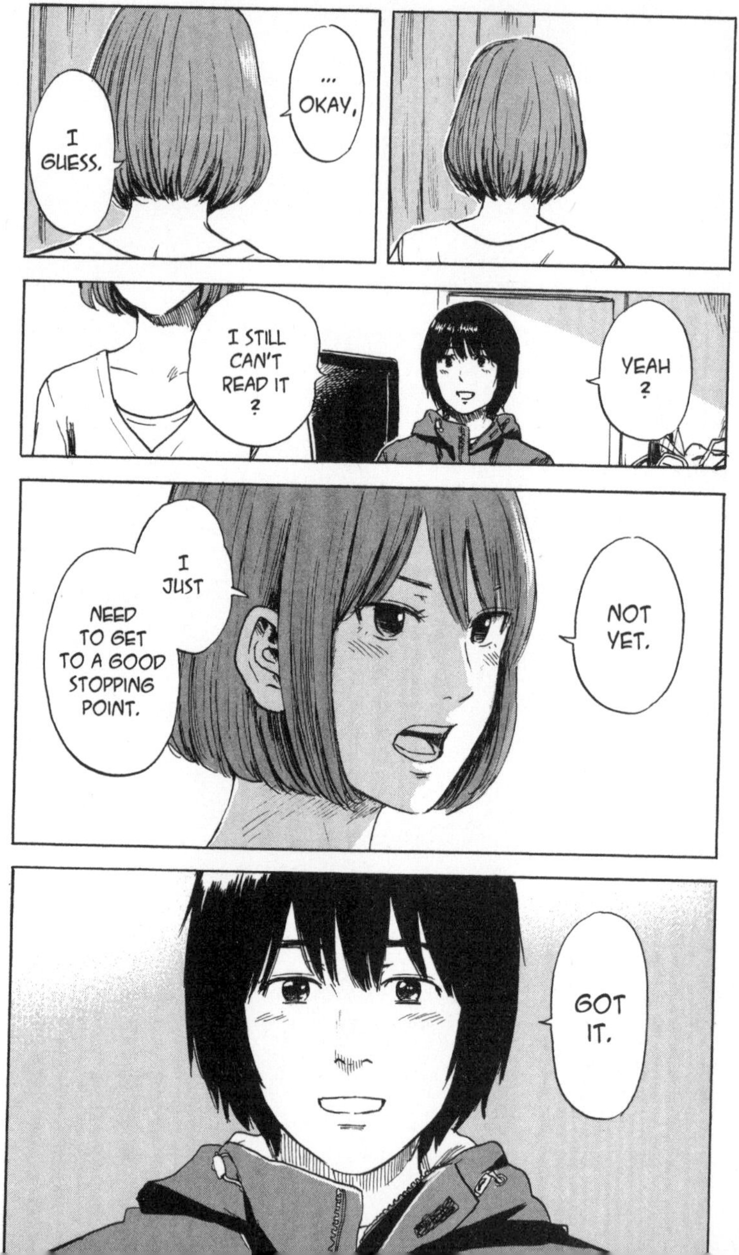
... OKAY,
I GUESS.
YEAH ?
I STILL CAN'T READ IT ?
NOT YET.
I JUST
NEED TO GET TO A GOOD STOPPING POINT.
GOT IT.

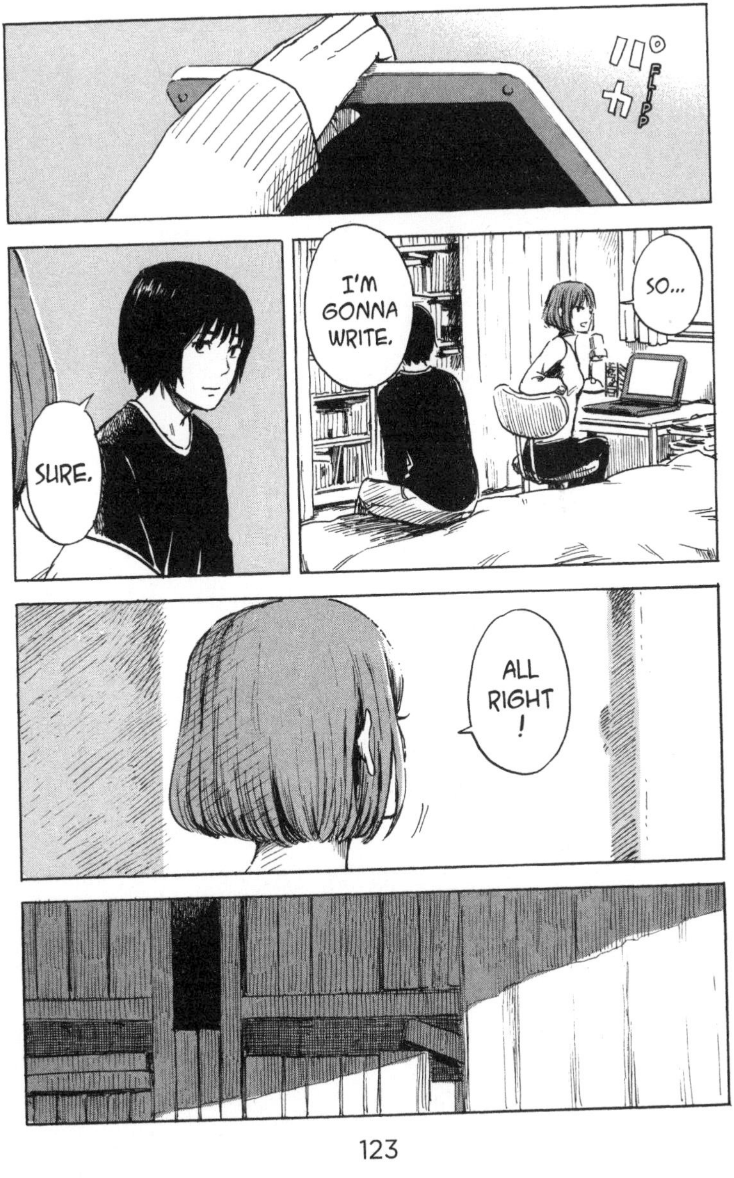
パカ
FLIPP
SO...
I'M GONNA WRITE.
SURE.
ALL RIGHT!

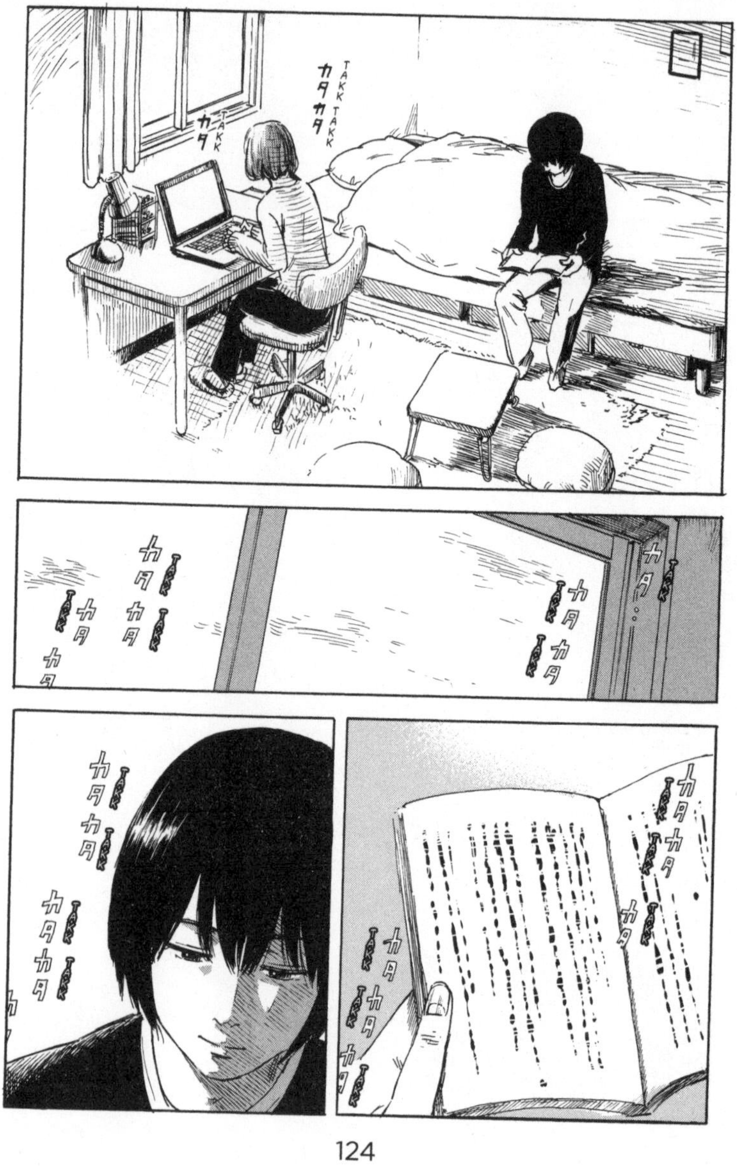
カタカタ
TAKK TAKK
カタ
TAKK
カタ
TAKK
カタ
TAKK
カタ
TAKK
カタ
TAKK
カタカタ
TAKK TAKK
カタ
TAKK
カタカタ
TAKK TAKK
カタカタ
TAKK TAKK
カタカタ
TAKK TAKK
カタ
TAKK
カタ
TAKK
カタ
TAKK
カタ
TAKK

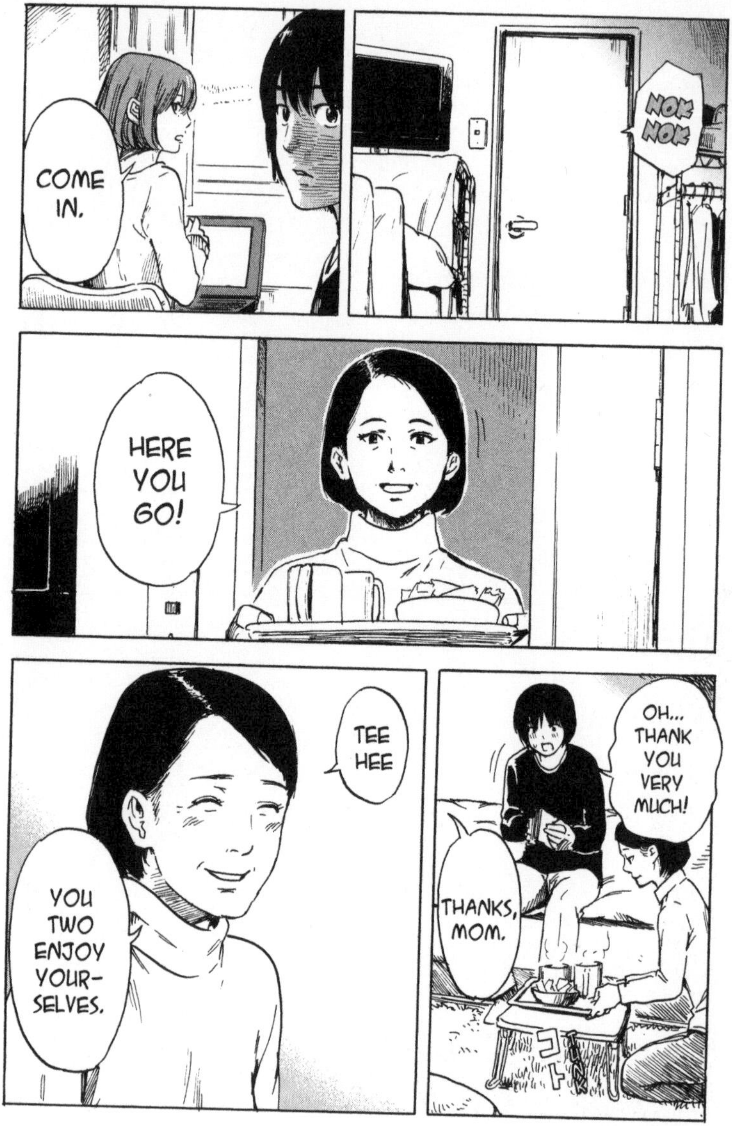
NOK NOK
COME IN.
HERE YOU GO!
OH... THANK YOU VERY MUCH!
THANKS, MOM.
コト
TEE HEE
YOU TWO ENJOY YOUR-SELVES.

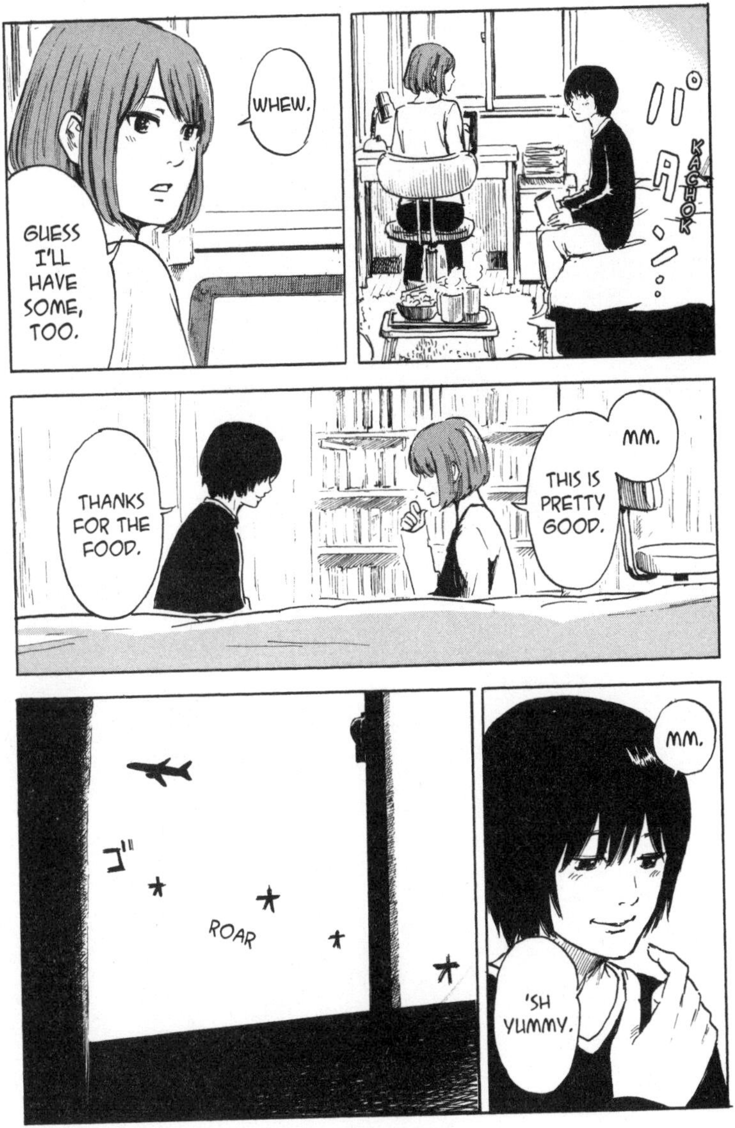
パ
KACHOK
WHEW.
GUESS I'LL HAVE SOME, TOO.
MM.
THIS IS PRETTY GOOD.
THANKS FOR THE FOOD.
MM.
'SH YUMMY.
ゴ
ROAR

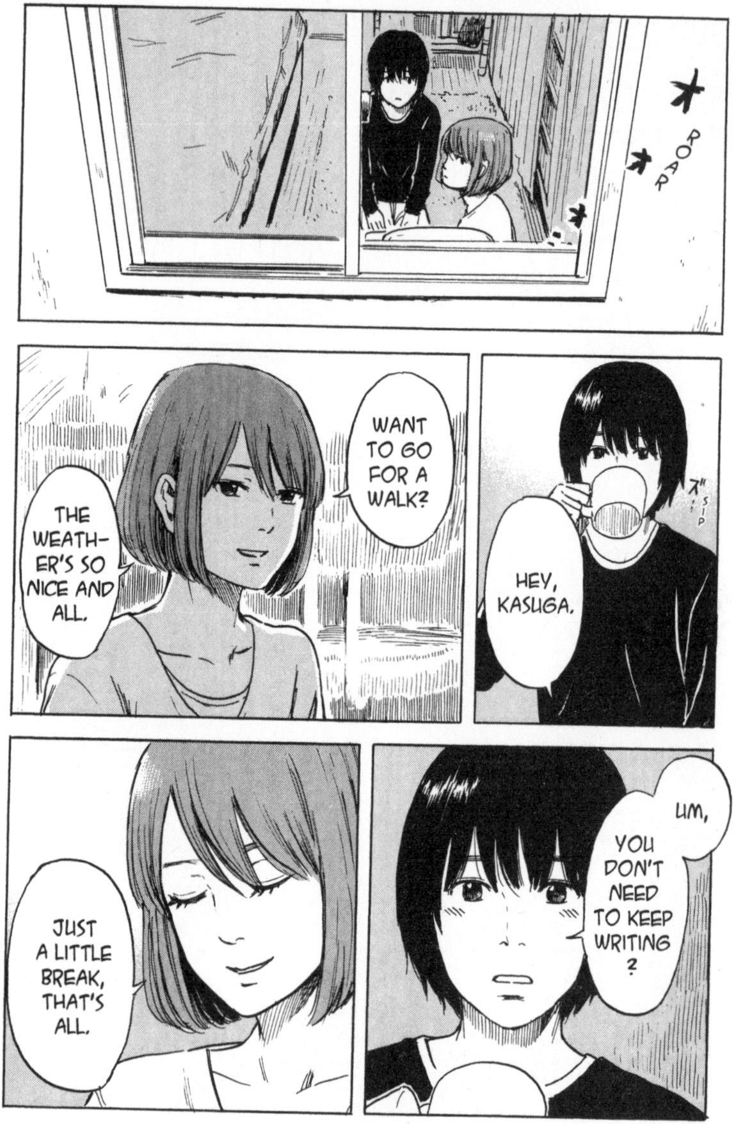
ROAR
SIP
HEY, KASUGA.
WANT TO GO FOR A WALK?
THE WEATHER'S SO NICE AND ALL.
UM, YOU DON'T NEED TO KEEP WRITING?
JUST A LITTLE BREAK, THAT'S ALL.

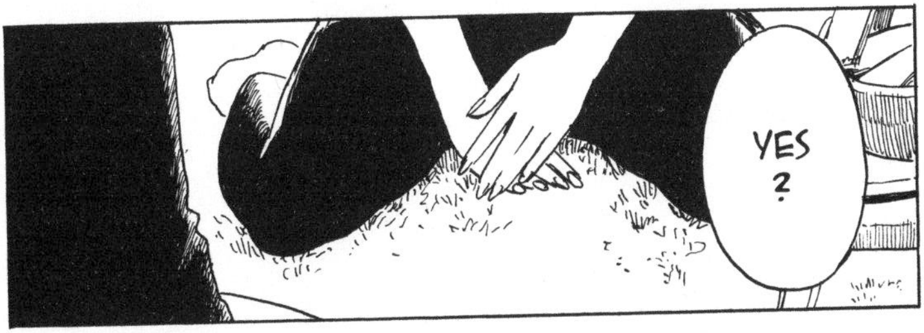
YES ?
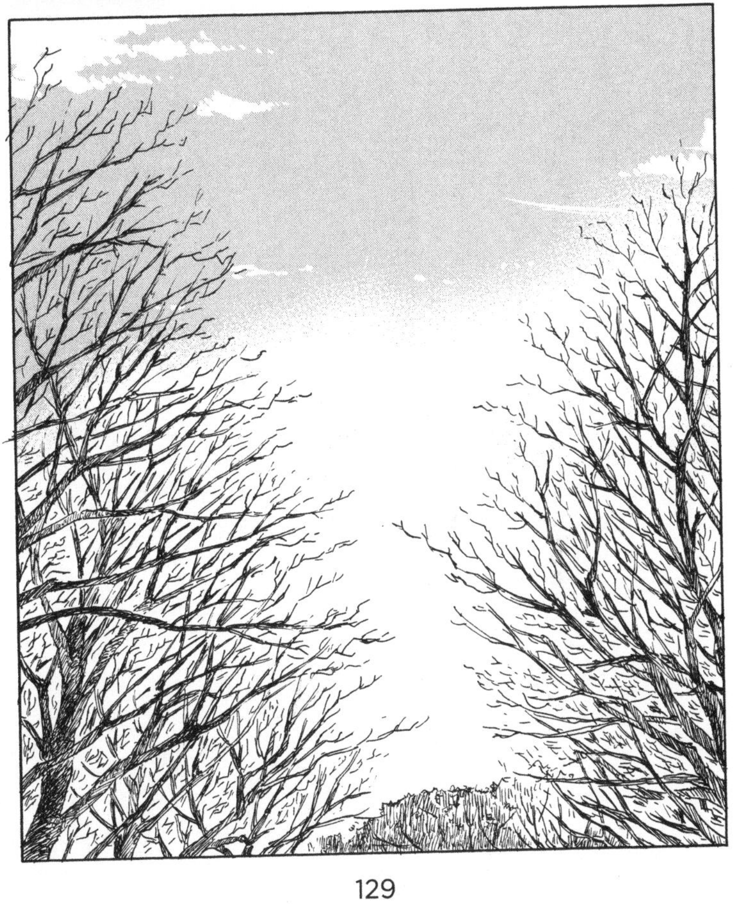

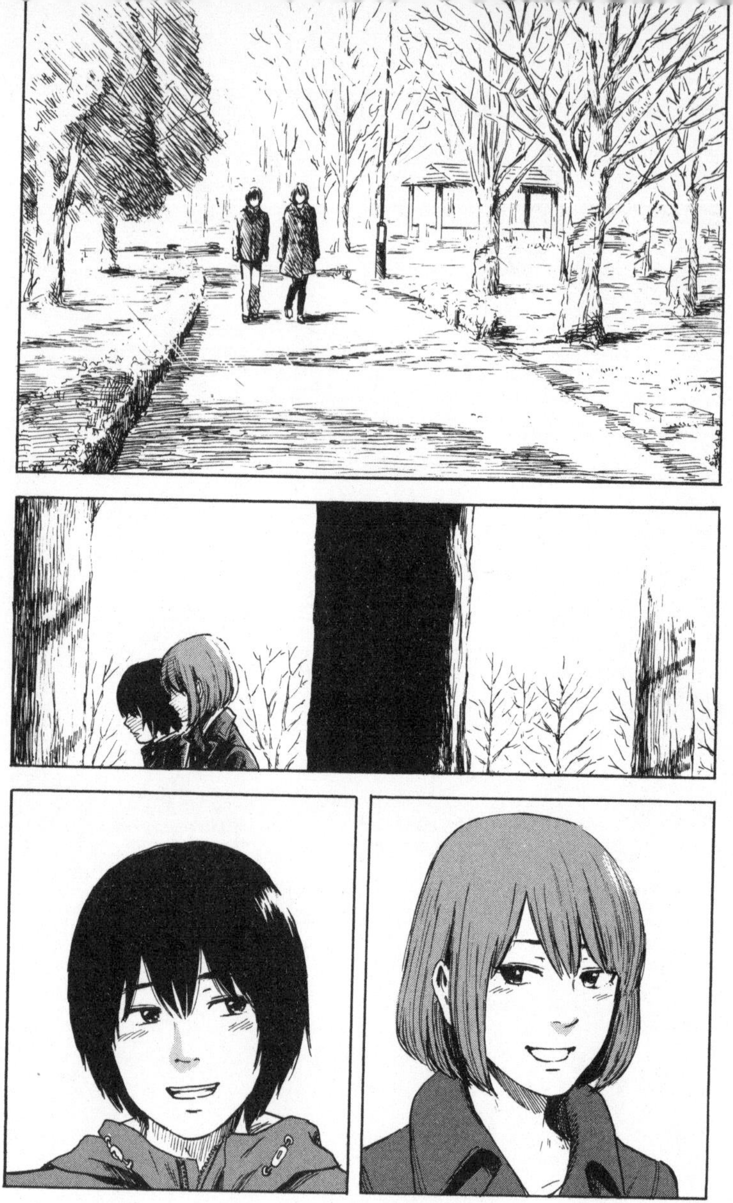

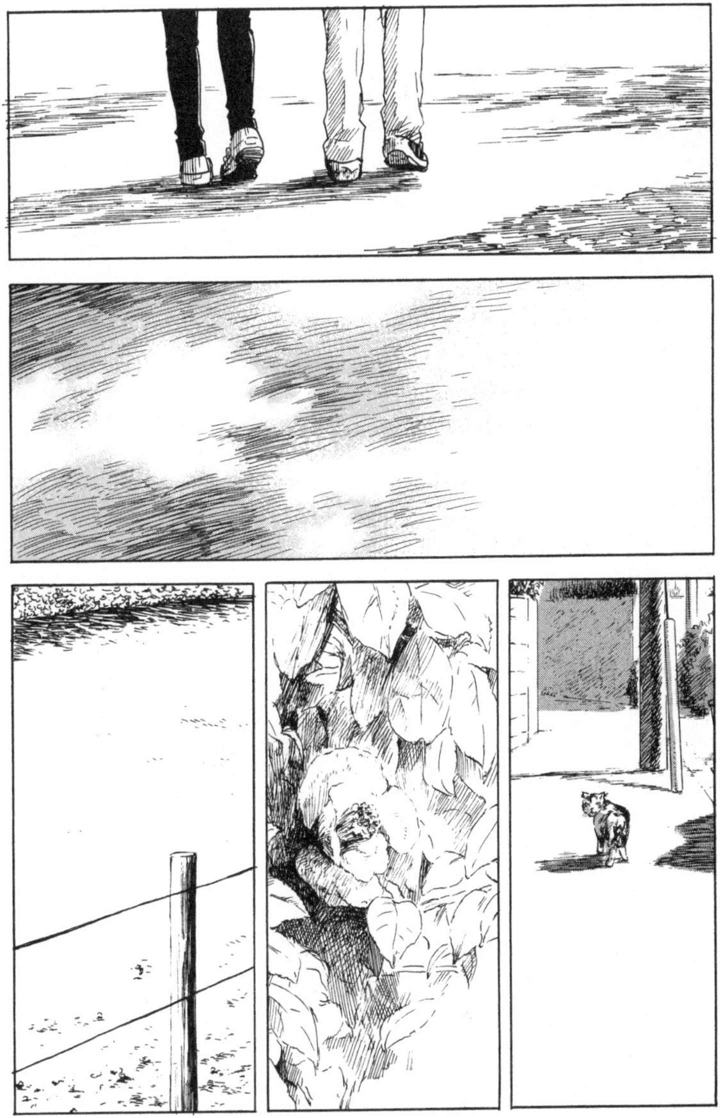

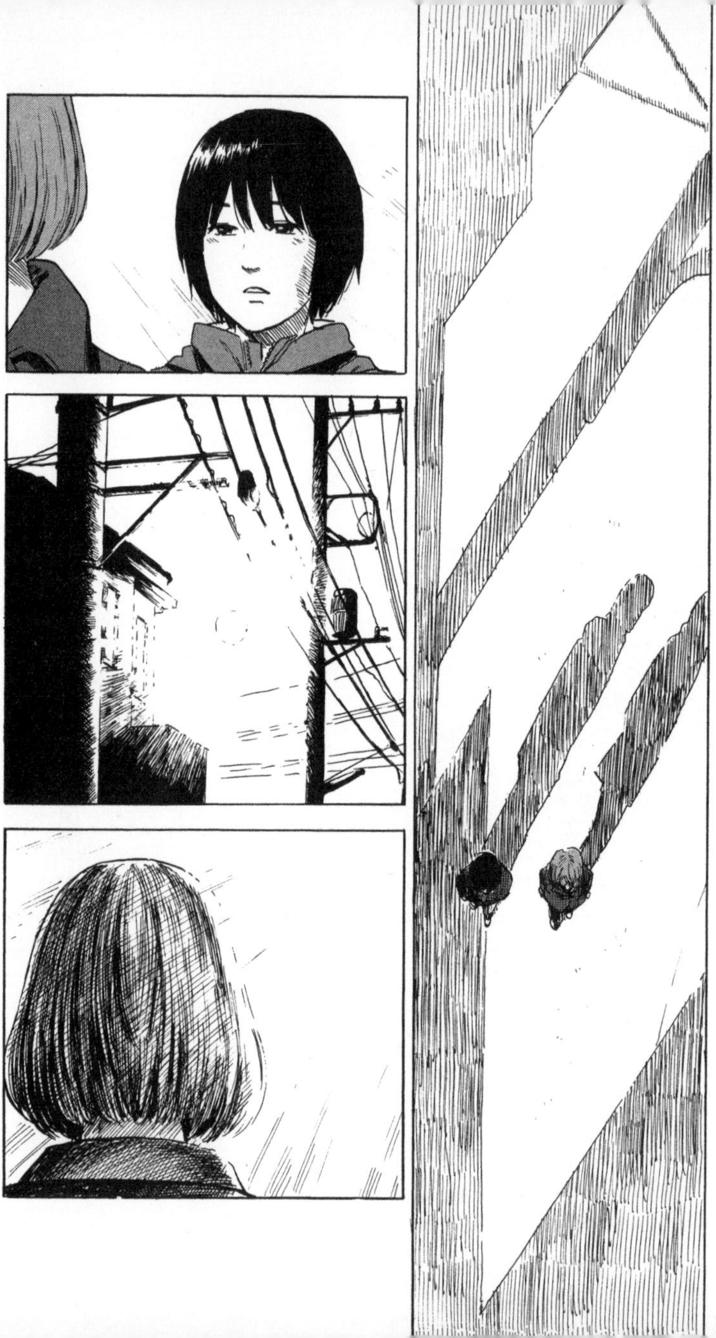

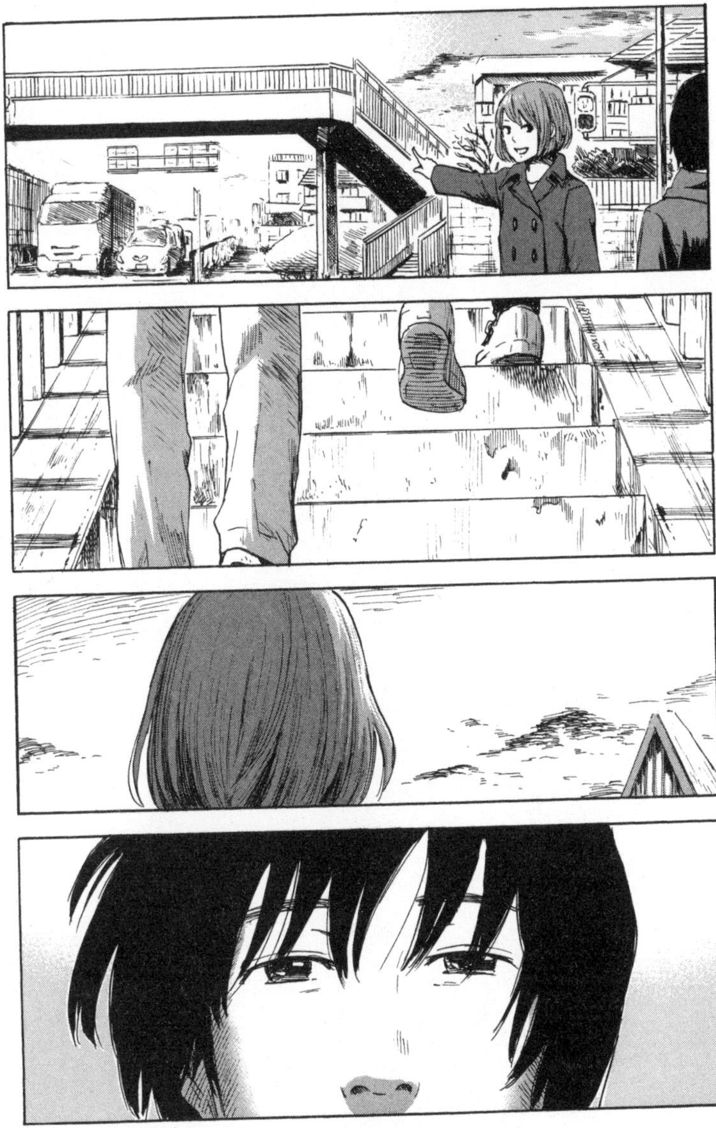

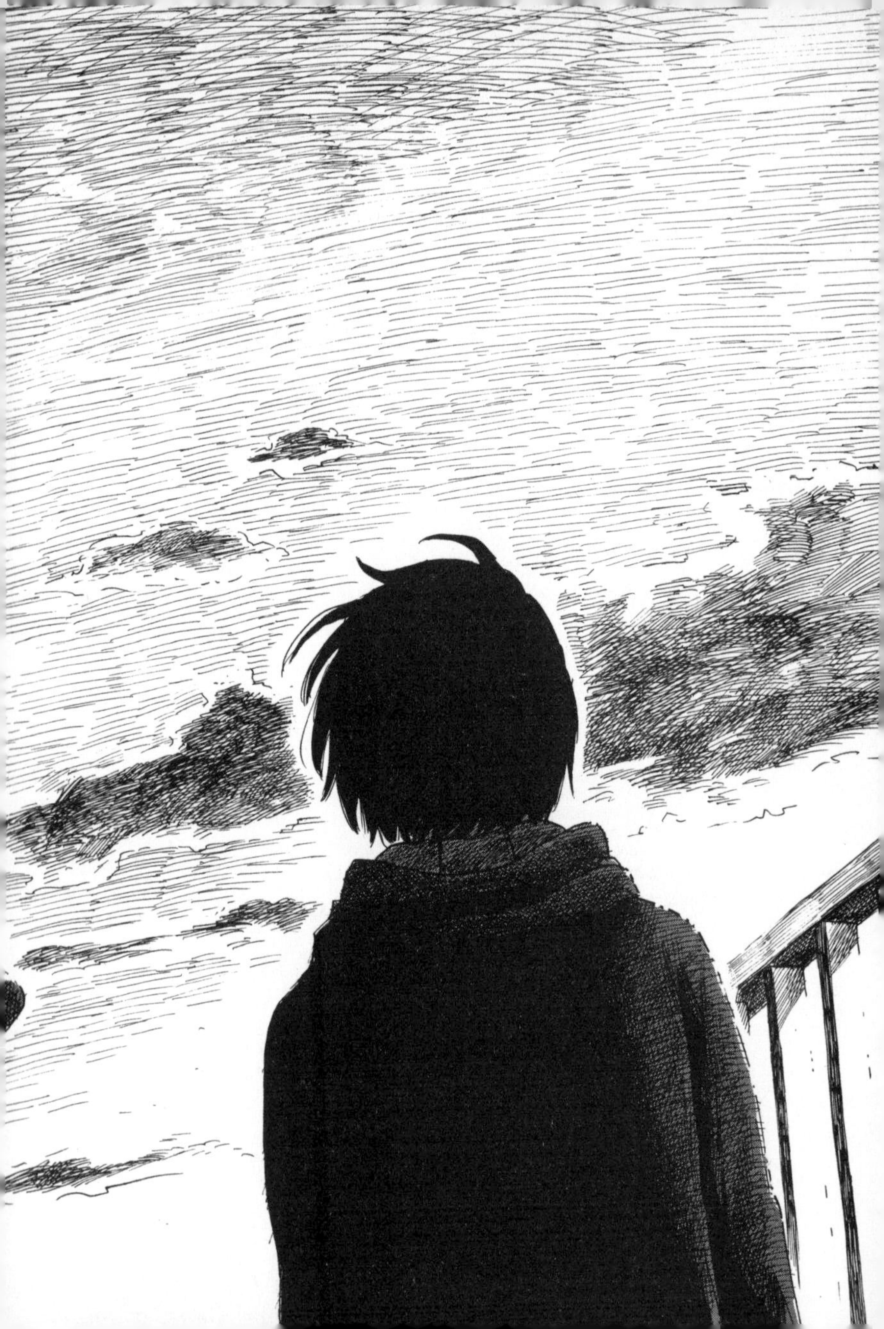

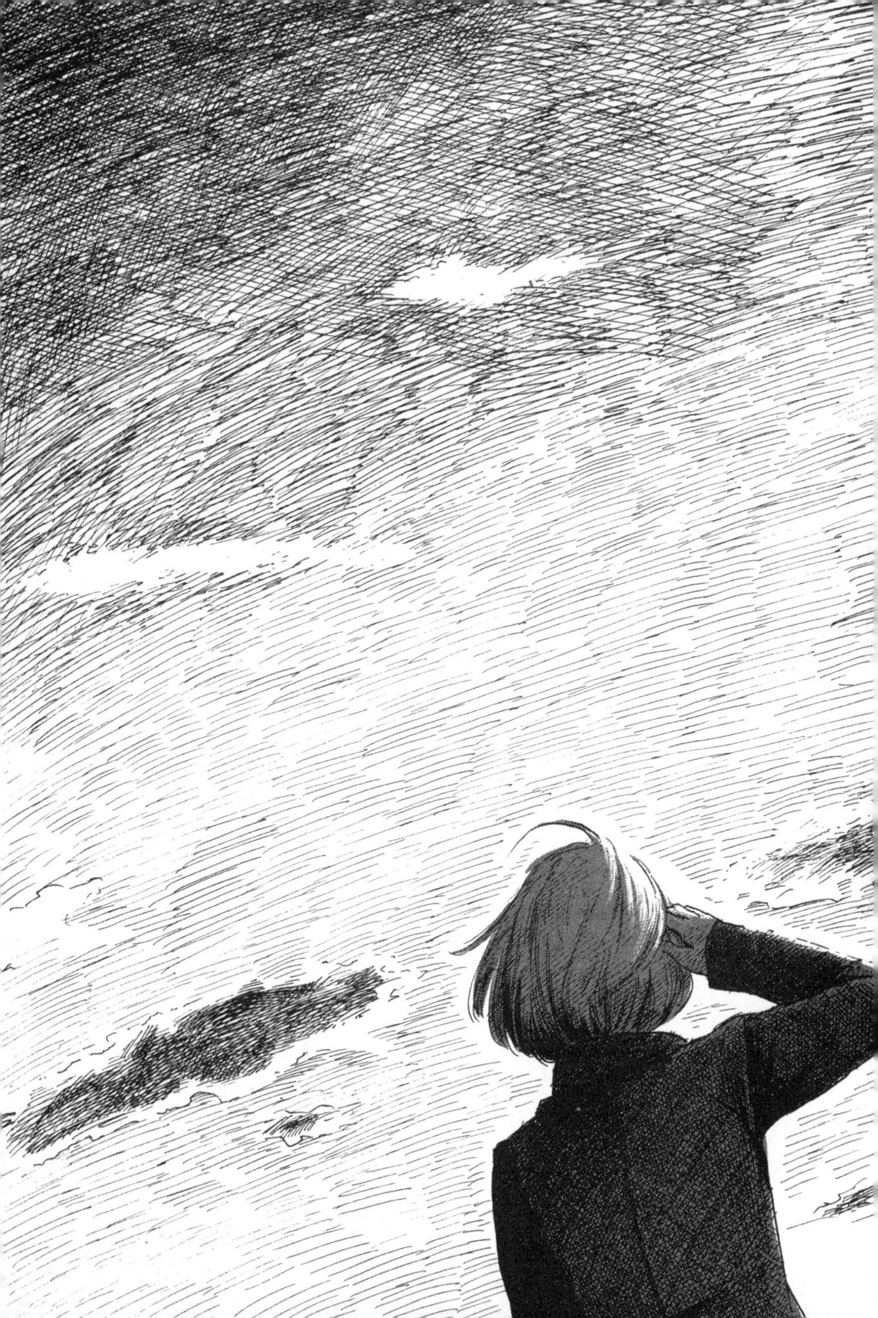

PRETTY, ISN'T IT?

IT IS ...

YEAH.

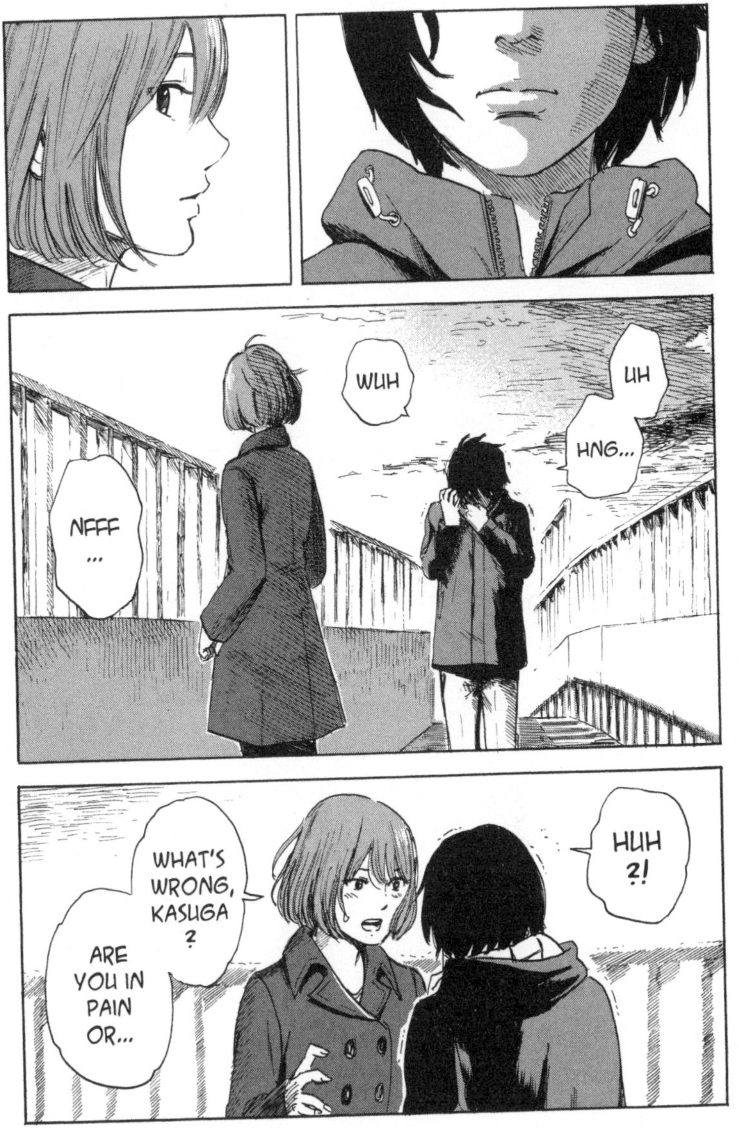
UH HNG...
WUH
NFFF ...
HUH ?!
WHAT'S WRONG, KASUGA?
ARE YOU IN PAIN OR...

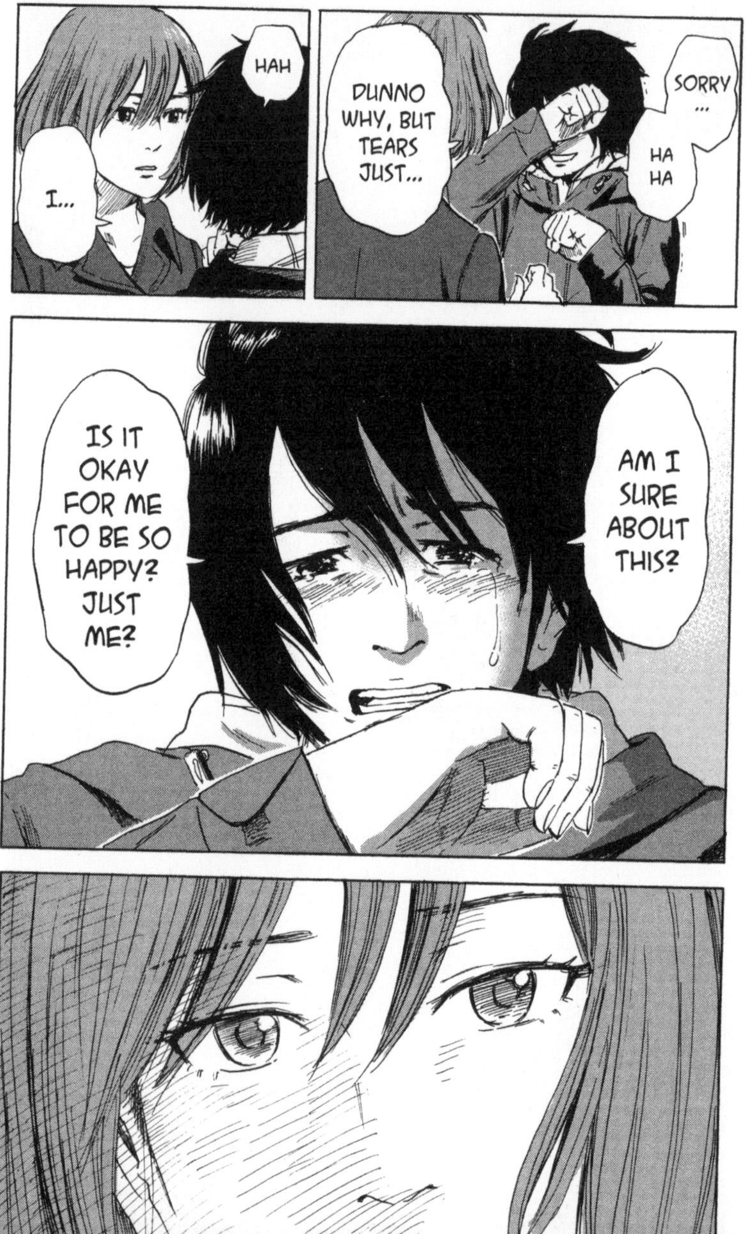
SORRY ...
HA HA
DUNNO WHY, BUT TEARS JUST...
HAH
I...
AM I SURE ABOUT THIS?
IS IT OKAY FOR ME TO BE SO HAPPY? JUST ME?

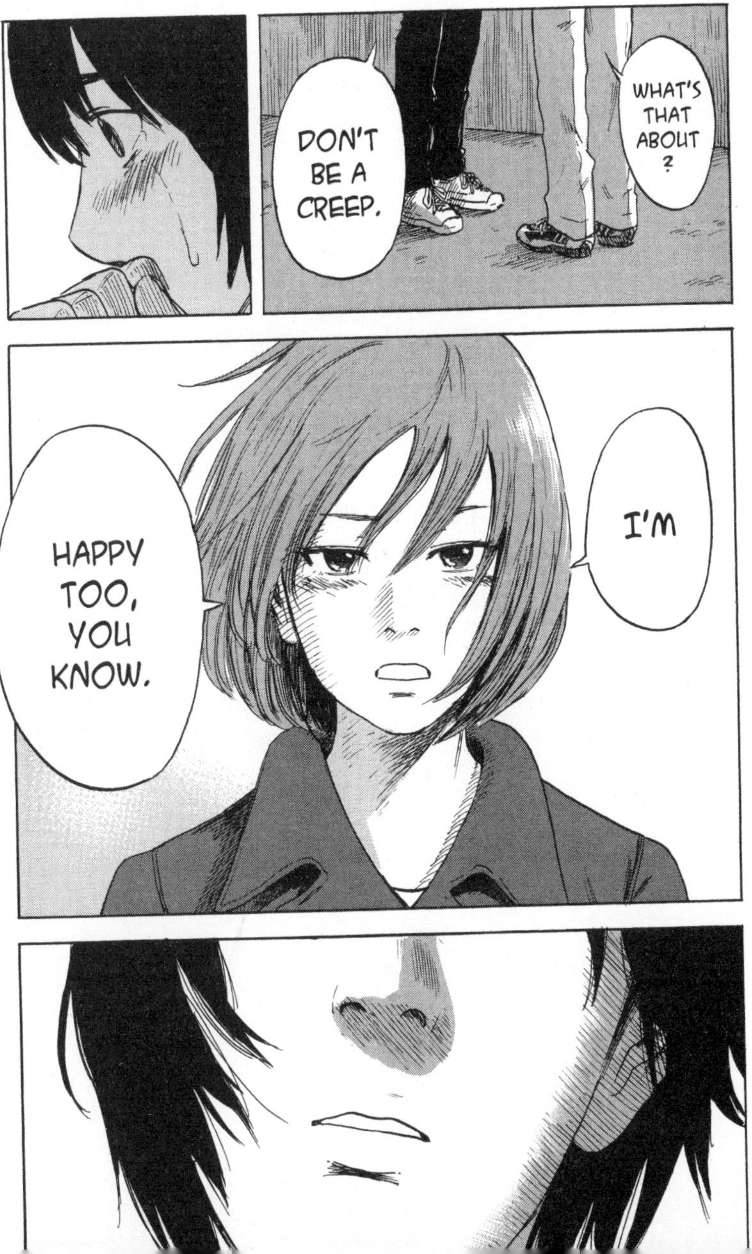
WHAT'S THAT ABOUT?
DON'T BE A CREEP.
I'M
HAPPY TOO, YOU KNOW.

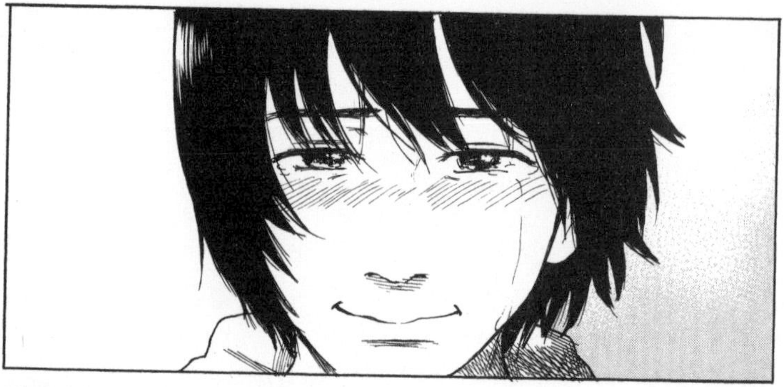

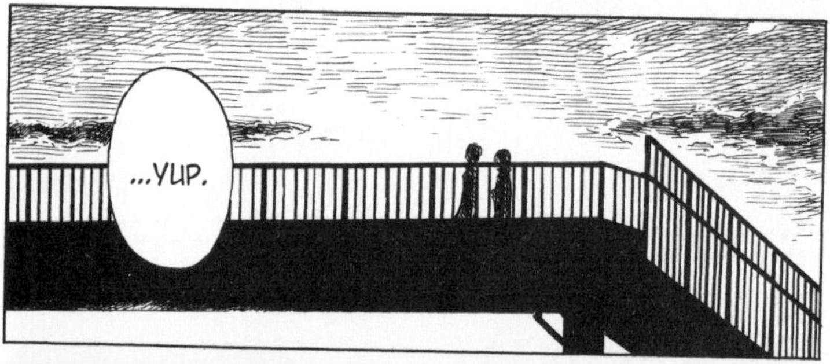
...YUP.

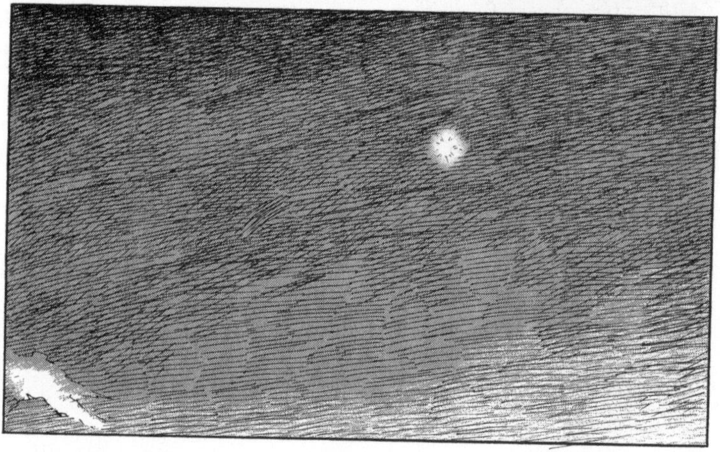

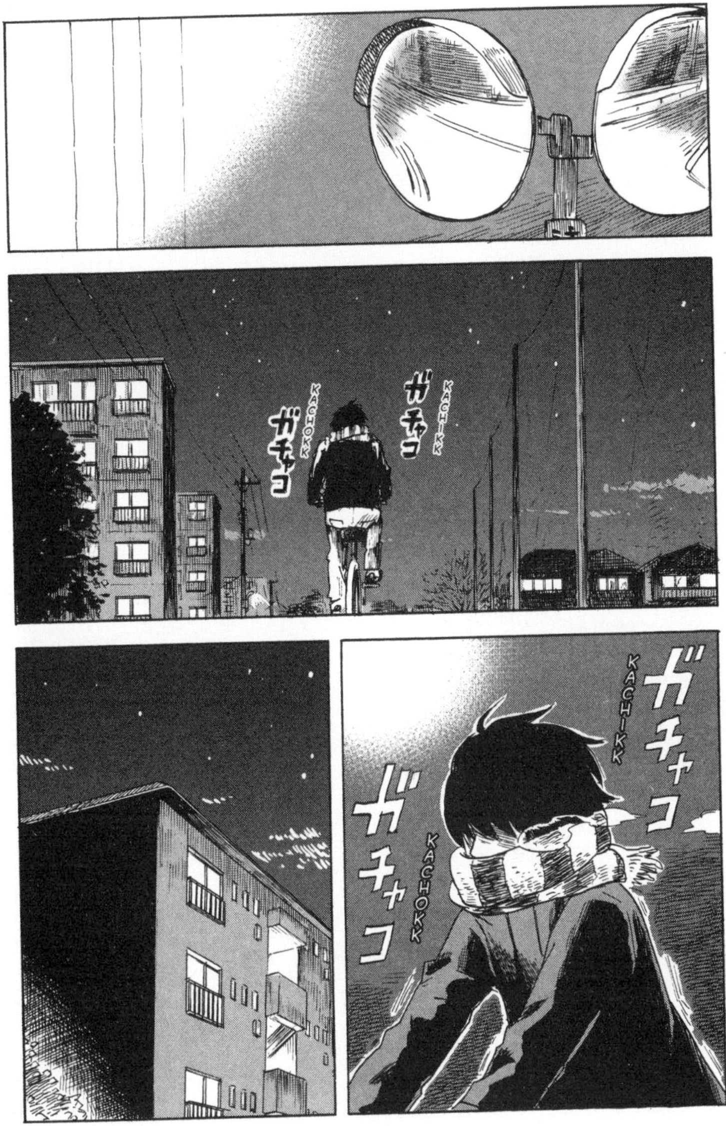
ガチャコ
KACHIKK
ガチャコ
KACHOKK
ガチャコ
KACHIKK
ガチャコ
KACHOKK

バタン
BTAM
ガラ…
RATTLE
WEL-COME HOME.

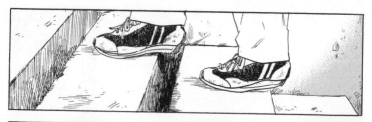

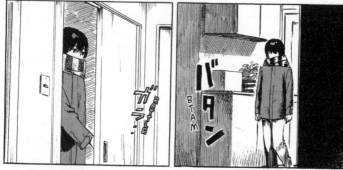

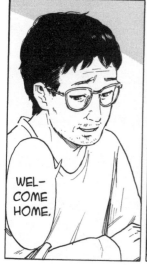

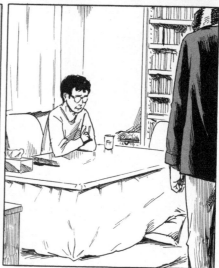

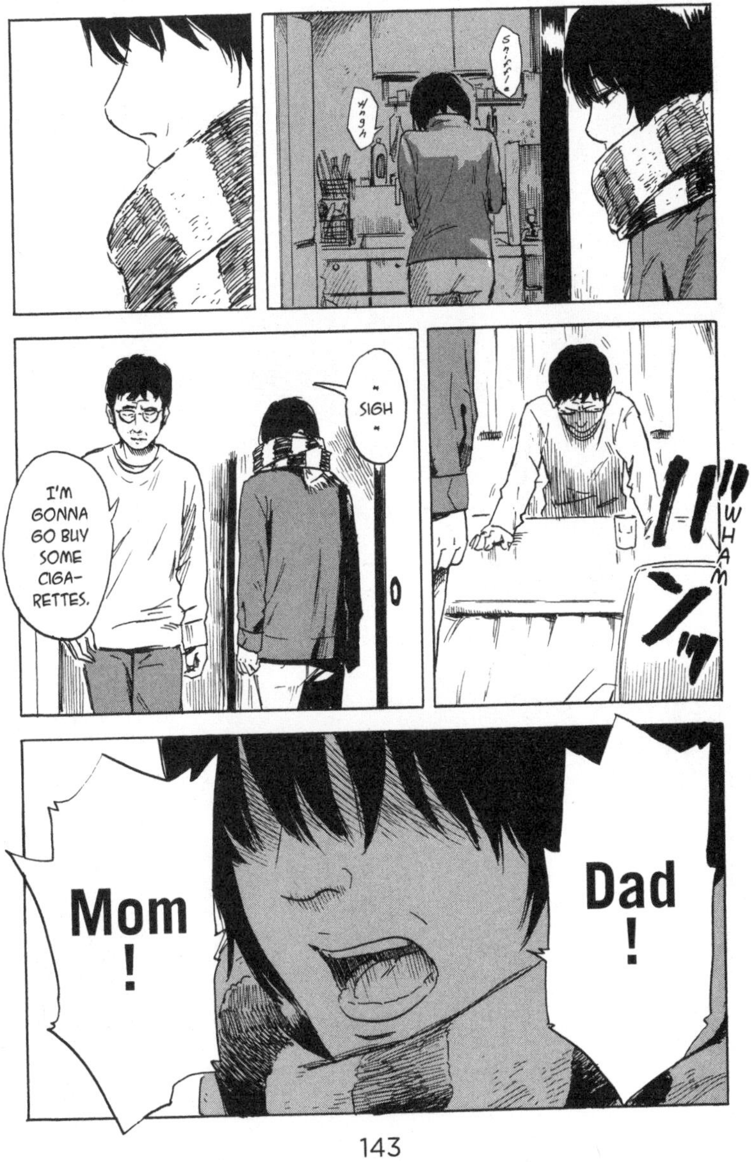
Sniffle
Hngh
WHAM
SIGH
I'M GONNA GO BUY SOME CIGA-RETTES.
Dad!
Mom!

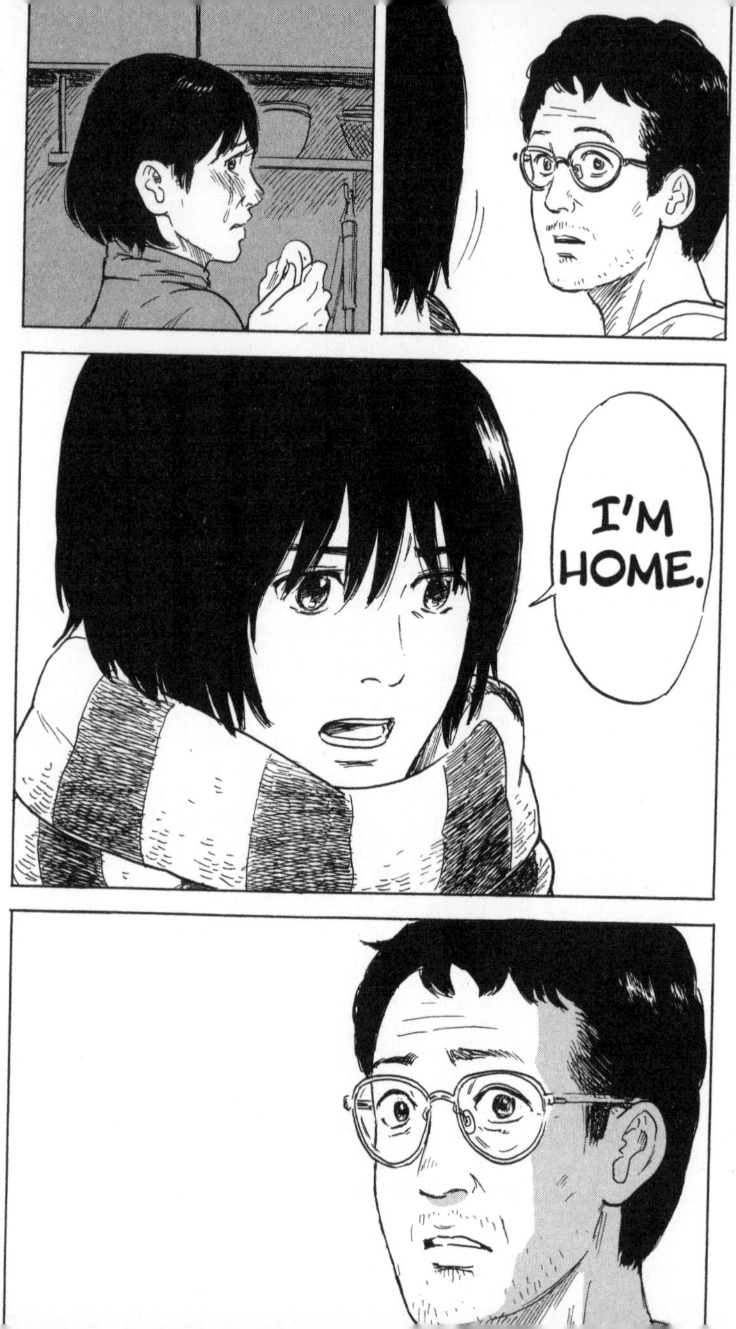
I'M HOME.

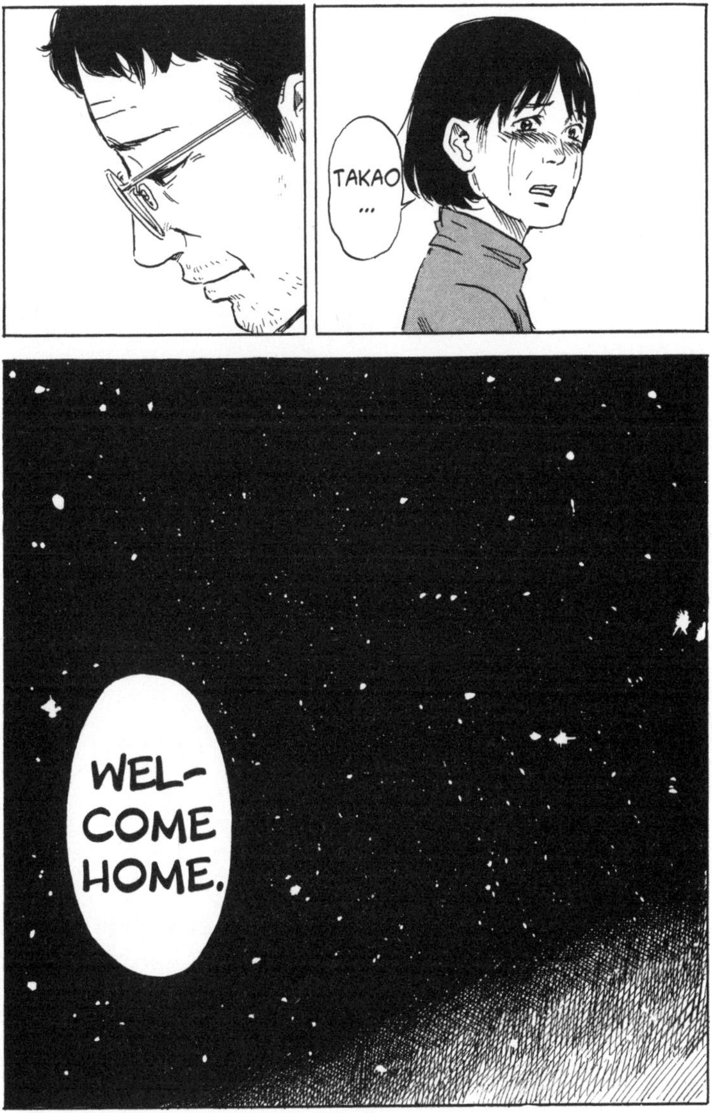
TAKAO ...
WEL-COME HOME.

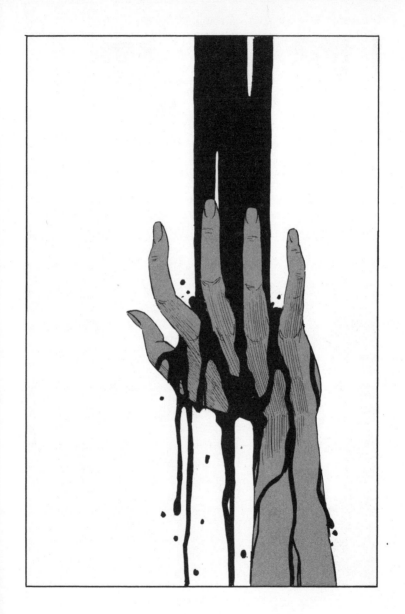

Chapter 47: Soon Homeward Now

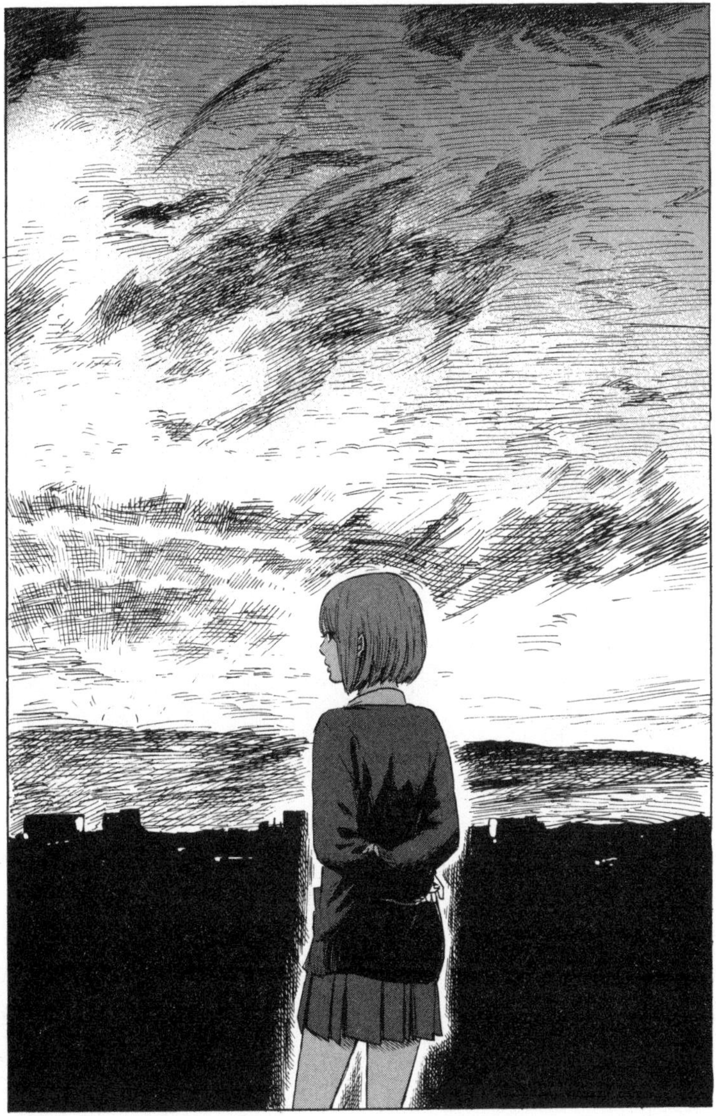

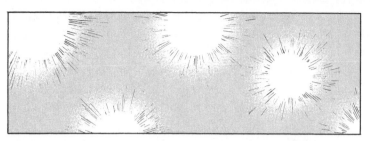

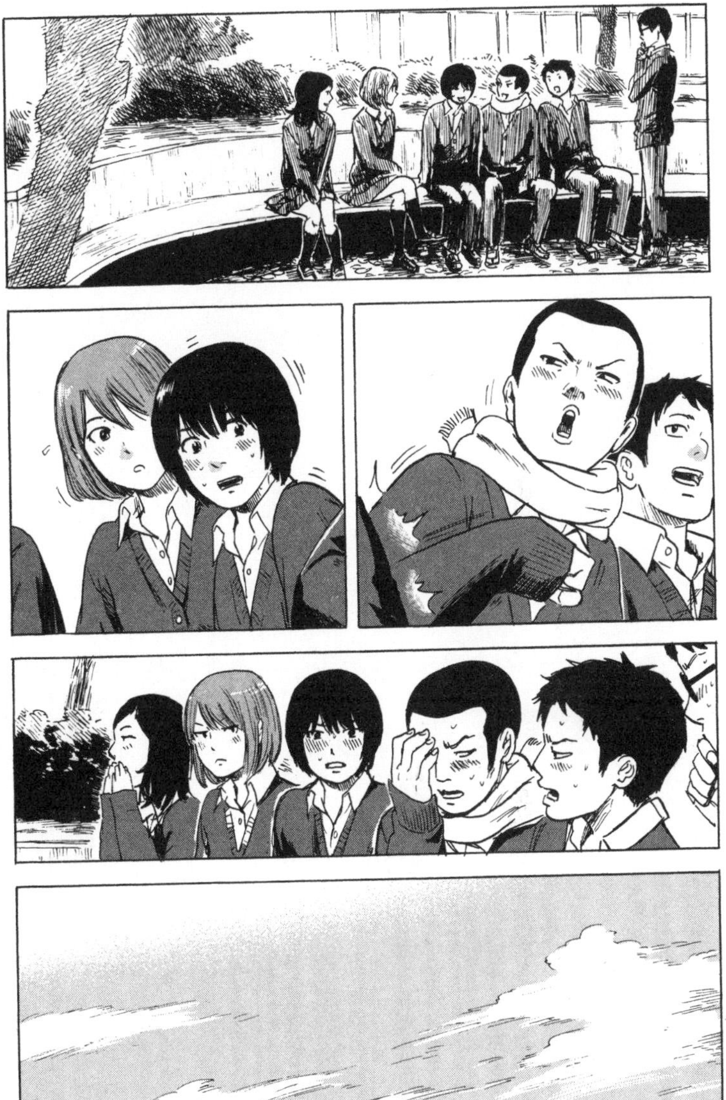

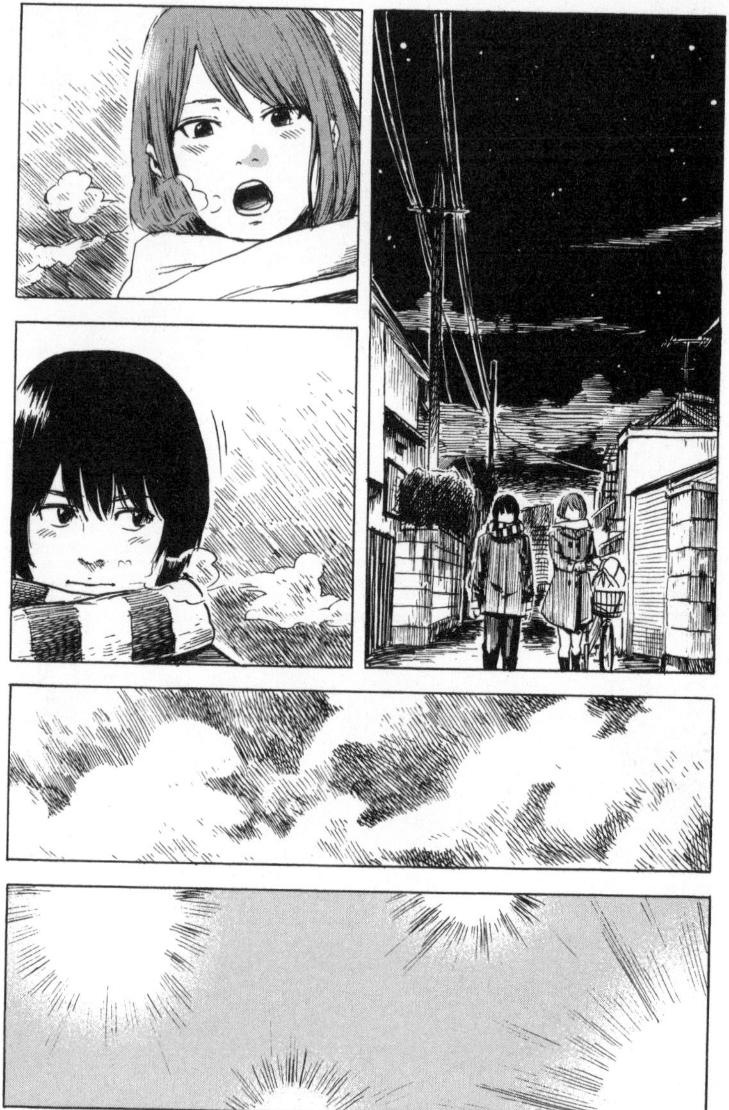

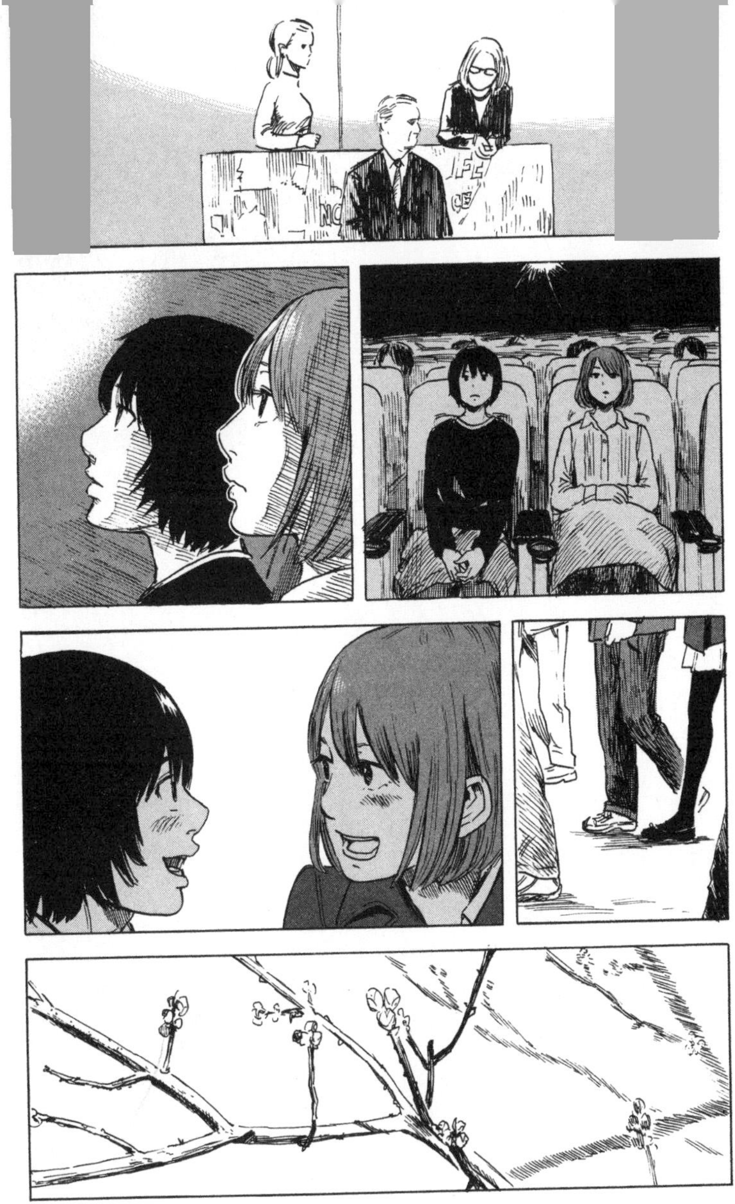

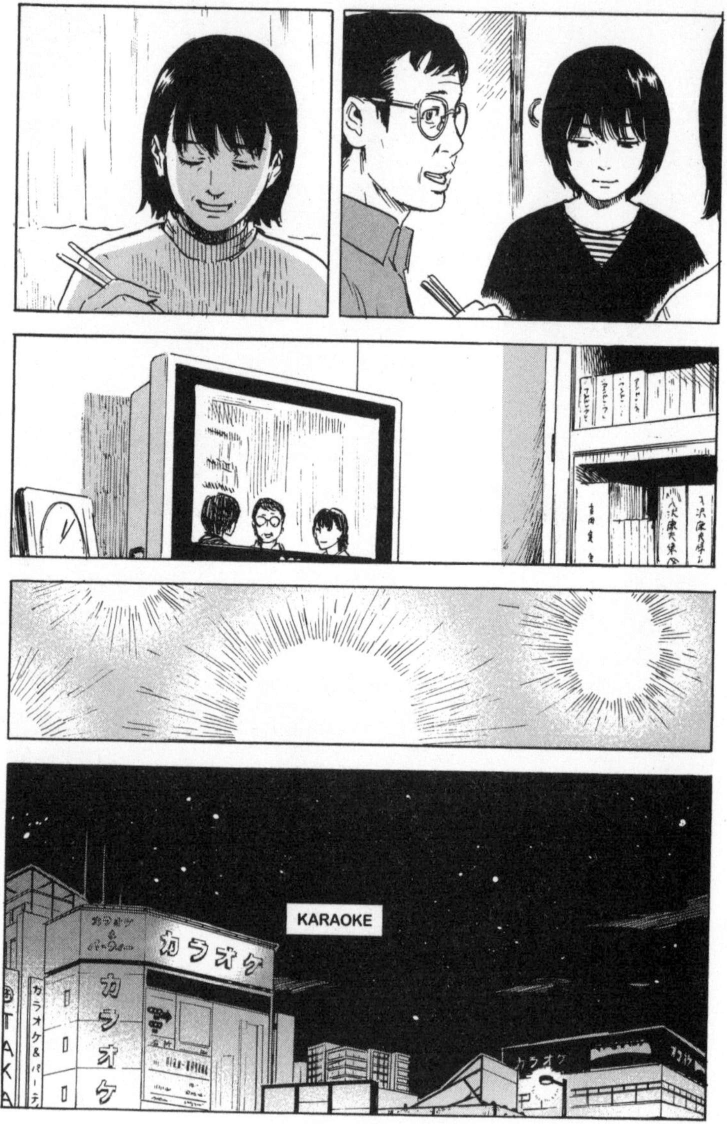
KARAOKE
カラオケ
カラオケ

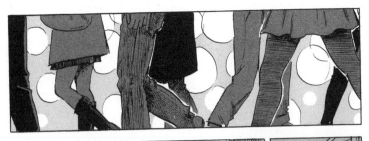

t's *Saki's tooth."*
     "Huh?!"

...en, through the
...oss from the mo...
...her in, like an oi...
     "Are you a ghos...

153

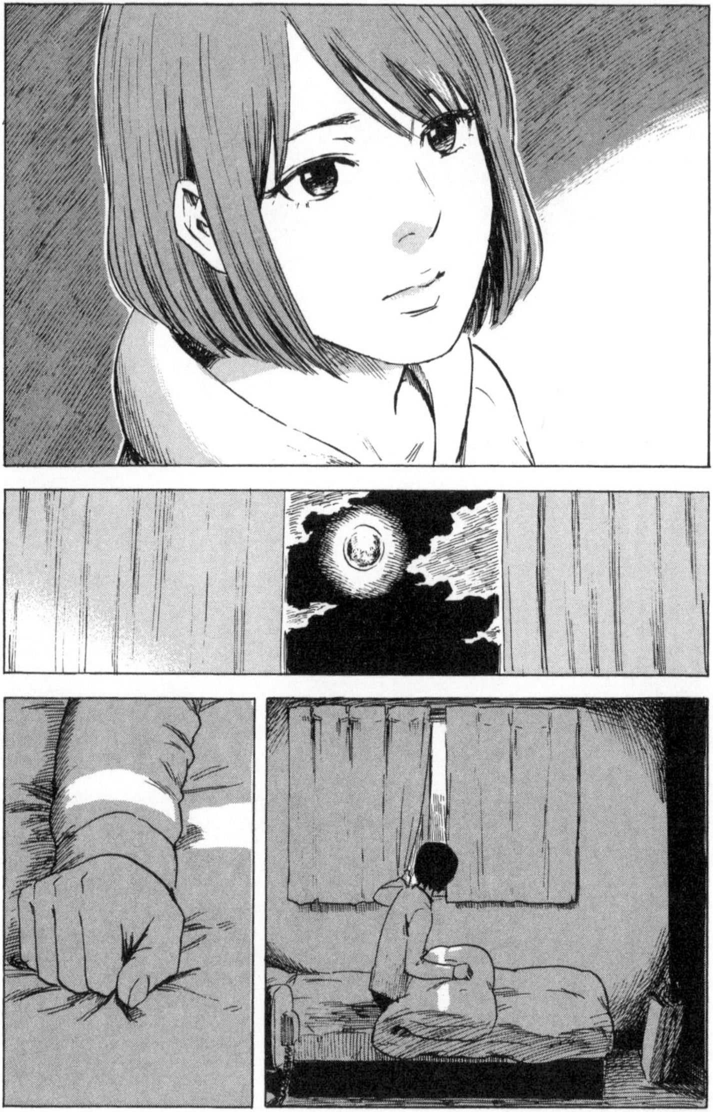

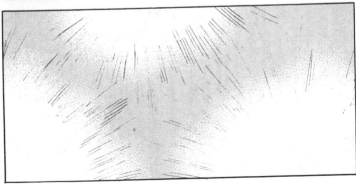

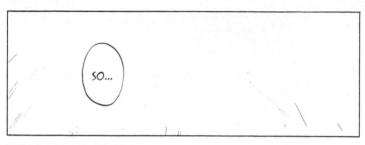

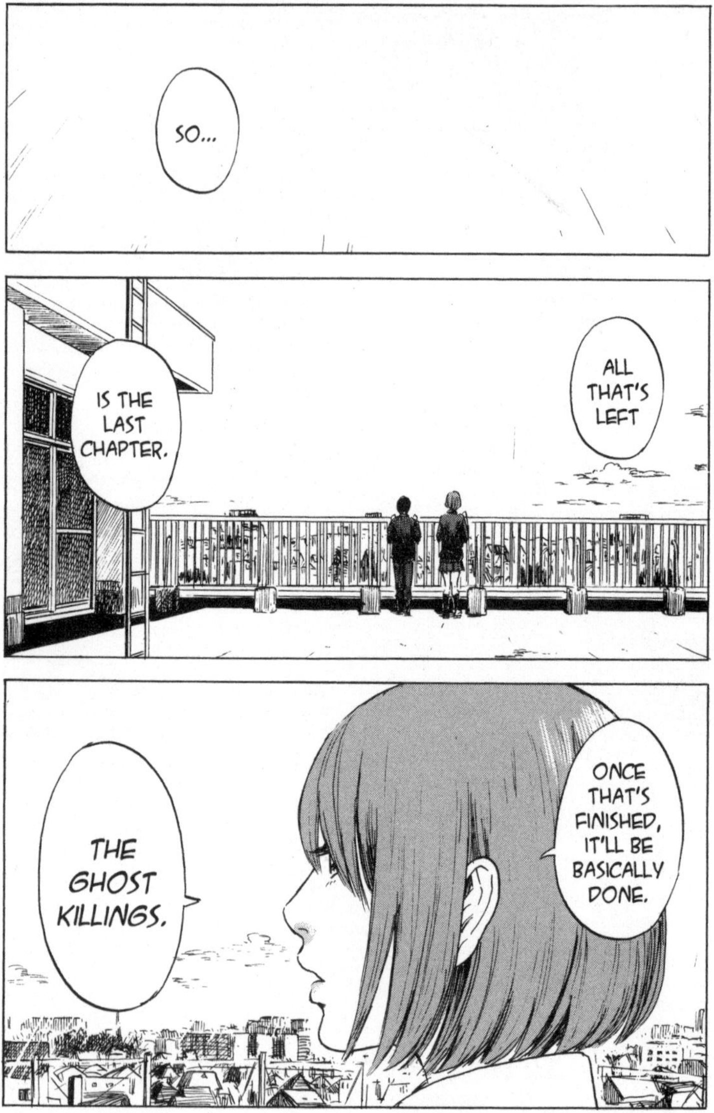
SO...
ALL THAT'S LEFT
IS THE LAST CHAPTER.
ONCE THAT'S FINISHED, IT'LL BE BASICALLY DONE.
THE GHOST KILLINGS.

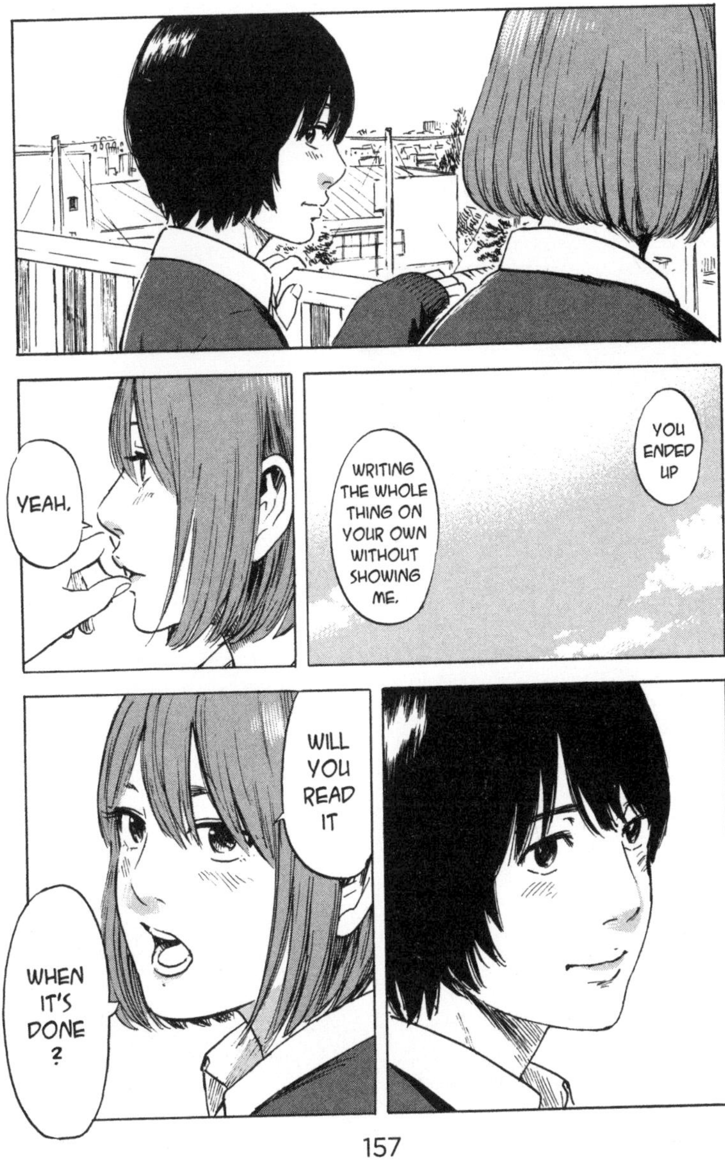
YOU ENDED UP
WRITING THE WHOLE THING ON YOUR OWN WITHOUT SHOWING ME.
YEAH,
WILL YOU READ IT
WHEN IT'S DONE ?

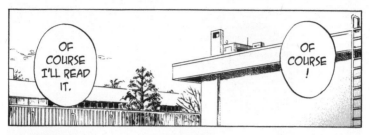

OF COURSE!
OF COURSE I'LL READ IT.
WHEW...
SO ENDS OUR 2ND YEAR OF HIGH SCHOOL.
YEAH.
FEELS LIKE IT WENT BY SO FAST.
HEY.
YOU'RE GOING TO COLLEGE, RIGHT, KASUGA?
HAVE YOU DECIDED WHERE TO APPLY?
MM...
NOT REALLY, NO...

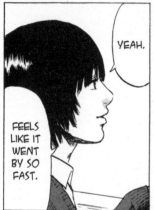

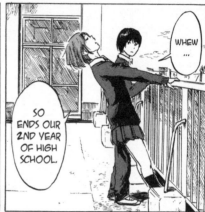

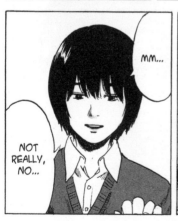

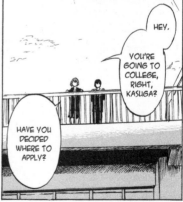

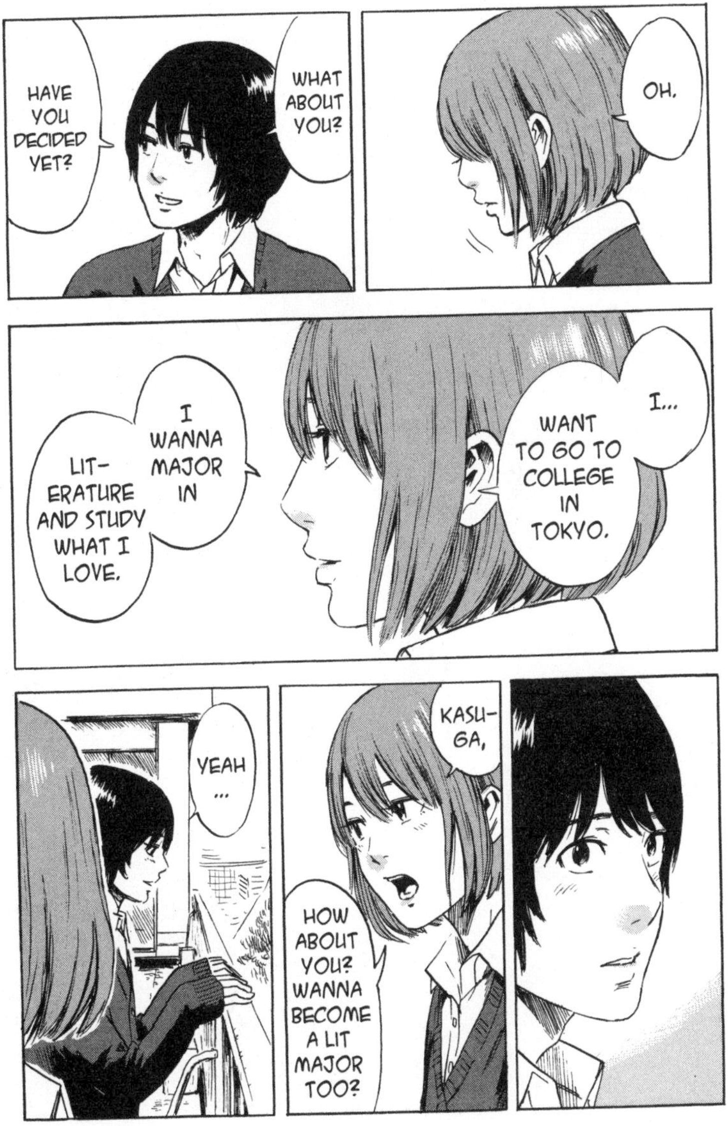
OH.
WHAT ABOUT YOU?
HAVE YOU DECIDED YET?
I...
WANT TO GO TO COLLEGE IN TOKYO.
I WANNA MAJOR IN
LIT-ERATURE AND STUDY WHAT I LOVE.
KASU-GA,
HOW ABOUT YOU? WANNA BECOME A LIT MAJOR TOO?
YEAH ...

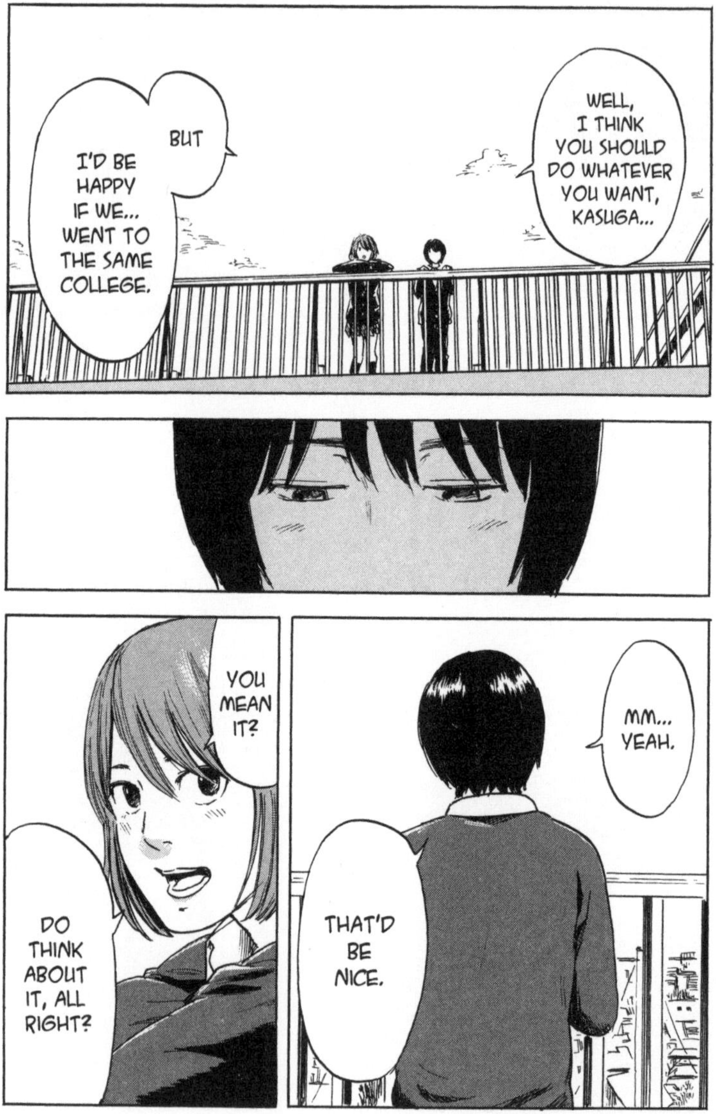
WELL, I THINK YOU SHOULD DO WHATEVER YOU WANT, KASUGA...
BUT
I'D BE HAPPY IF WE... WENT TO THE SAME COLLEGE.
MM... YEAH.
THAT'D BE NICE.
YOU MEAN IT?
DO THINK ABOUT IT, ALL RIGHT?

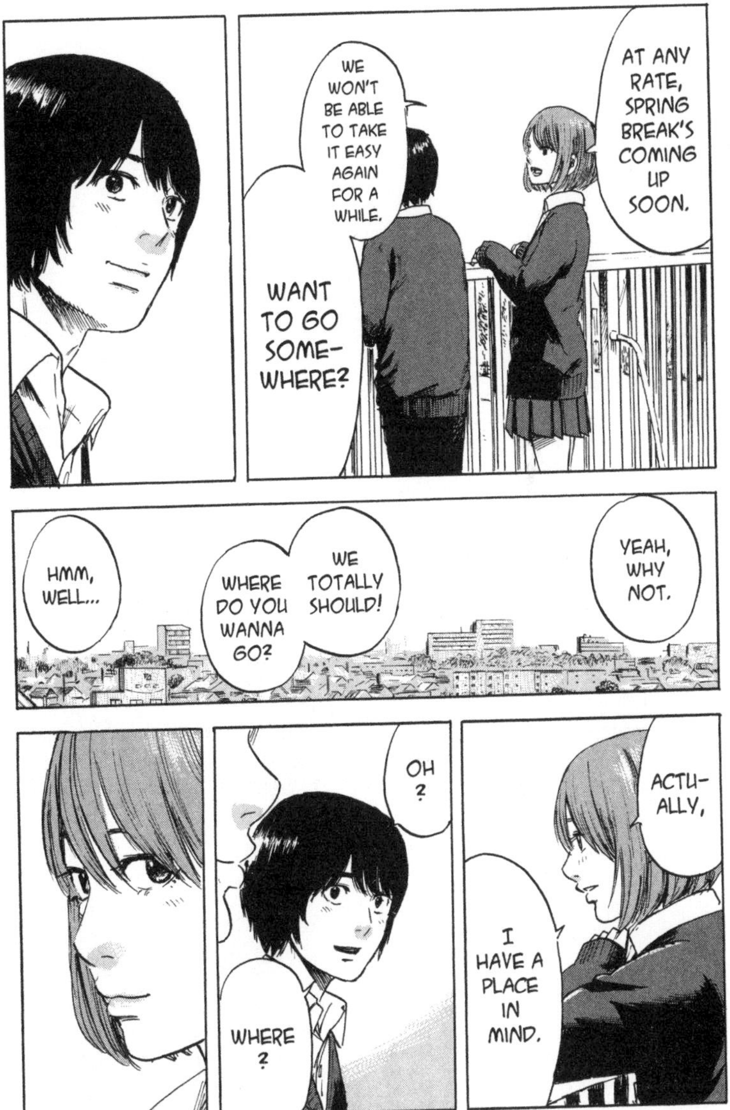
AT ANY RATE, SPRING BREAK'S COMING UP SOON.
WE WON'T BE ABLE TO TAKE IT EASY AGAIN FOR A WHILE.
WANT TO GO SOMEWHERE?
YEAH, WHY NOT.
WE TOTALLY SHOULD!
WHERE DO YOU WANNA GO?
HMM, WELL...
ACTUALLY,
I HAVE A PLACE IN MIND.
OH?
WHERE?

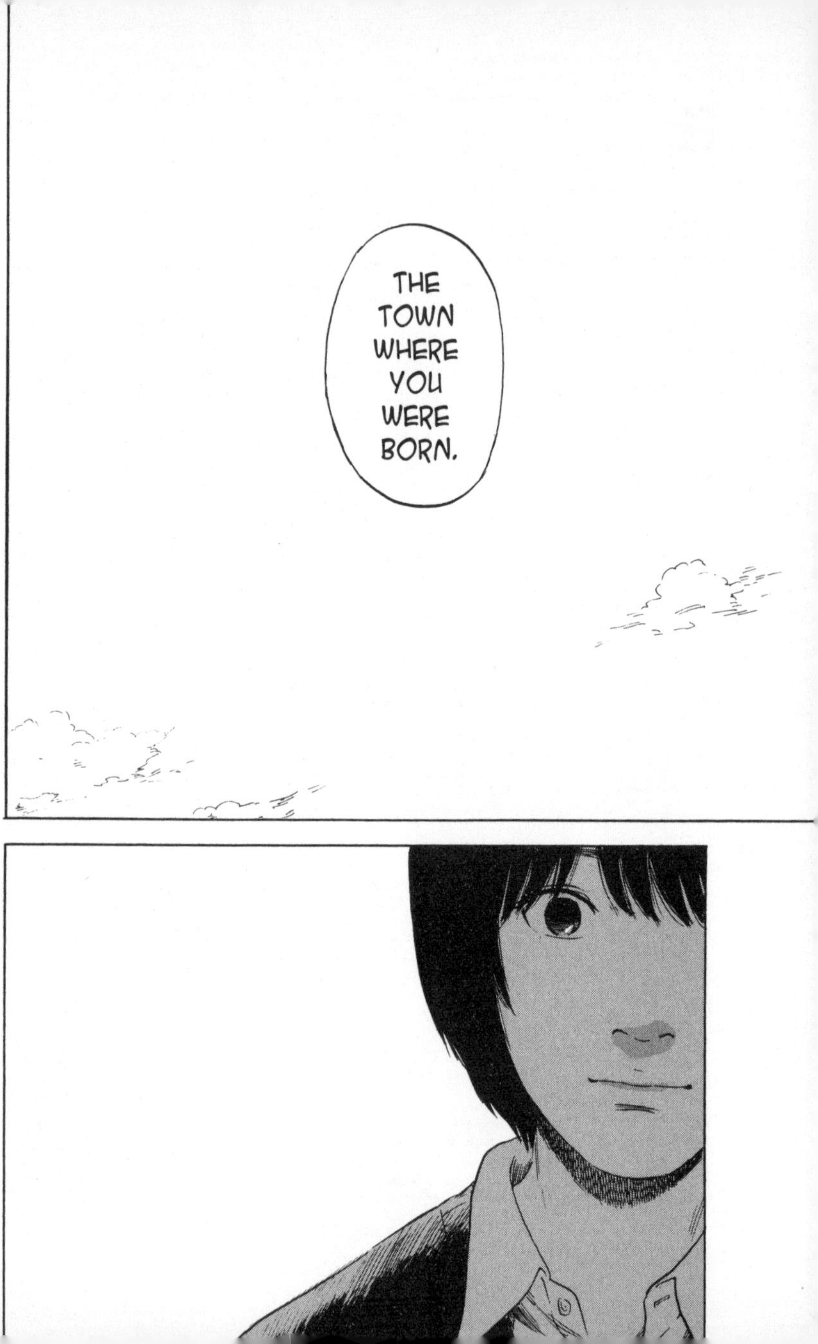
THE TOWN WHERE YOU WERE BORN.

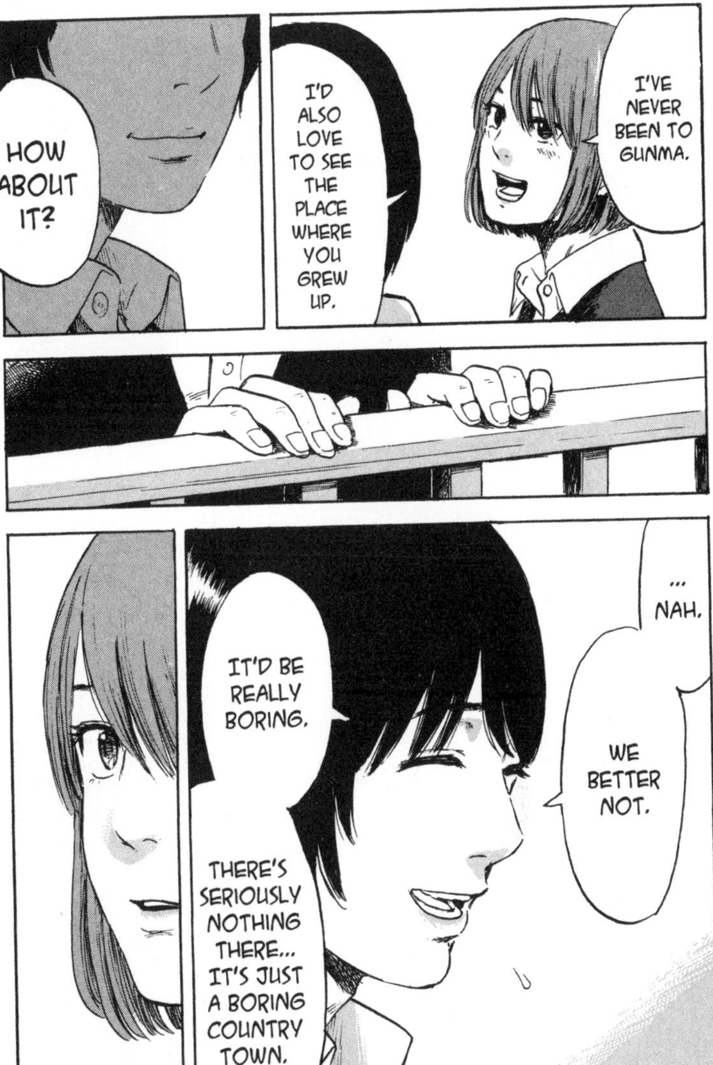
I'VE NEVER BEEN TO GUNMA.
I'D ALSO LOVE TO SEE THE PLACE WHERE YOU GREW UP.
HOW ABOUT IT?
... NAH.
WE BETTER NOT.
IT'D BE REALLY BORING.
THERE'S SERIOUSLY NOTHING THERE... IT'S JUST A BORING COUNTRY TOWN.

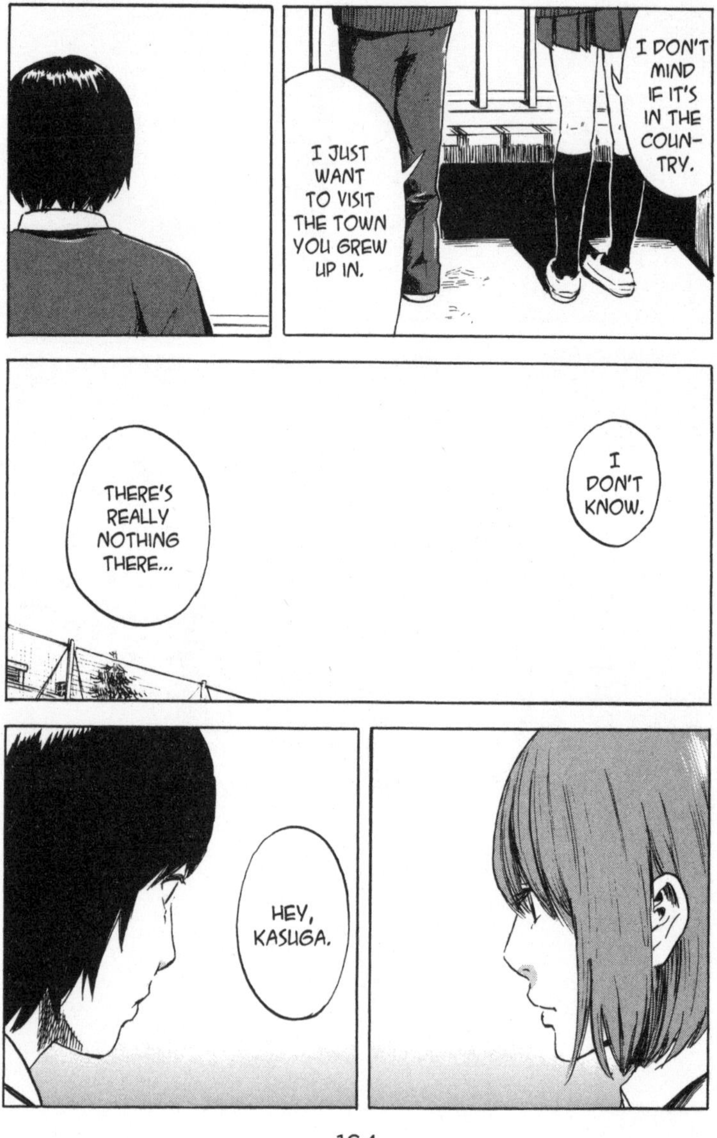
I DON'T MIND IF IT'S IN THE COUN-TRY.
I JUST WANT TO VISIT THE TOWN YOU GREW UP IN.
I DON'T KNOW.
THERE'S REALLY NOTHING THERE...
HEY, KASUGA.

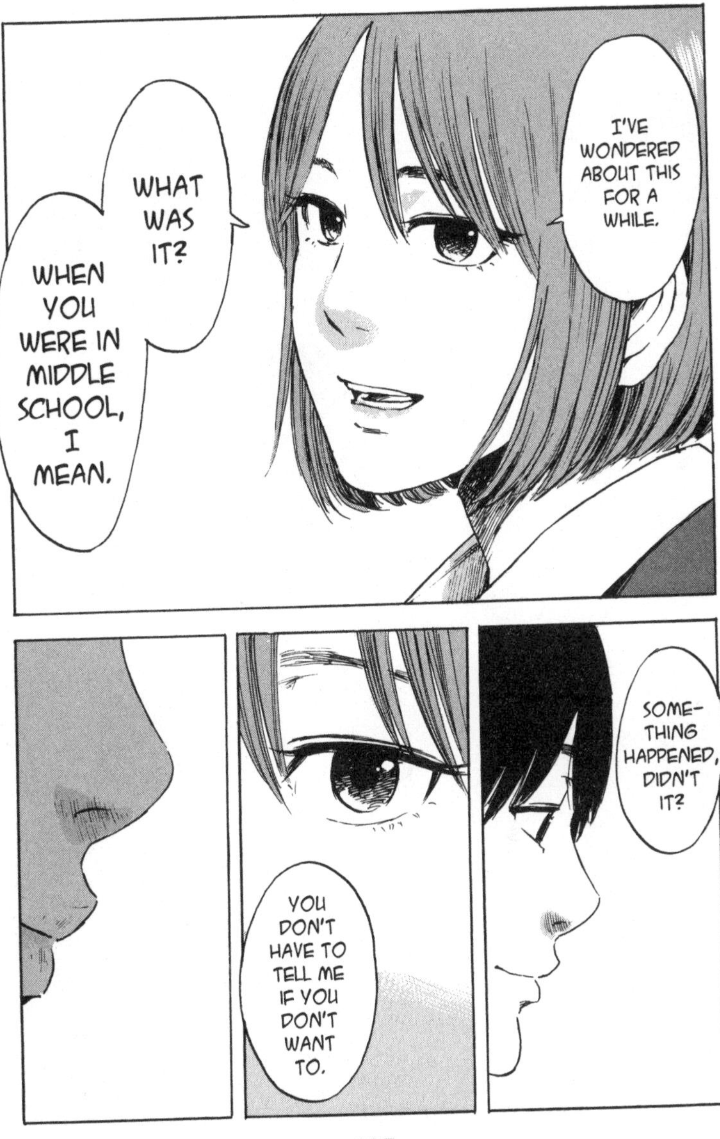
I'VE WONDERED ABOUT THIS FOR A WHILE.
WHAT WAS IT?
WHEN YOU WERE IN MIDDLE SCHOOL, I MEAN.
SOME-THING HAPPENED, DIDN'T IT?
YOU DON'T HAVE TO TELL ME IF YOU DON'T WANT TO.

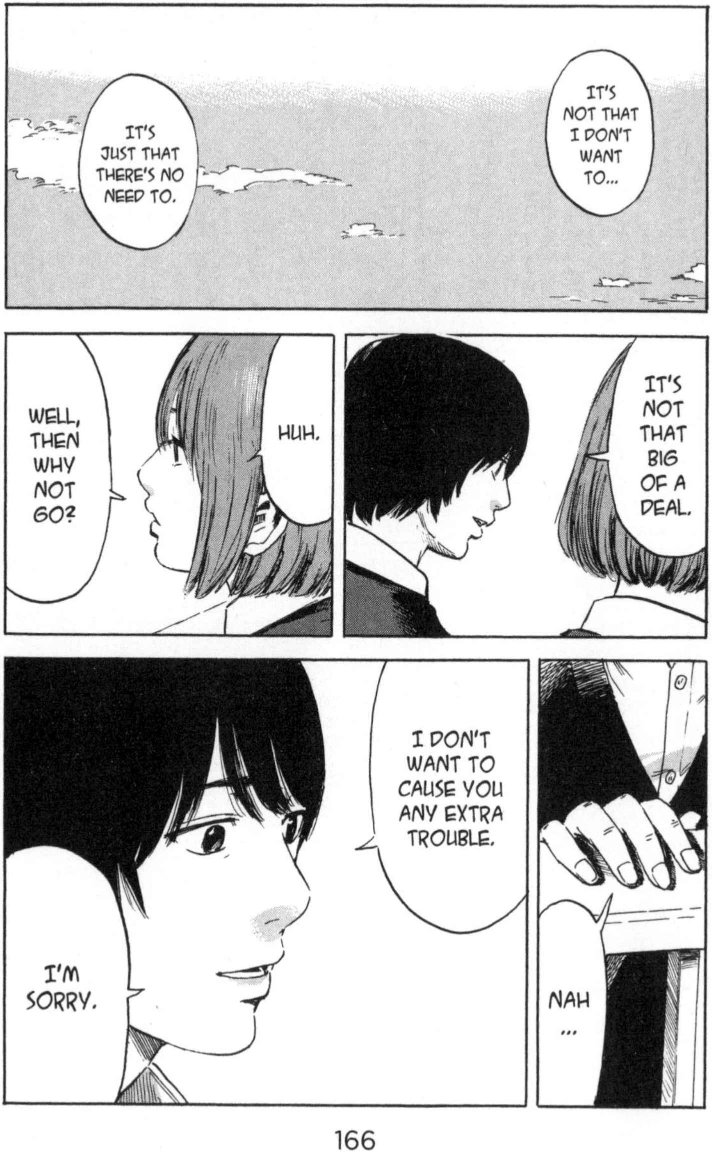
IT'S NOT THAT I DON'T WANT TO...
IT'S JUST THAT THERE'S NO NEED TO.
IT'S NOT THAT BIG OF A DEAL.
HUH.
WELL, THEN WHY NOT GO?
NAH ...
I DON'T WANT TO CAUSE YOU ANY EXTRA TROUBLE.
I'M SORRY.

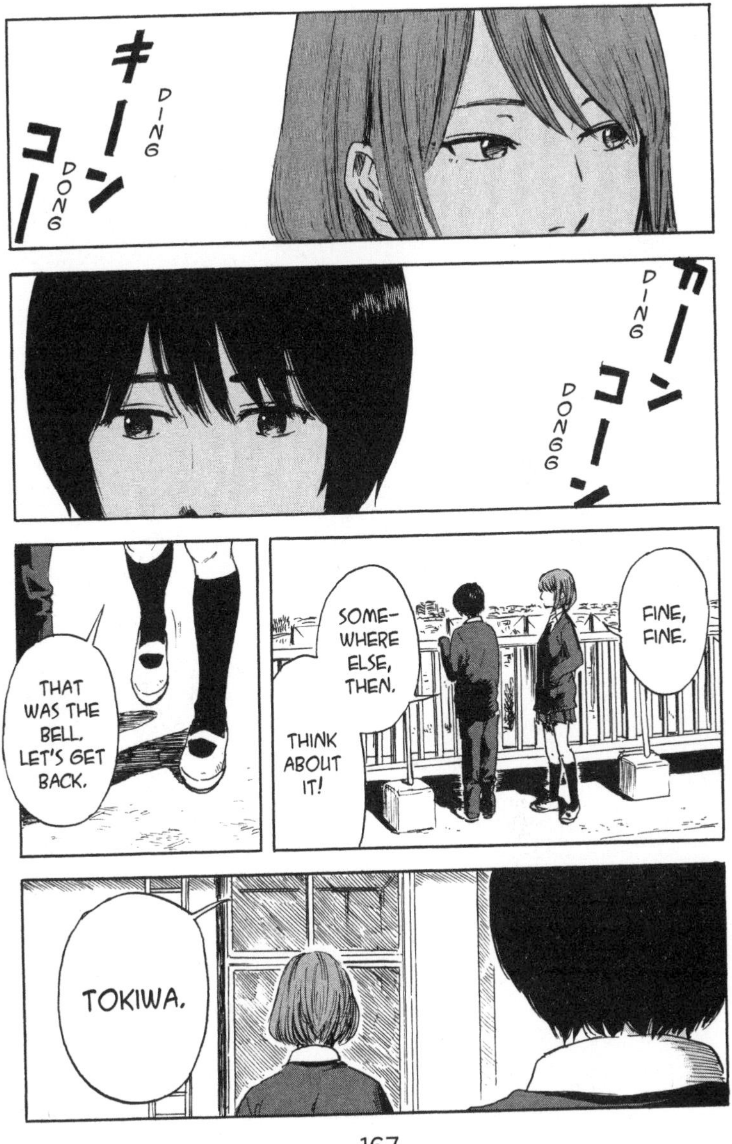
キーンコーン
DING
DONG
カーンコーン
DING
DONGG
FINE, FINE.
SOME-WHERE ELSE, THEN.
THINK ABOUT IT!
THAT WAS THE BELL. LET'S GET BACK.
TOKIWA.

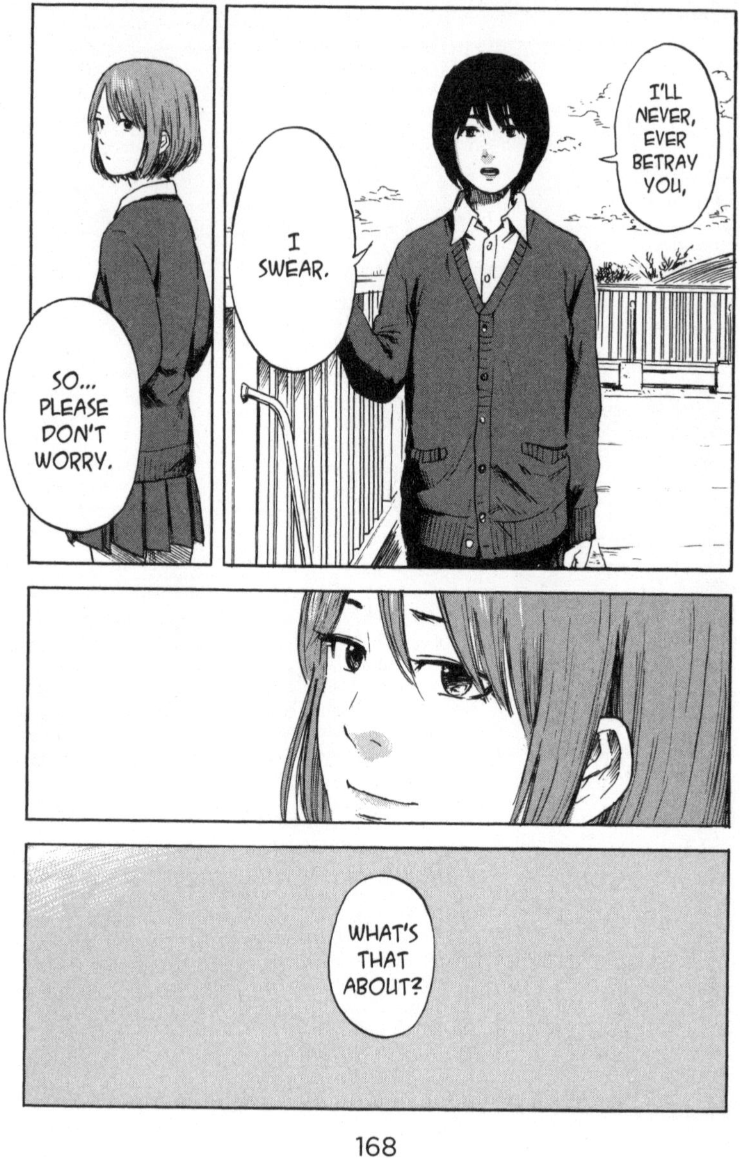
I'LL NEVER, EVER BETRAY YOU,
I SWEAR.
SO... PLEASE DON'T WORRY.
WHAT'S THAT ABOUT?

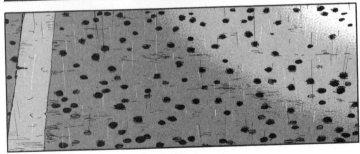

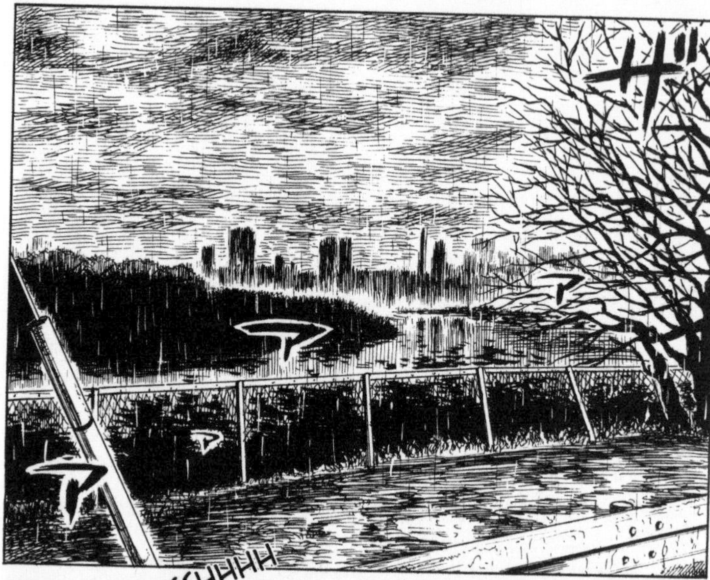
ザッ
FSSSHHHH
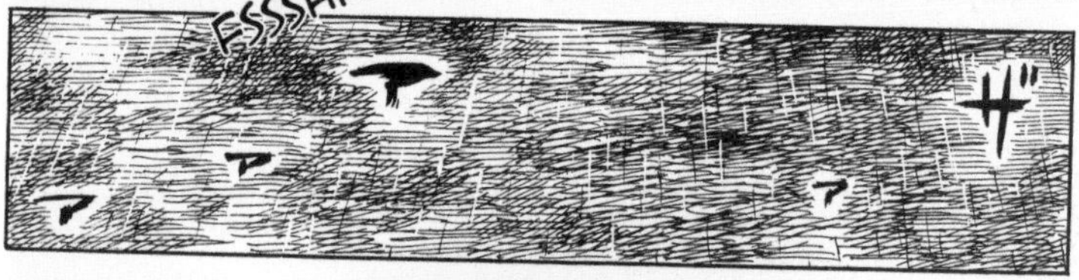
ザ
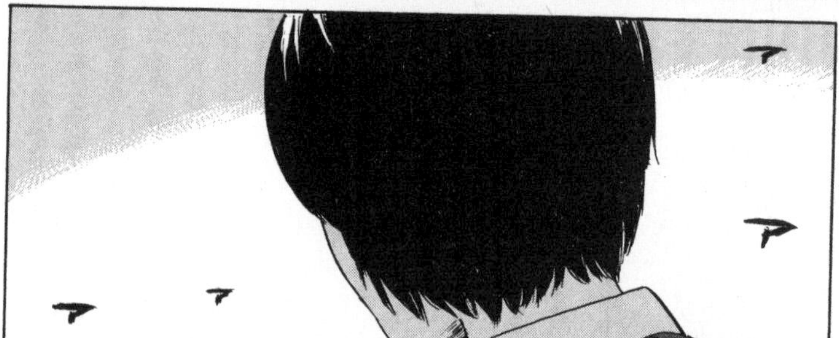

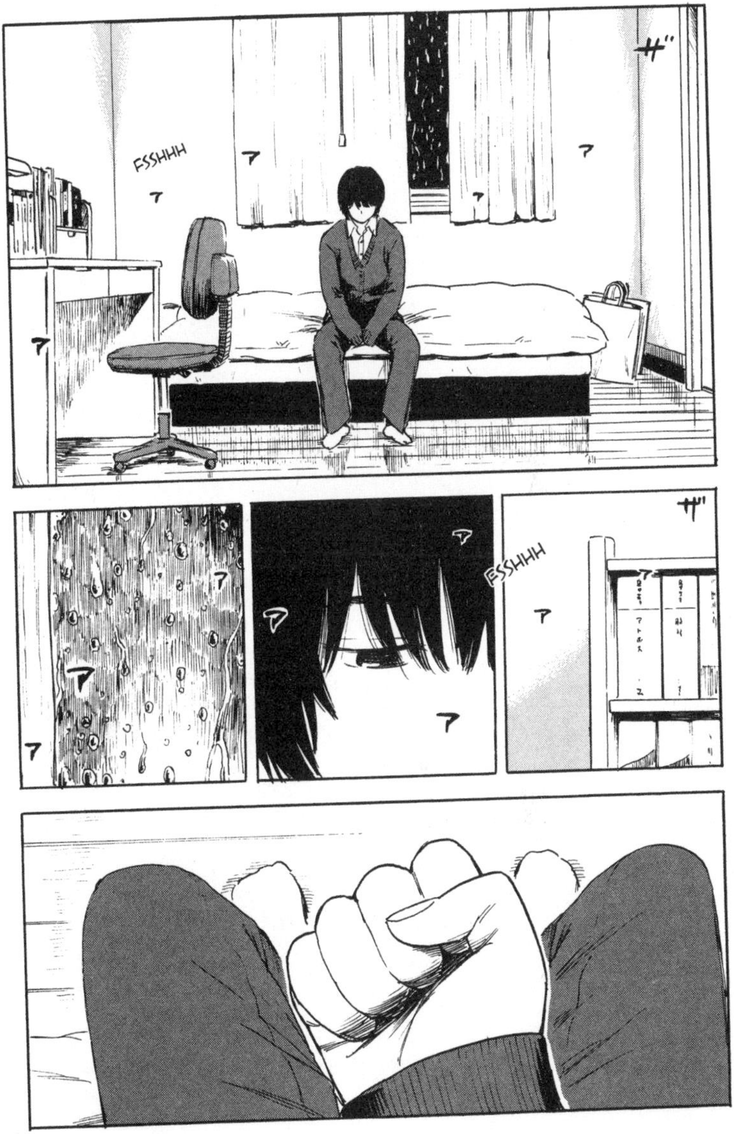
ザ"
ア
ア
ア
FSSHHH
ア
ア
ザ"
FSSHHH
ア
ア
ア
ア
ア
ア
ア

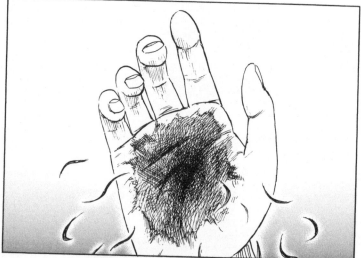

172

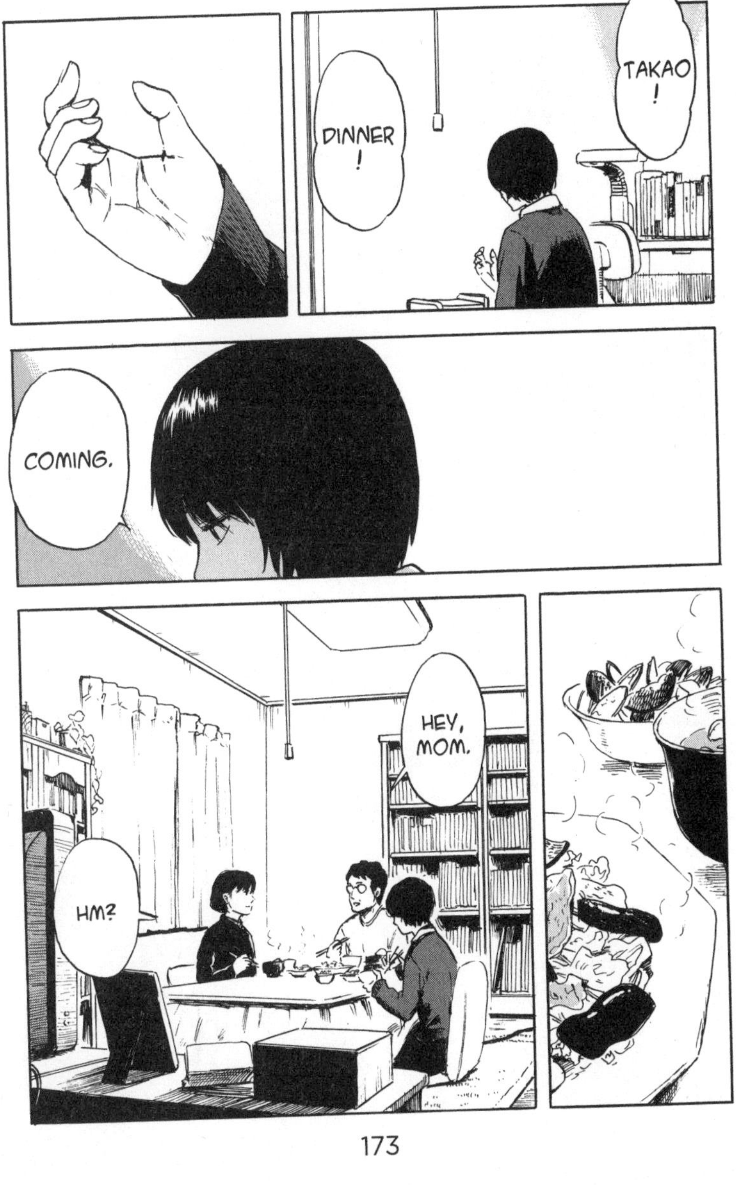
TAKAO!
DINNER!
COMING.
HEY, MOM.
HM?

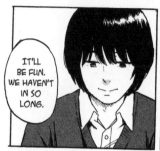

WANNA EAT OUT THIS SUNDAY?
SOME-WHERE NICE.
NOPE. WASTE OF MONEY.
IT'LL BE FUN. WE HAVEN'T IN SO LONG.
YES?
WE'LL BRING TAKAO, TOO.
HUH?
OH, SURE.
WHAT'S WRONG, TAKAO?
DID SOME-THING HAPPEN?

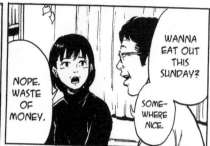

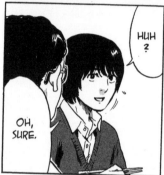

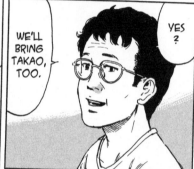

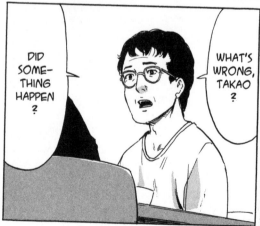

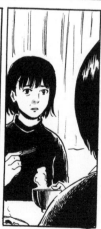

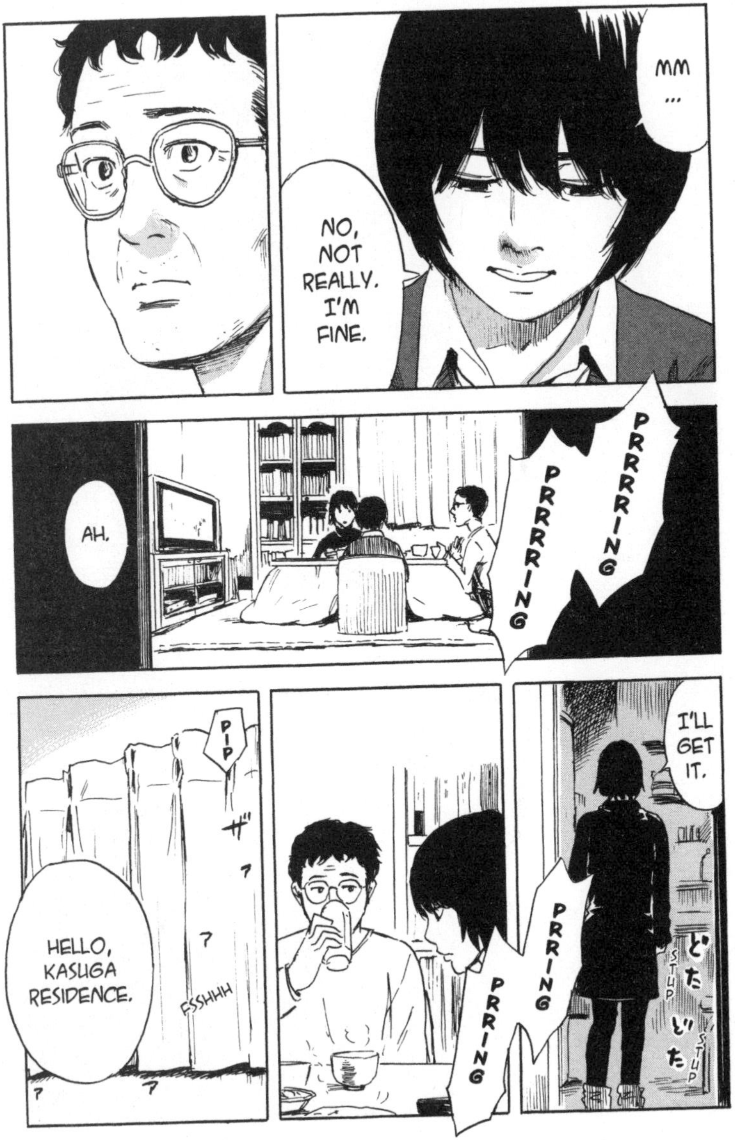
MM ...
NO, NOT REALLY. I'M FINE.
PRRRRING
PRRRRING
AH.
I'LL GET IT.
PRRING
PRRING
どたどた
STUP STUP
PIP
ザァ
HELLO, KASUGA RESIDENCE.
FSSHHH

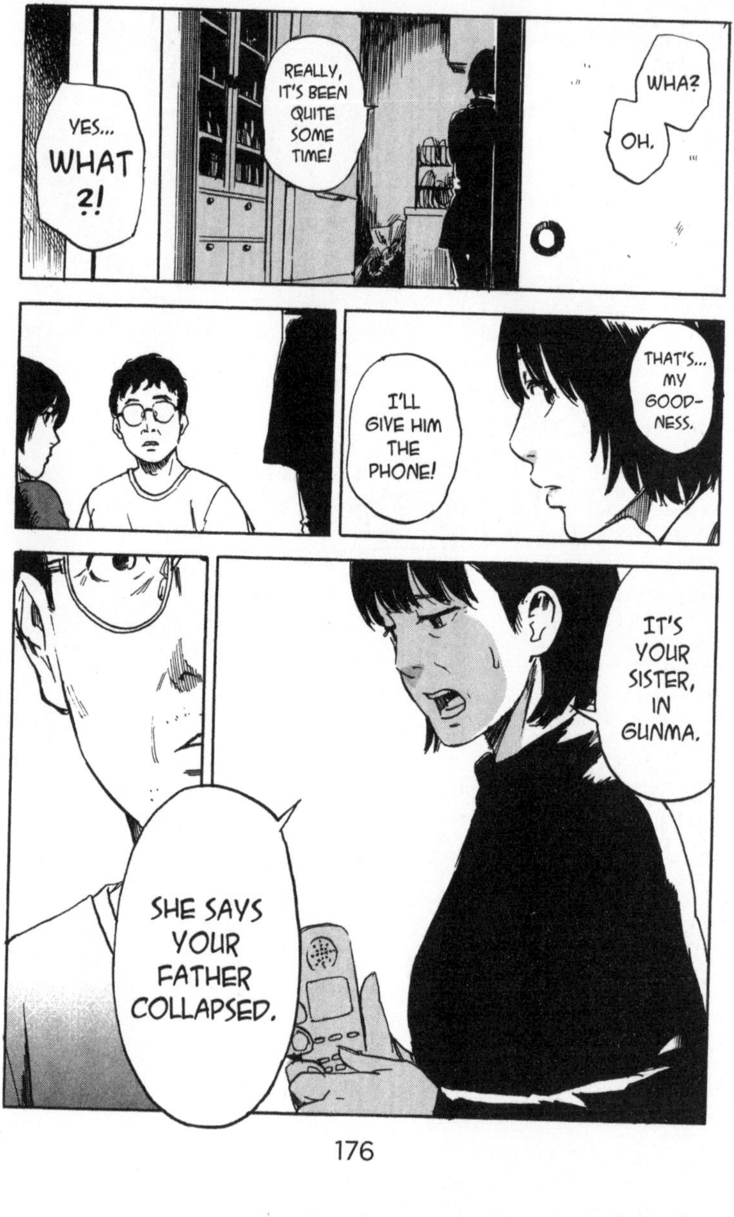
WHA?
OH.
REALLY, IT'S BEEN QUITE SOME TIME!
YES... WHAT?!
THAT'S... MY GOODNESS.
I'LL GIVE HIM THE PHONE!
IT'S YOUR SISTER, IN GUNMA.
SHE SAYS YOUR FATHER COLLAPSED.

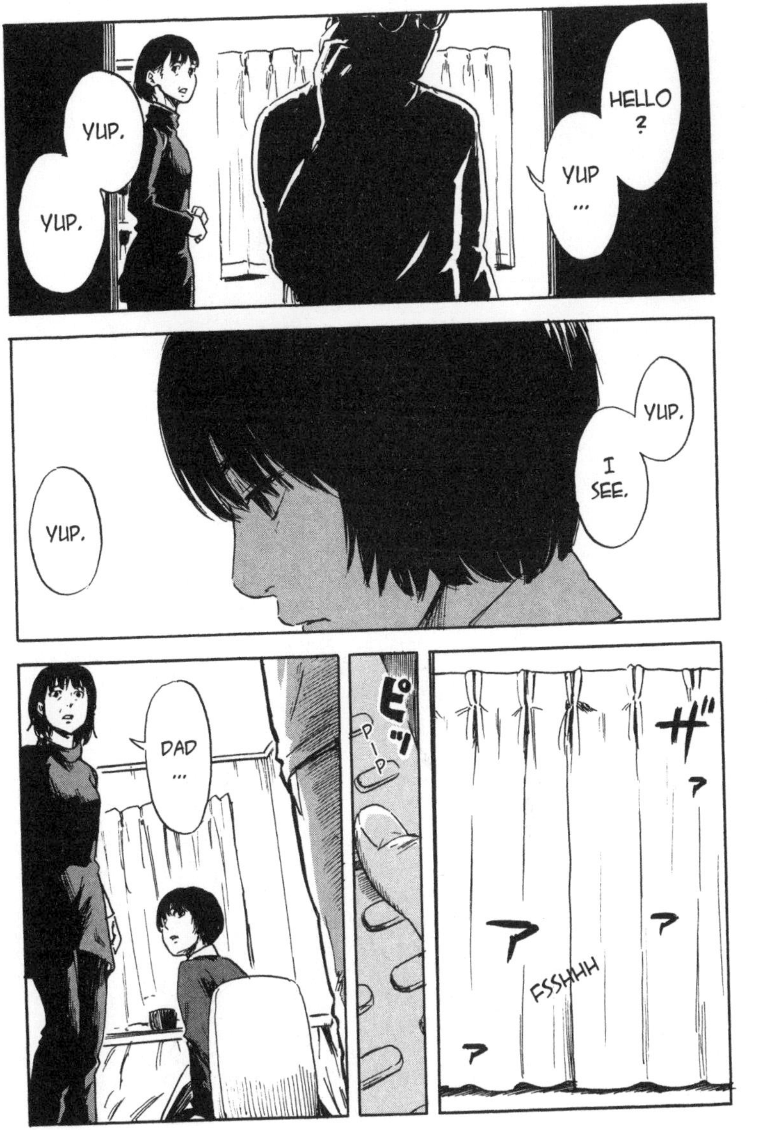
HELLO?
YUP...
YUP.
YUP.
YUP.
I SEE.
YUP.
ザァァァァ
FSSHHH
ピッ
P-P
DAD...

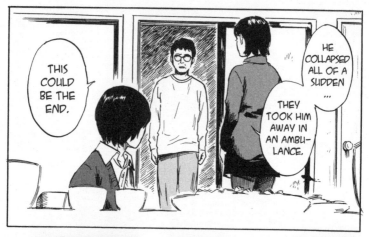

HE COLLAPSED ALL OF A SUDDEN ...
THEY TOOK HIM AWAY IN AN AMBULANCE.
THIS COULD BE THE END.
NO ...
I'LL GO... TOMORROW.
I'LL COME, TOO.
NO, UH... DON'T BOTHER.

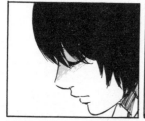

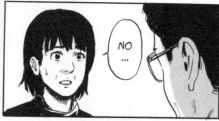

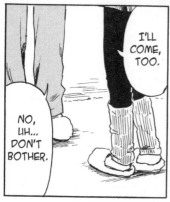

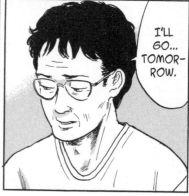

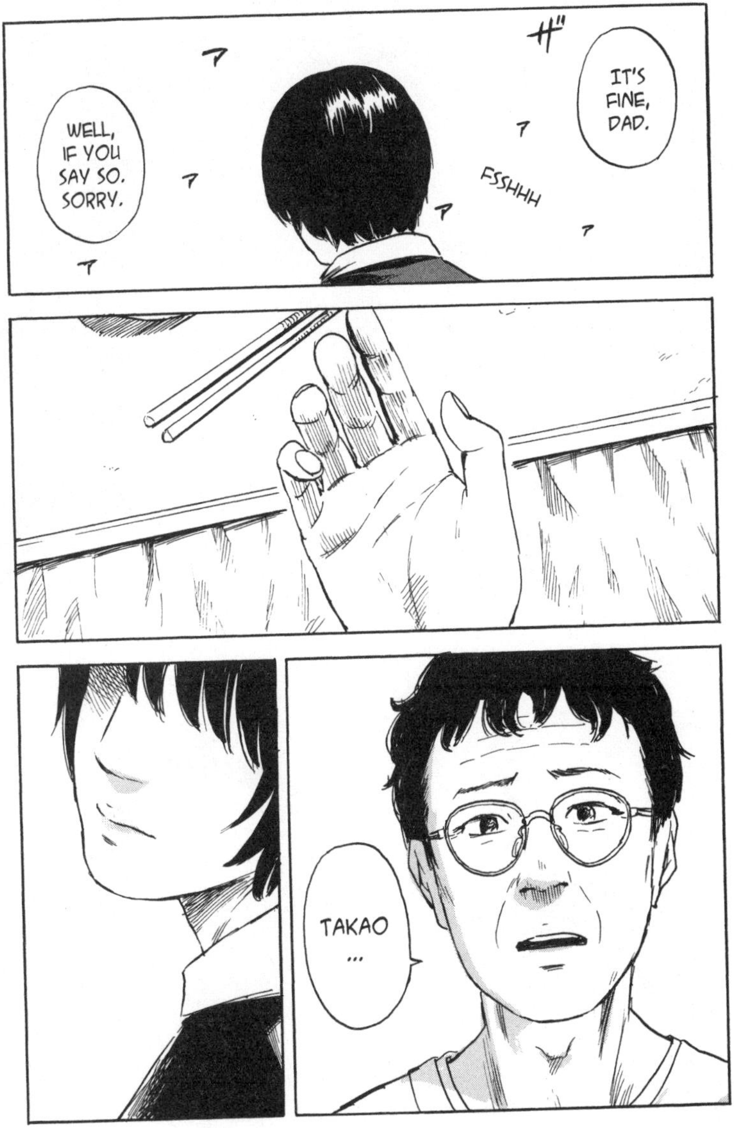
IT'S FINE, DAD.
FSSHHH
WELL, IF YOU SAY SO. SORRY.
TAKAO ...

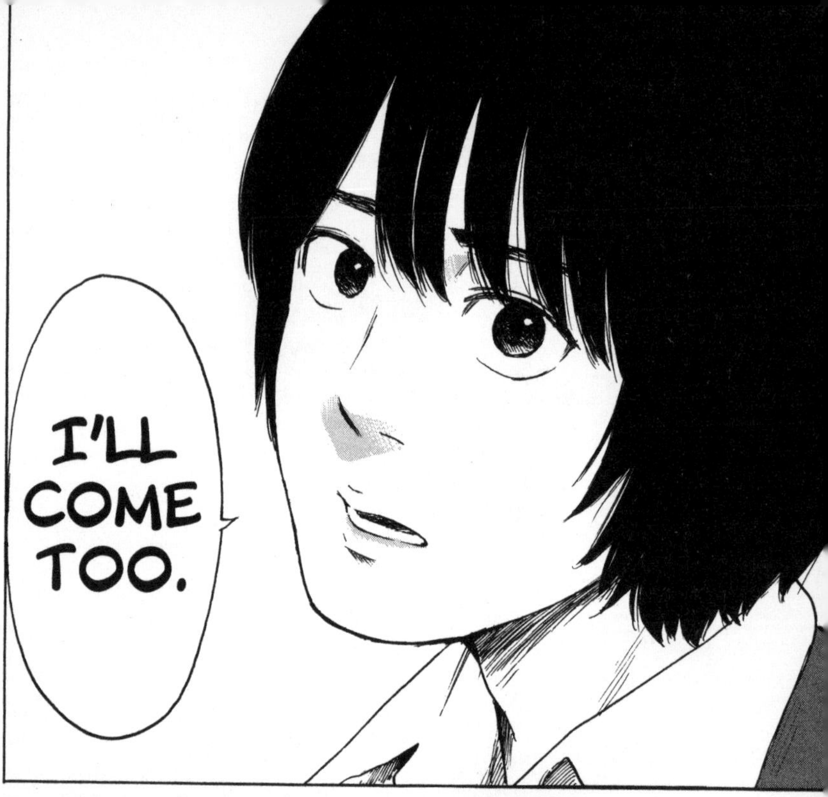
I'LL COME TOO.
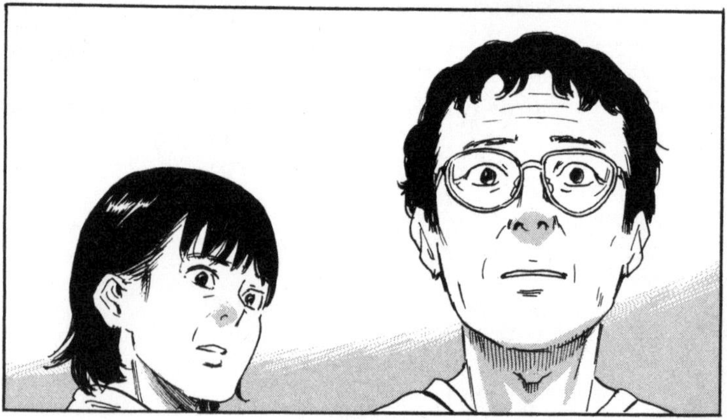

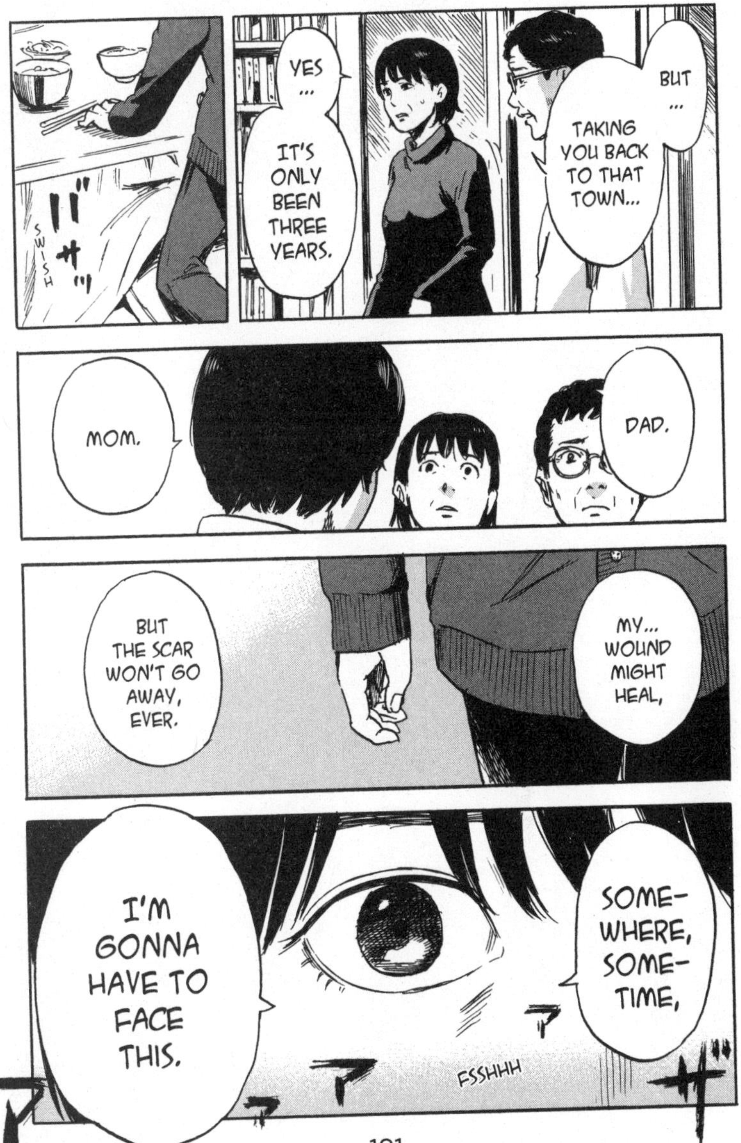
BUT ... TAKING YOU BACK TO THAT TOWN...
YES ... IT'S ONLY BEEN THREE YEARS.
SWISH
DAD.
MOM.
MY... WOUND MIGHT HEAL,
BUT THE SCAR WON'T GO AWAY, EVER.
SOME-WHERE, SOME-TIME,
I'M GONNA HAVE TO FACE THIS.
FSSHHH

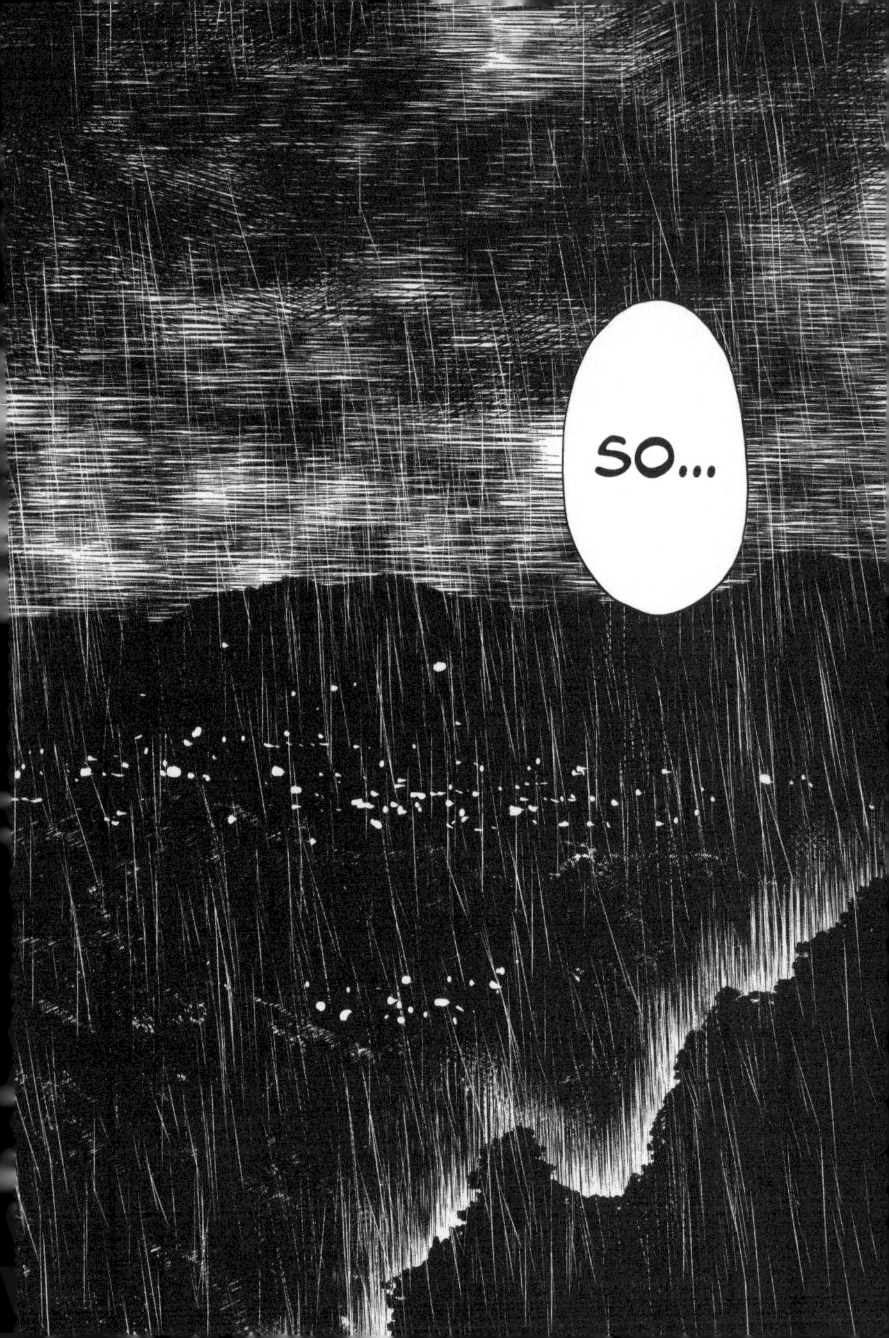
SO...

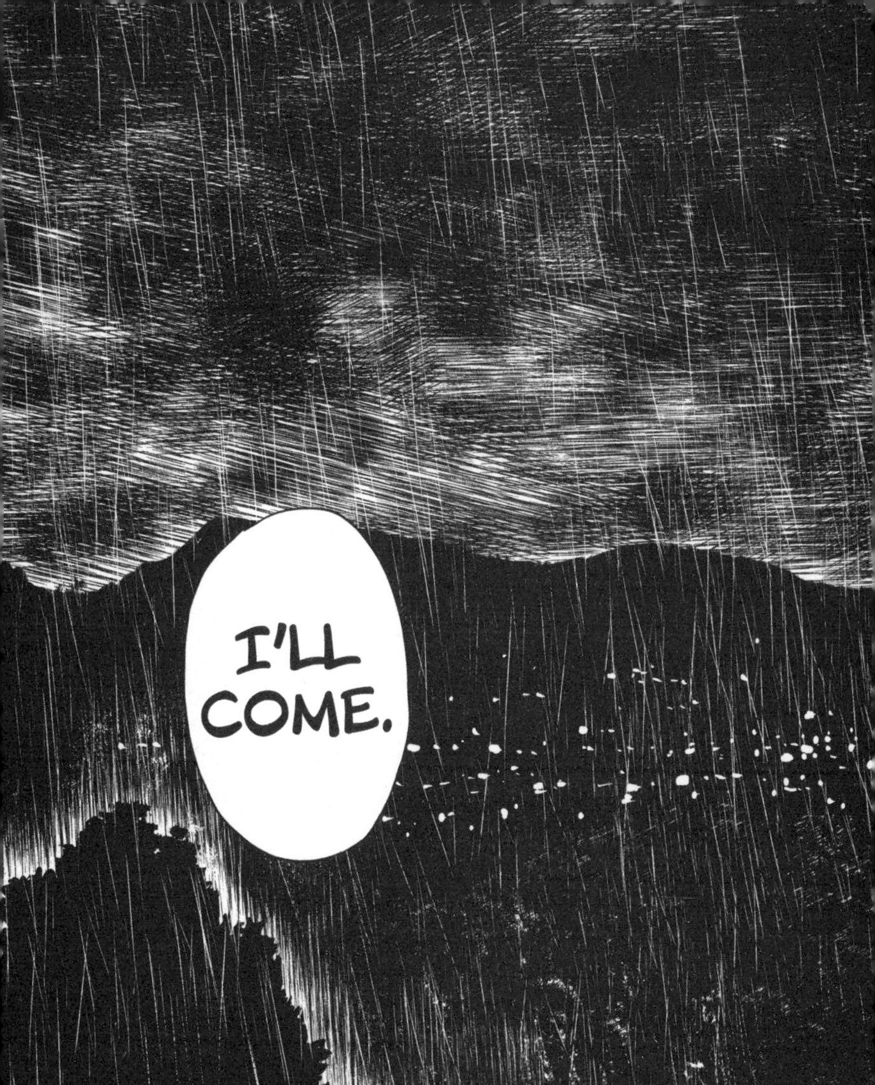
I'LL COME.

Continued in volume 10

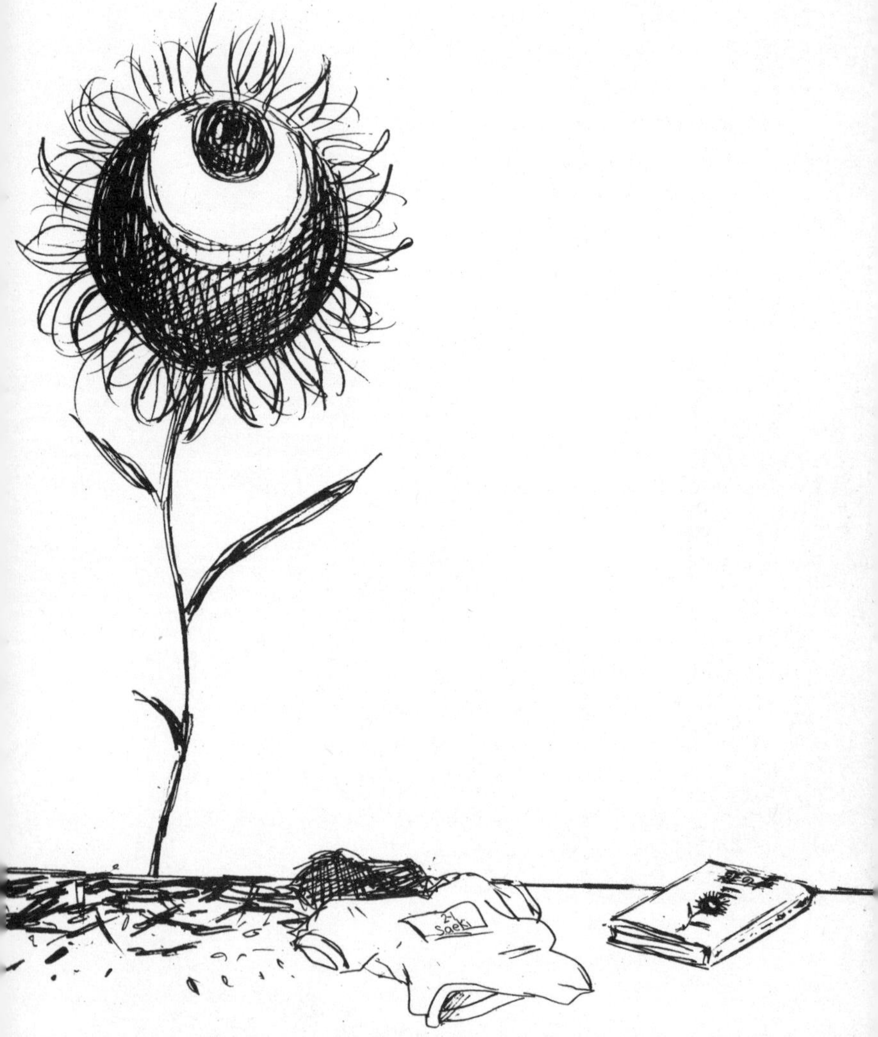
2-1
Saeki

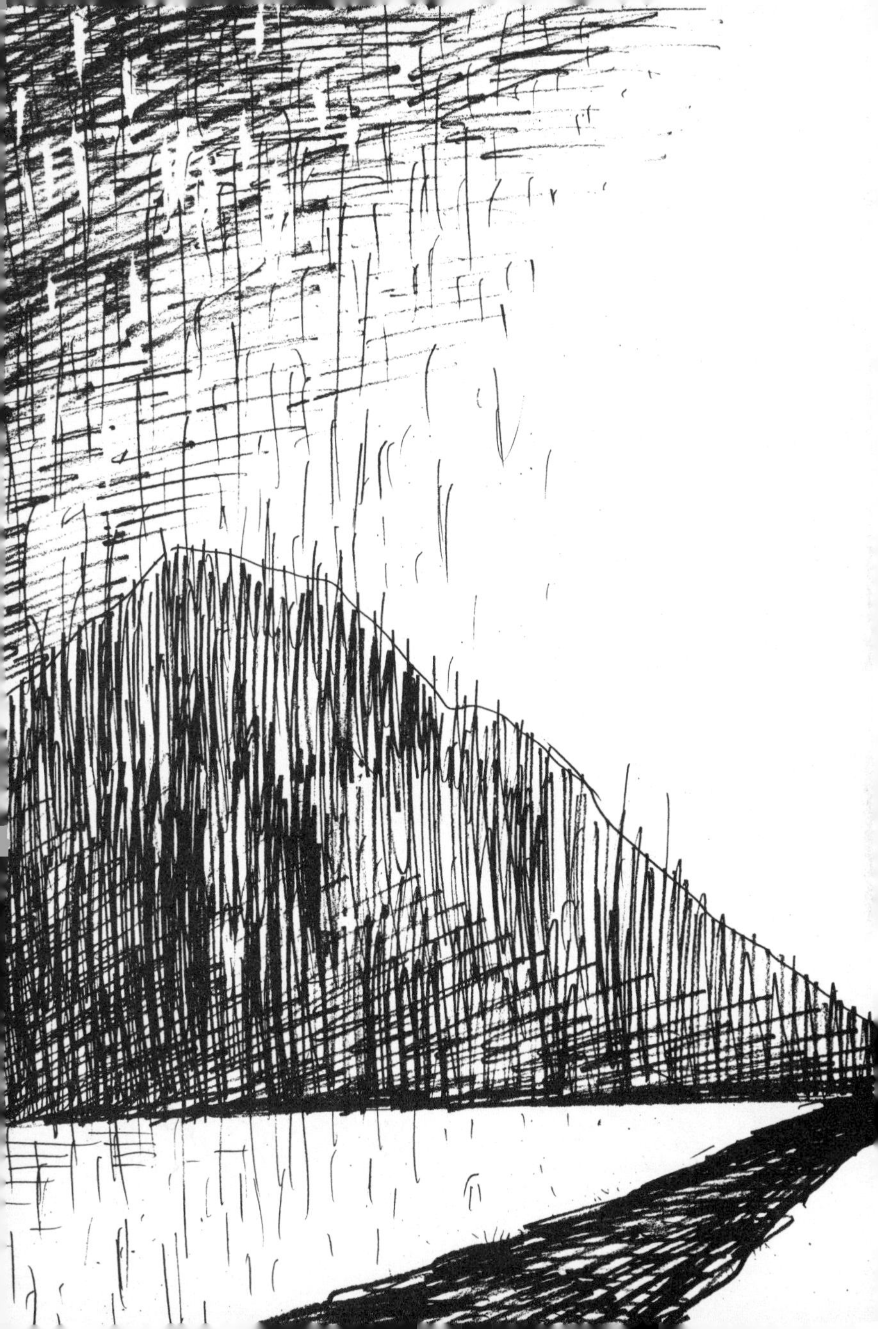

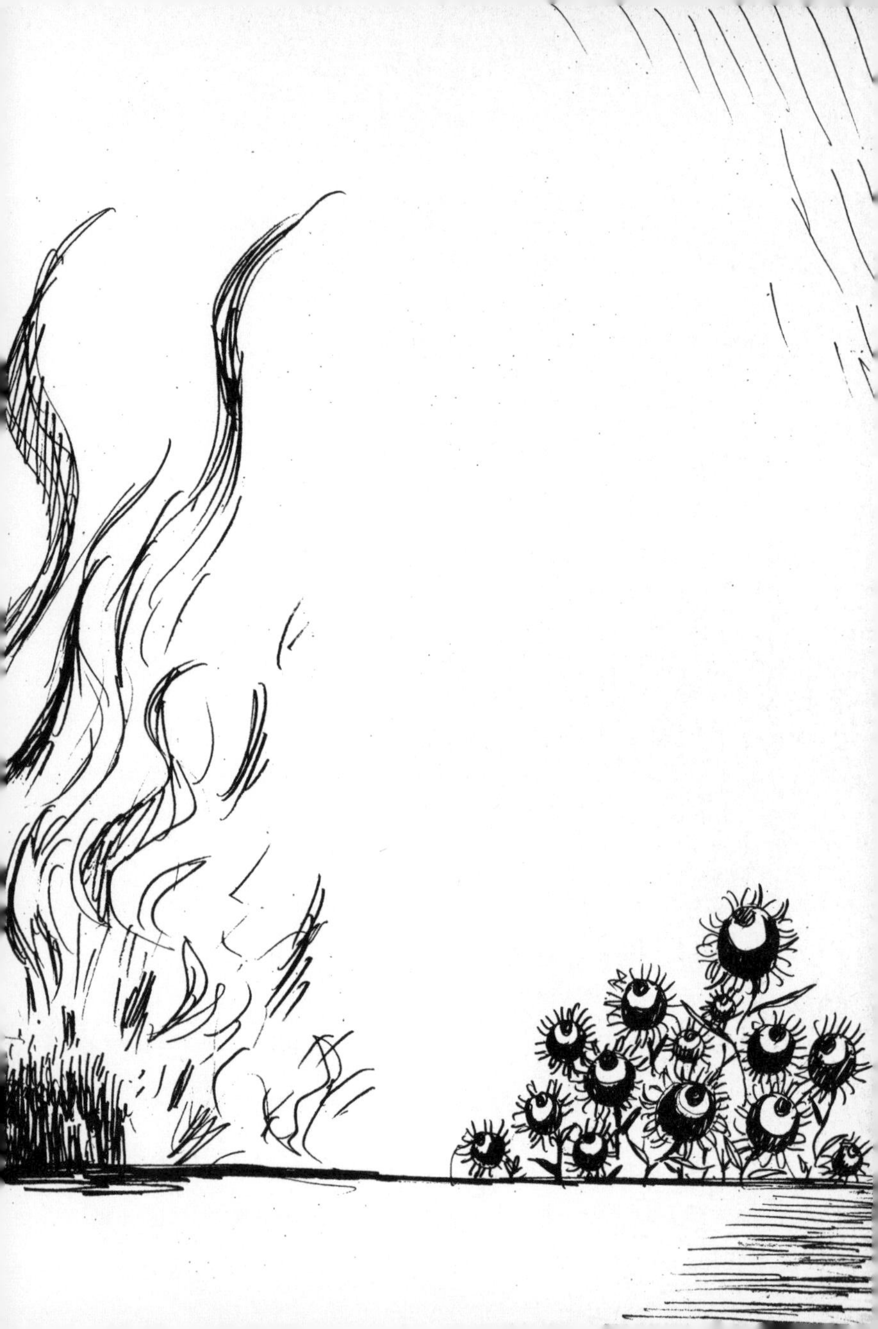

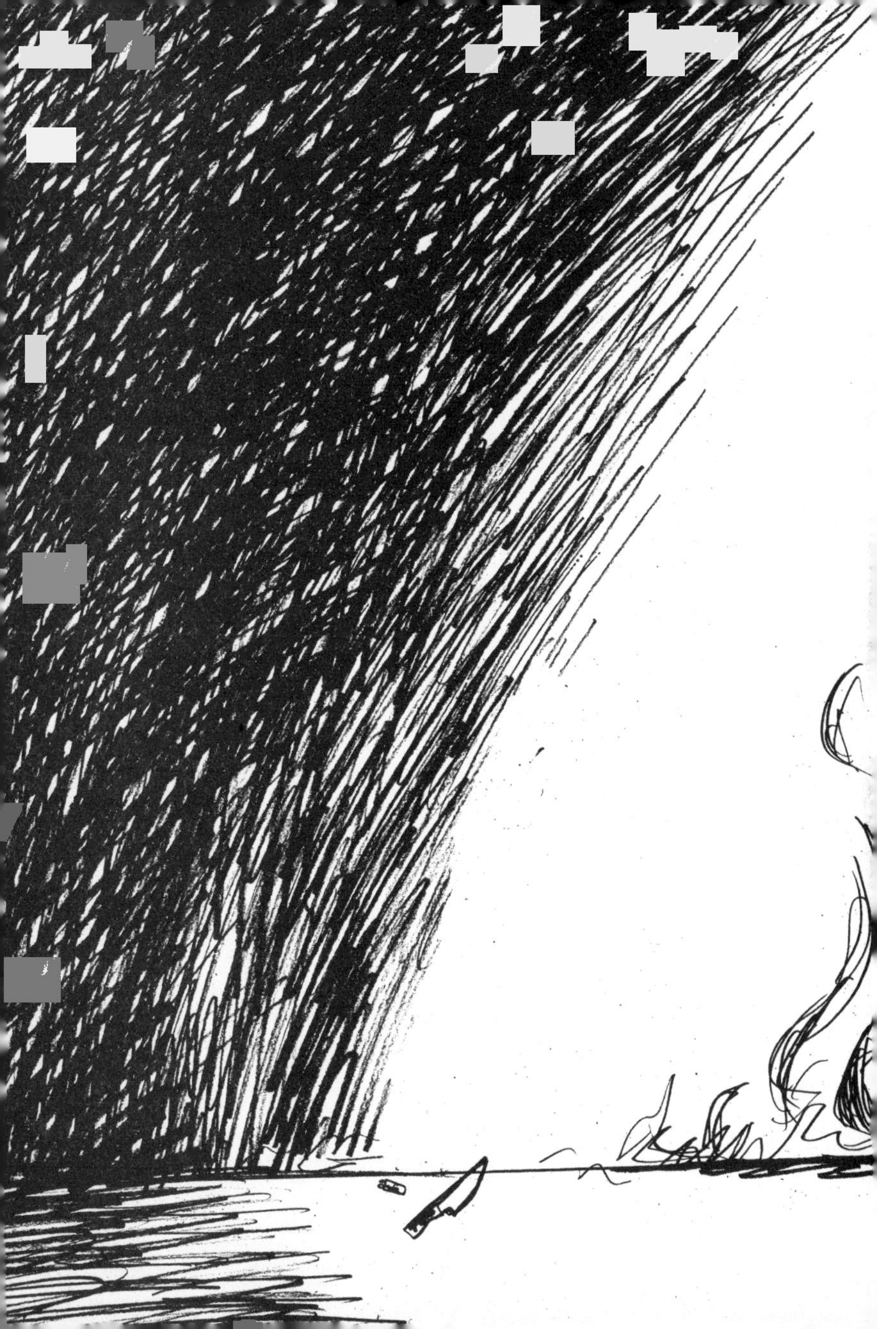

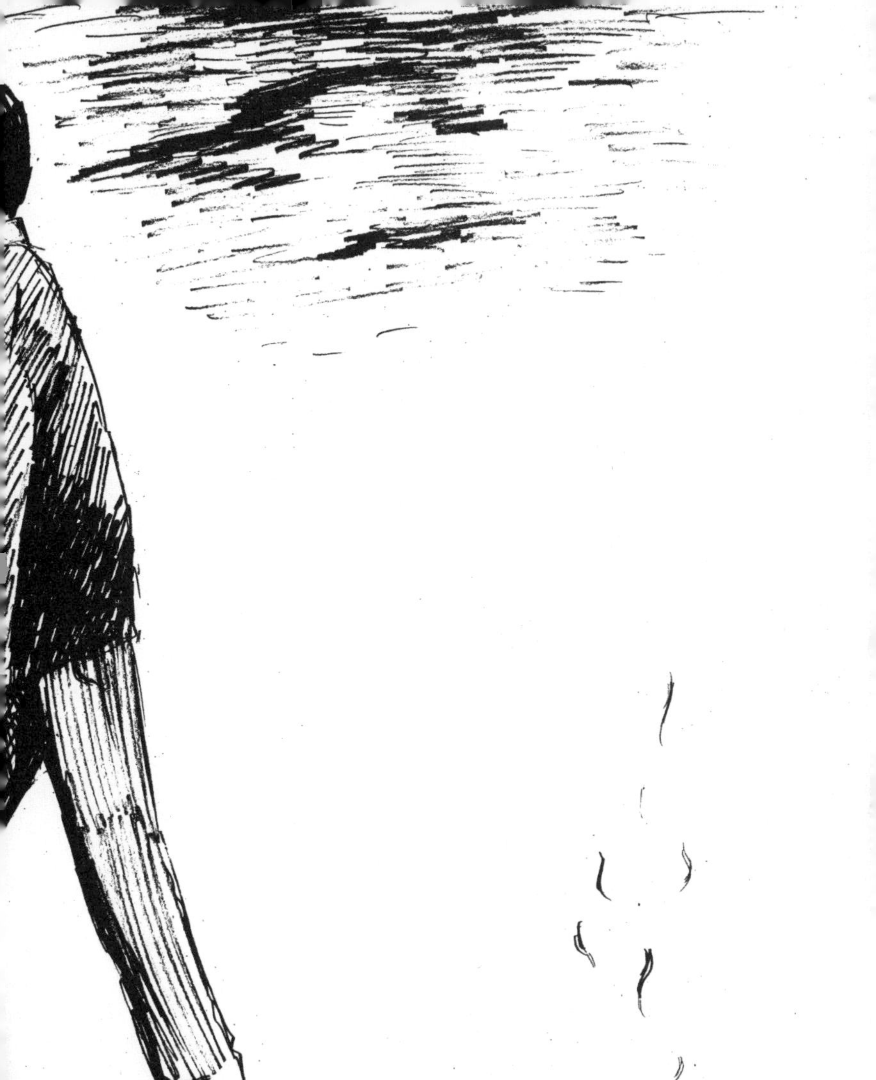

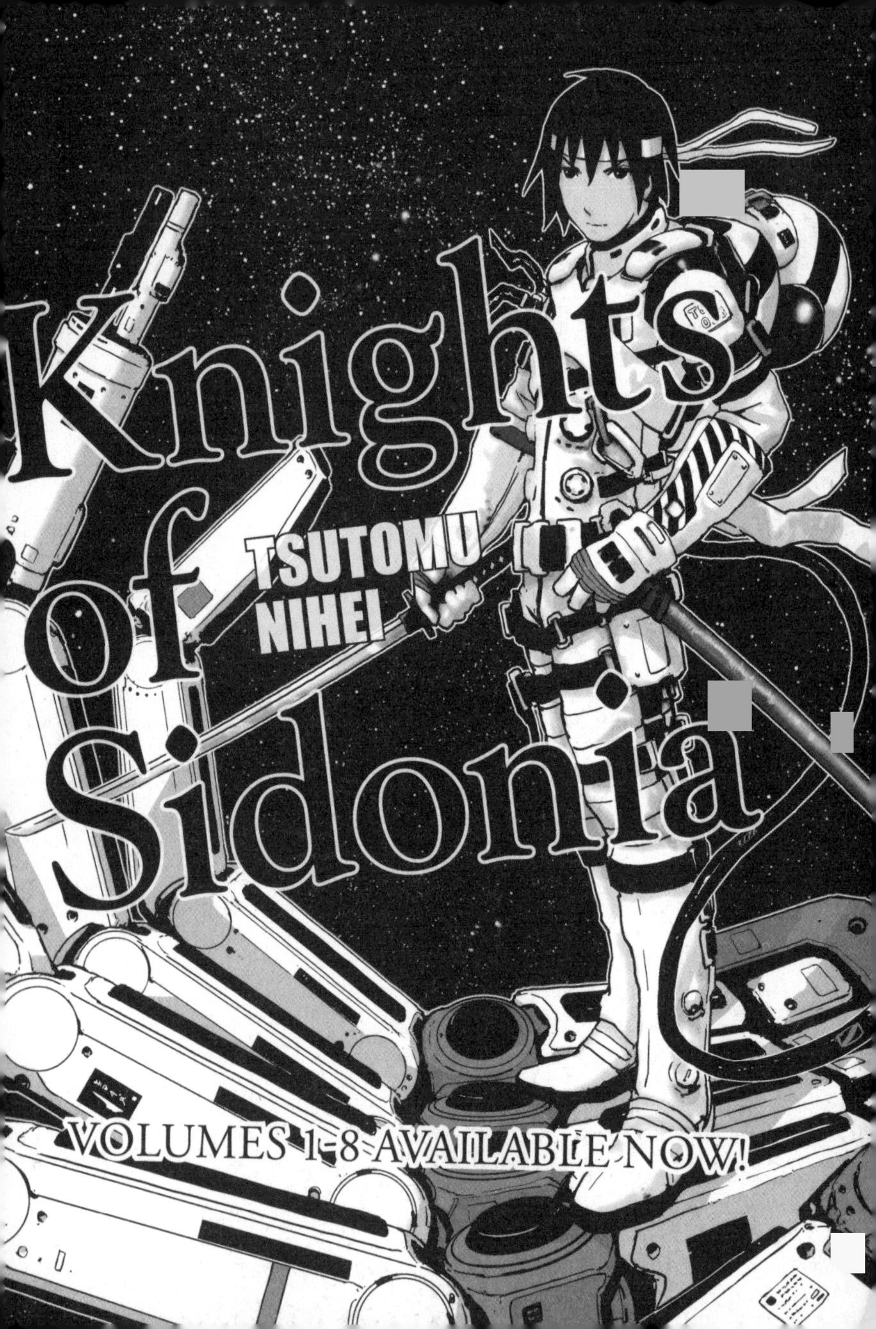

Knights of Sidonia
TSUTOMU NIHEI
VOLUMES 1-8 AVAILABLE NOW!

CORE EXPOSED

Outer space, the far future.

A lone seed ship, the *Sidonia*, plies the void, ten centuries since the obliteration of the solar system. The massive, nearly indestructible, yet barely sentient alien life forms that destroyed humanity's home world continue to pose an existential threat.

Nagate Tanikaze has only known life in the vessel's bowels deep below the sparkling strata where humans have achieved photosynthesis and new genders. Not long after he emerges from the Underground, however, the youth is bequeathed a treasured legacy by the spaceship's coolheaded female captain.

Meticulously drawn, peppered with clipped humor, but also unusually attentive to plot and structure for the international cult favorite, *Knights of Sidonia* may be Tsutomu Nihei's most accessible work to date even as it hits notes of tragic grandeur as a hopeless struggle for survival unfolds.

"One of *Knights of Sidonia*'s chief strengths is that it doesn't bog down the intrigue of its world with too much unnecessary, bloated dialogue... It's definitely a solid pick-up for Vertical; there's not really anything else in their catalog like it. Dig into the first volume and see if Nihei's gorgeously depicted wreck of a sci-fi future doesn't secure an immediately tight grip."

— *Otaku USA*

"*Knights of Sidonia* is off to a solid start with its first volume... All in all it's a promising and entertaining offering and one that's left me chomping at the bit for the next volume."

— *Comic Book Resources*

The Flowers of Evil, volume 9

Translation: Paul Starr
Production: Risa Cho
          Nicole Dochych

Copyright © 2014 Shuzo Oshimi. All rights reserved.
First published in Japan in 2013 by Kodansha, Ltd., Tokyo
Publication for this English edition arranged through Kodansha, Ltd., Tokyo
English language version produced by Vertical, Inc.

Translation provided by Vertical, Inc., 2014
Published by Vertical, Inc., New York

Originally published in Japanese as *Aku no Hana* by Kodansha, Ltd., 2013
Aku no Hana first serialized in *Bessatsu Shonen Magazine*, Kodansha, Ltd., 2009.

This is a work of fiction.

ISBN: 978-1-939130-28-0

Manufactured in Canada

First Edition

Vertical, Inc.
451 Park Avenue South
7th Floor
New York, NY 10016
www.vertical-inc.com